James Harrod
of Kentucky

James Harrod of Kentucky

Kathryn Harrod Mason

COMMONWEALTH BOOK COMPANY
St. Martin, Ohio

Copyright © 1951 by Kathryn Harrod Mason.
Originally published in 1951 by Louisiana State University Press in its *Southern Biography Series*.

Copyright © 2022 by Commonwealth Book Company.

All rights reserved. No part of this book may be reproduced in any form or by any means without the prior written consent of the publisher, excepting brief quotes used in reviews. Printed in the United States of America.

ISBN: 978-1-948986-45-8

Cover: Kentucky Landscape, by James Pierce Barton [1817–1891].

Title page photograph: Blockhouse in Fort Harrod.

To
John Brown Mason

PREFACE

A SSEMBLING materials for a biography of an early American is always complicated because of the lapse of time. In the case of frontiersmen such as James Harrod the problem is still more difficult, since they often came from obscure families and were generally second-generation pioneers. Record keeping in the wilderness was scanty at best, inaccurate, and confused, while spelling of proper names was done largely "by ear." Even those frontiersmen who possessed the necessary skill wrote little because paper was scarce, time for reflection even scarcer, and opportunities for mail delivery dependent on itinerant travelers.

The author is deeply indebted to numerous people who opened their records for her use, particularly to members of the Harrod-Moore family, who made it possible to obtain for the first time a clear picture of this pioneering group. Special thanks and appreciation are due Mrs. Bernice Lewis Swainson, Piedmont, California, for long hours of consultation and for making available hundreds of newly discovered records, and particularly for her assistance in establishing much genealogical data. Mr. Walter F. Harrod, Nottinghamshire, England; Mrs. Myrtle W. Richey and Mrs. John H. Cary of Washington, Pennsylvania; Mrs. Helen Denny Howard, Waynesburg, Pennsylvania; Mr. William R. Anthony, Memphis, Tennessee; Mrs. W. R. Patterson, Oroville, California; Dr. F. P. Strickler and Dr. D. W. Chamberlin of Louisville, Kentucky; Mrs. Maude Darling, Crete, Nebraska; and Mr. James D. Harrod, Midway City, California, were also among the members of the family who furnished data. Colonel J. Franklin Bell, USAR, Washington, D. C., provided the maps and supervised their preparation. He gave many hours of study to geographical problems connected with the movements of the Harrod brothers.

Others, not descendants of the Harrods, also contributed records either directly or through Mrs. Swainson. Among them are: Mr. Howard L. Leckey, Waynesburg, Pennsylvania, who traced landholdings and family relationships through his collection of records on two hundred western Pennsylvania pioneers; Mr. Earle R. Forrest of Washington, Pennsylvania, who furnished illustrative material; Major George C. Chinn, USMC, a long-time student of Harrodsburg records, Mrs. T. F. Sandusky, the late Mr. James Taylor Cooke, Mr. D. M. Hutton, editor of the Harrodsburg *Herald,* and members of his staff—all of Harrodsburg, Kentucky; and Mr. Cass K. Shelby of Hollidaysburg, Pennsylvania, who cleared up the relationship between the Harrods and the Shelbys.

I am happy to acknowledge the debt I owe numerous scholars and research workers in the state and private offices where I have worked, especially Miss Alice E. Smith, Curator of the Draper Collection, Wisconsin Historical Society, Madison, Wisconsin; Miss Ludie J. Kinkead, Filson Club, Louisville; Mrs. Jouett Taylor Cannon and her assistant, Mr. Bayless Hardin, Kentucky State Historical Society, Frankfort, Kentucky; Miss Margaret Finch of the National Archives, Washington, D. C.; Miss Nell Nugent of the Virginia Land Office and Mr. J. J. Van Shreeven of the State Library, both of Richmond, Virginia; the county clerks and custodians of records in various pension and land offices in Pennsylvania, Maryland, Virginia, West Virginia, Kentucky, Ohio, Indiana, and Illinois; staff workers in numerous libraries including the Library of Congress, Virginia State Library, New York Public Library, Oberlin College Library, and the library of the Maryland State Historical Society in Baltimore.

The writings of outstanding specialists on early American history and thought have contributed immeasurably to my understanding of this segment of the frontier. I am particularly indebted to several of these scholars for their personal interest and suggestions. Professor Max Savelle of the University of Washington assisted me through the inspiration of his course at Stanford on the Colonial Mind and through his published writings. He read and criticized the manuscript and was kind enough to write the introduction. Dr. Clarence E. Carter, Editor in Chief of the Territorial Papers of the United States, Washington, D. C., also read the entire manuscript and contributed many hours of consultation and critical discussion. Professor Thomas Perkins Abernethy, Chairman of the Corcoran School of History at the University of Virginia, read the study several times and was particularly helpful because of his intimate knowledge of the Virginia frontiers. Dr. St. George L. Sioussat, former Director of the Manuscript Division, Library of Congress; Professor Merrill Jensen of the University of Wisconsin; Dr. John H. Powell, former Assistant Librarian of the Philadelphia Free Library; and Miss Elizabeth Hooker, research assistant of the Land Tenure Section, Bureau of Agricultural Economics, Washington, read portions of the manuscript and furnished helpful criticism.

I am indebted to the D.A.R. library in Washington for their help in locating materials as well as for permission to examine the brooch said to have belonged to Ann Harrod.

Mrs. Alberta Powell Graham and Mrs. Catherine Cate Coblentz, writers, Washington, D. C., will be gratefully remembered for their long and helpful interest in this manuscript.

The Editor of the Southern Biography Series, Professor T. Harry Williams, Louisiana State University, was of great assistance. His wide knowledge and his meticulous editorial work have contributed immeasurably to whatever value the study may possess.

The author alone is responsible for any errors of fact that may have passed unnoticed, as well as for the conclusions expressed.

Oberlin, Ohio KATHRYN HARROD MASON
January 16, 1948

CONTENTS

	Preface	vii
	Introduction	xv
I	For King and Country (1754-1755)	1
II	The Road Builders (1756-1767)	17
III	The Western Fever (1767-1773)	30
IV	The First Kentucky Settlement (1774)	42
V	Virginia's Private War (1774)	53
VI	A Last Farewell (1775)	68
VII	Transylvania (1775)	80
VIII	Virginia Creates a County (1776)	91
IX	Two Rescues (1776-1777)	101
X	The Siege of Fort Harrod (1777)	110
XI	A Clouded Sky (1777)	121
XII	A Secret Well Kept (1778)	130
XIII	Captain Jim Takes a Wife (1778)	143
XIV	The Monongahelans (1778-1779)	156
XV	The Hard Winter (1779-1780)	170
XVI	The 1780 Campaign	181
XVII	Crossroads (1781-1782)	194
XVIII	Colonel Jim—Kentucky Citizen (1783-1784)	204
XIX	Family Business (1785-1786)	213
XX	Tragedy and Mystery (1786-1792)	225
	Epilogue	237
	Appendix	243
	Critical Essay on Authorities	245
	Index	255

ILLUSTRATIONS

facing page

Indians Delivering up English Captives to Colonel Bouquet in 1764	26
General James Ray	88
William Harrod's Commission from the Virginia Committee of Safety	98
Blockhouse in Fort Harrod (restored)	112
Interior of Fort Harrod (restored)	116
Westward to the Mississippi (map)	140
First page of John Filson, *The Discovery, Settlement and Present State of Kentucke*	164
Crossing the Alleghenies (map)	176
John Filson's map of Kentucky	208
Letter from James Harrod to William Clark, 1785 (only known existing letter written by Harrod)	222

INTRODUCTION

HISTORY is a process.

It is the process, constantly going on, of growth, expansion, and refinement in human society and culture. For a human society is like an organism whose seed contains within itself the essential elements of growth. Once planted in a congenial environment, it must draw upon the environment for its sustenance in order to grow; at the same time, it survives best where it adapts itself most effectively, and the result of this adaptation is something which is outwardly, if not essentially, new.

Of course, human society is made up of individuals; and individual reactions, individual character, and individual ideals have an enormous influence upon the peculiar shape that the culture of any new society will take. This was markedly true in the case of the Harrods and of that particular brand of the American way of life that grew up in Kentucky.

The formation of the American way of life was brought about in the first place by the interaction of three powerful forces. The first of these was the force of the people themselves. For the people who first settled on these shores were Europeans: first the English, then Scotch, Irish, Germans, and French, all men and women of sturdy, rugged racial stock. But these Europeans, accustomed to life under the conditions of Europe, were compelled to adapt themselves to the new land physically, economically, socially, politically, and intellectually. The most obvious cases of adaptation were in Virginia, where the cultivation of tobacco induced a form of economy and social organization unknown to the mother country; in the West Indies, where the soil, climate, and geographic forms of the Windward and Leeward Islands operated to form an economy and a society that were different, again, from those both of England and Virginia; and in New England, where the economic line of least resistance led men into the fishing industries and their economic correlates, shipbuilding and commerce.

Thus the second great force operating to differentiate the American societies from those of Europe was the environment: the land itself, soil conditions, climate, fauna, flora, and natural resources. But these sectionally differentiated American societies probably could not have differed so greatly from each other or from their parent society had it not been for the great differences in the ideas and ideals that directed the lives of the individuals who composed them. Who, for example, could question the force of the influence exercised upon the formation of New England society by Puritanism, or deny the obvious power of that set of ideas upon American history from that day to this? Or who could question the extreme historical significance of inherited ideas relative to representative government in Virginia that resulted in the famous assembly that sat at Jamestown in the summer of 1619? Or the historic significance of the body of thought wrapped up in the phrase "no taxation without representation"—a body of thought which caused so much strife throughout the colonial period and played so important a role in the precipitation of the American Revolution? The basic force at work to produce a new way of life was embodied in the people, and the great molding crucible was the environment. But the factor which first gave direction to the growth of the new communities was the guiding power of ideas.

That is not to say, however, that the ideas of the founders of American societies formed an inflexible and unbreakable cast to control and contain the development of the new America. Quite the contrary, indeed; for all, or nearly all, of the predominating ideas used in shaping the foundations laid by the first settlers were quickly modified, even within the first generation of settlers, to make them more applicable to the conditions of the new land. Such, for example, was the introduction of the idea of territorial basis for political representation, the idea of written constitutions, or the change in Puritan ideas represented by the halfway covenant and the ultimate secularization of the Puritan ideal.

At the same time, new ideas and institutions appeared to give direction to the growth of the new societies. Such, for example, was the acceptance and establishment of slavery in Virginia, with a consequent rationalization of the peculiar social stratification resulting from it; such, also, was the set of ideas embodied in the institution known as the New England town meeting.

These ideas and institutions, whatever their remote roots, were essentially new. But once established they became firmly fixed in the minds of the inhabitants of those areas, simply by reason of the fact that their results were so very satisfactory. Thus, if old, inherited ideas were a strong force in the formation of an American way of life, new ideas, at first devised to meet a need in a new situation, added their force in guiding the lines of historical development in the American colonies. Once firmly established, however, these new institutions and ideas became fairly fixed, and extremely difficult to overthrow. In other words, they soon became a conservative force operating to preserve the forms that had been established in the first era of settlement.

It should be noted especially that both the modification of old ideas and the invention of new ones to meet the needs of adaptation in the new land took place in the course of the experience of the people on the land, and were both a part of that experience and a result of it. Thus those characteristics of the American way of life which are most American, and which differentiate it from the way of life of every other people in the world, are derived from the experience of the people on the soil. No matter what its racial, social, or intellectual background, the American way of life is rooted in America.

II.

Thus the process of building new institutions and ideals did not stop with the settlement of Virginia or Massachusetts. On the contrary, it is one of the most profound characteristics of American history that the process of planting, growth, and differentiation of institutions repeated itself over and over again as population moved westward.

The first of these repetitions took place in the first half of the eighteenth century, when the "Old West" was laid down. Here the process of founding, growth, and differentiation took place in a new environment. The people here were Scotch-Irish, Germans, and some of the descendants of the original English planters. These people, in large part, were new. And if they were not very different racially from the original English, they were certainly very different in language, in culture, and in their heritage of political and social ideals. The environment, too, was new; for these people moved into the lands along the upper reaches of the coastal rivers, into the piedmont of the Allegheny ranges, and even into the great valley of the Allegheny highland itself. Thus the conditions to which these new people had to adapt themselves were new.

But the ideas these "newlanders" brought with them, as they moved slowly westward into the mountains, were filtered through the already established ideas of the old communities of the seaboard. At the same time, the sharp original differentiation between Germans and Scotch-Irish on the one side and the English of the seaboard was considerably softened by the admixture of men of pure English blood who moved westward with them. Thus, the process of differentiation in the Old West was in part directed and controlled by the patterns of society and of mind already established along the seaboard.

The Old West was nevertheless sharply differentiated from

the Old East. It demanded more political and economic equality, and it demanded easy money with which to pay its debts to the hard-money East. Less sophisticated, less well educated, and less "enlightened" than the East, it developed its own brand of supercharged emotional religion.

Examination of expressions of the economic, social, political, religious, and cultural outlook of the Americans of the eighteenth century thus reveals a complex American mind in which there already appears a conservative, static eastern mood, derived in part from the ideals of the static culture inherited from the seventeenth-century founders and in part from the new conservatism of the tidewater wealthy of town and plantation. Already, too, this native American conservatism was being challenged, about the middle of the eighteenth century, by the more progressive mood of the Old West. The conservatism of the tidewater sought to preserve a set of habits and institutions that had proved their worth in the crucible of the first American experience, while the challenge of the West arose out of a new and different experience. The mood of the West was a mood that was new because, taken all together, the experience of the Westerners was new. The way of life of the West was new and stood in contrast, even conflict, with the Old East precisely because the total experience of the new frontiersmen was different from the total experience of the old.

A new world had again made a new culture. The derivation of a culture from the interaction of men, cultural heritage, and environment had repeated itself, but in new terms. And history, in America, had shown itself to be a process of renewal, or re-creation.

III.

Then it happened again. For the people of the East and the piedmont moved westward again, this time down the westward slopes of the mountains, along the courses of the "western waters." This time the people were not new; for they were the children and the grandchildren of the English, the Germans, and the Scotch-Irish of both the Old East and the Old West: they were the first offshoot of the original American melting pot.

But the environment was new. For the region into which they moved was now the Ohio Valley, the basin of "La Belle Rivière"—the beautiful river. Their heritage was new, too, in the sense that it was now non-European. This migration, indeed, was the first large-scale migration of a native American set of ideas and ideals. As always, the heritage of ideas that crossed the mountains in the knapsacks of the Harrods and their followers was soon modified under the stress of the new environment. But they were American when they crossed the mountains; and if they were modified, as they inevitably had to be, they were modified within the basic American pattern. They were made, if anything, more American.

The new frontier of Kentucky, and the repetition of the process of culture building that took place there, did not produce a phenomenon that stood isolated and alone. For just as the Old West had exercised its force upon the ideas and institutions of the Old East to make them more fluid and more equalitarian, just so the culture area of the Ohio Valley soon began to exercise its influence upon both the Old East and the Old West. The founding of Kentucky meant the founding of a new culture section within the broad American pattern that already included New England, the Middle Atlantic area, the Old South, and the Old West. It was a new culture area which was to exert a profound and persistent influence upon the evolution of the increasingly complex pattern of American life.

IV.

But these were the broad, deep, and silent processes of American history of which the ordinary citizen is conscious only barely, if at all. For him, and especially for the pioneer who really starts the process, the compelling drive is the im-

INTRODUCTION   xxi

mediate job to be done. The first pioneer may have a vision of the future, and Jim Harrod and his brothers probably did have such vision. But most of their time and that of their comrades was occupied with the hard tasks of surveying lands, cutting down trees and building cabins, planting corn and vegetables, hunting, tending cattle and swine, fighting Indians and, eventually, Englishmen, finding salt, taking the products of their farms to market, and keeping order among themselves. Eventually the community of Harrodsburg, founded by James Harrod, was flanked by other towns. Eventually, too, those towns joined forces to fight their common enemies and later united to win their independence from the parent Virginia and to set up a constitution and a government of their own.

Here in Kentucky the process of re-creation was repeated. James Harrod and his brothers, and the few men and women who came with them and after them, brought a heritage of ideas and institutions from the Old East that they planted in the wilderness of the West. There that seed took root and grew, and the culture that resulted from its growth and adaptation to the new land was different from the parent culture. While clearly, almost fiercely, American, within the broad pattern of American culture, Kentucky was a new society, sharply different from its parent society and from the other communities that together formed the United States of America.

Throughout the early stages in the process of foundation, growth, and differentiation of a society in Kentucky, one of the giants of strength and leadership was James Harrod. And in him, as in all great leaders of the people, the profound forces of history become personalized. Every problem, every step in the experience of this new community, from the first trip over the mountains to the establishment of the state constitution, is touched, and influenced, by the experience and the intelligence of this one individual.

It is needless to say, of course, that if he had not done it someone else would have. The fact is that he did it, and he unquestionably left his stamp upon the history of the state to whose founding and early growth he contributed so much. Without the deep-running forces of the American westward movement his career as one of the founders of a great commonwealth could not have been. On the other hand, it is equally obvious that without the imprint of his individual force and character the society that grew there could never have been exactly as it was.

MAX SAVELLE

Chapter I
FOR KING AND COUNTRY
(1754-1755)

Over the hills with heart we go
To Fight the proud insulting foe,
Our country calls and we'll obey,
Over the hills and far away.[1]

THE WIDOW'S sons were born to danger. When John Harrod died in 1754, the struggle against the French and Indians for possession of the Ohio Valley had already begun, and a second generation of Western pioneers became soldiers by birth and circumstance. But when the wars were over they had attained the goal for which their young manhood was spent—land. Born in the years between 1728 and 1750, Harrod's boys found their activities molded by the fast-moving events that followed. From the Potomac to the Mississippi these six brothers, particularly James and William, played a significant role in the drama of the western movement. Together their lives represent the frontier in all its exciting aspects.

The father was hardly in his grave before John, Jr., volunteered for an expedition under the youthful Lieutenant Colonel George Washington, who was on his way to assert Virginia's domination over the Forks of the Ohio. This was not the eighteen-year-old Harrod's first military service. For several years he had been a militia private in upper Maryland, where he learned the rudiments of Indian fighting, scouting,

[1] Recruiting song, Baltimore *Maryland Gazette*, September 19, 1754.

and trailmaking—activities which he hoped would guarantee possession of the land his father had settled.[2]

Washington, too, was interested in Western land and only a year before had passed through this area on a mission to the French commander at the Forks of the Ohio (Duquesne). Numerous companies of speculators had plans for acquiring tracts west of the mountains, but the Ohio Company of Virginia, of which Lawrence and Augustine Washington were members, spearheaded the movement for settling there.[3] When the Company declared that under a grant from the Virginia Council they would bring in two hundred families to the Forks of the Ohio, the French announced that they owned by conquest and occupation all the territory on the river and throughout its tributaries to their sources. They erected a chain of forts from the Great Lakes down to the Ohio and furnished the Indians with guns and powder to help drive the speculators away. Washington had failed in his mission to convince the French that the land belonged to Virginia by virtue of her charter, and now a year later, at the instigation of Governor Robert Dinwiddie, he was recruiting an ex-

[2] Rachel Henton's Book, manuscript, in private possession of Judge Albert C. Cole, Peru, Ind.; Darling Papers, in private possession of Mrs. Maude Darling, Crete, Neb.; *Journal of the House of Burgesses* (Williamsburg, 1766), November 12, 19, 1766, pp. 18, 27. (This citation and all subsequent ones to the *Journal of the Virginia Convention*, the *Journals of the Council of Virginia*, the *Journal of the Senate of Virginia*, the *Journal of the Virginia House of Delegates*, etc., are *not* variant titles of the work, J. P. Kennedy and H. R. McIllwaine (eds.), *Journals of the House of Burgesses of Virginia*, cited in the Critical Essay on Authorities. They are instead the original editions of those various journals, printed immediately following the close of each session of the respective bodies and now located in the Library of Congress Rare Book Division. They carry no name of editor, and in most cases even the place of publication is not entirely clear. They will be referred to herein by date of session rather than by page numbers.)

The name Harrod is frequently misspelled in family and official records, appearing as Harwood, Herod, Horod, Haward, and Howard. Even today, members of the same branch of this family spell the name differently.

[3] Lawrence H. Gipson, *The British Empire Before the American Revolution* . . . (Vols. I-III, Caldwell, Ind., 1936; Vols. IV-VI, New York, 1939-1946), Vol. IV *(Zones of International Friction; North America South of the Great Lakes Region, 1748-1754)*, 228-29. For a detailed study of the Ohio Company's activities, see Kenneth P. Bailey, *The Ohio Company of Virginia and the Westward Movement, 1748-1792* (Glendale, Calif., 1939).

pedition to occupy the Ohio Company's new fort at the mouth of Redstone Creek on the Monongahela, from which point he hoped to drive the French from the Forks of the Ohio.[4] John Harrod and his friends liked and respected the dignified commander; furthermore they wanted to see the highly touted land the traders were always talking about.

But the expedition proved a disastrous one.[5] Washington's small army, which John Harrod joined at Wills Creek, moved over the newly cut Nemacolin Trail with the greatest difficulty. While the men sweated and groaned, the wagons broke down or became mired in spite of all the efforts of the soldiers to put the crude path in condition. When they reached the western slope of the Alleghenies, they received reports that the French troops at the Ohio had been strongly reinforced. It appeared that the Indians on whom they had counted as allies were deserting to the enemy.

At the Great Meadow—a level bottom traversed by a small creek and surrounded by heavy woodland—the commander ordered his men to erect a fortification. They set to work on an irregular square with strong picketing and three bastion gates, the whole to be surrounded by trenches. Washington was pleased with the new Fort Necessity and in his report to Governor Dinwiddie declared it "a good Intrenchment, and ... a charming field for an Encounter."[6]

While waiting for promised reinforcements from Virginia, Washington advanced with part of his army to Trader Gist's plantation near a mountain later named Braddock. He achieved a minor victory over the French and Indian force that had been lying in wait for him on the heights west of Laurel Hill, but news of the advancing French from Fort Duquesne compelled an order for retreat to the Great Meadow palisade.

The men hurried through the dark silent forest with its

[4] Gipson, *British Empire*, VI *(The Great War for the Empire; The Years of Defeat)*, 23; Justin Winsor, *The Mississippi Basin* (Boston, 1895), 254.
[5] Gipson, *British Empire*, VI, 28-32; Darling Papers.
[6] Quoted in Gipson, *British Empire*, VI, 30.

giant deciduous trees matted at the tops by overgrowth of vine and moss. Exhausted from lack of food and continuous march, they lined up in battle formation outside of the new fort at the Meadow. When the advanced French contingent began firing, the colonials jumped into their water-filled trenches and fired back. Amid rain and galling fire they kept on shooting until they were ordered to retreat to the fort.

After a day-long fight, Washington gave up the unequal struggle. When the French took over the next morning, the Indians rushed in the gates to pillage the colonials' baggage, shoot down their cows and horses, and kill a few men into the bargain. The soldiers recognized them as Shawnee, Delawares, and Mingos and pleaded with them to spare their goods; "but all the answer they got," according to one of Harrod's friends, "was calling them the worst name their Language admits of . . . ."[7]

John Harrod, who was among the many wounded, had to be carried by his tottering comrades a few miles a day to the Wills Creek camp. He and the other volunteers were too bewildered to question the wisdom or tactics of the sad expedition, but this they believed: Lieutenant Colonel Washington had behaved courageously throughout, and come what may they would join him any time he was ready to drive those French from the Ohio land. Soldiering was now in their blood. They had found a good colonial leader, and he was their idol. They did not know that they had fired the first shots in a larger conflict that would settle the fates of two empires and control their own destinies for thirty years to come.

It was not merely by accident that John had become a soldier. His earliest memories were of Indian conflict. Many times his father had told him of early days on the Susquehanna frontier where, along with other men from Pennsylvania and the shores of Maryland, he had tried to establish a home. About ten years after he had migrated from Bedfordshire, England, with his father and several of his brothers,

---

[7] *Ibid.*, 41-42.

John, Sr., was married and living in an isolated cabin near the river.[8] Here disaster struck. The young husband returned from a hunting trip to find that Indians had burned his house and killed his wife. Not far downstream he discovered her left hand, minus her wedding ring, lying in a canoe with part of the household stuff. Neighbors had rescued the babies, Thomas and John.[9] The father told how, soon after this tragedy, he had taken his sons to Baltimore to stay with his mother's family.[10] Then John Harrod met Sarah Moore, who was to become his second wife. Her father, James Moore, was a wealthy planter living near the mouth of Gunpowder River, by the thriving little town of Joppa. It was evident that Sarah's dignified mother, Frances Gay, would have preferred a young merchant or professional man for a son-in-law, but John had won the love of this high-spirited girl, and marry her he did.[11]

For the present John could offer Sarah little but hope. His father, James, would inherit a large landed estate in England—someday;[12] meanwhile, there was the new land being opened for settlement west of the Blue Ridge in the Valley of Virginia. So Sarah and John started out on horseback along the east bank of the Susquehanna to Harris' Ferry (Harrisburg), where they joined other families crossing the river and passing through the Conococheague Valley into Maryland again, down to Harper's Ferry and into the upper Shenandoah Valley—a place known to the Indians as the "daughter of the stars."[13]

Here the Harrods found the Vanmetres, the Shelbys, the

[8] Records of Walter Harrod, Nottinghamshire, England; Rachel Henton's Book. According to an interview in 1932 with a descendant, John Harrod, of Pewee Valley, Kentucky, the name of the first wife of John Harrod was Caroline Downey, "a black-haired, black-eyed Scotch-Irish girl." This Confederate veteran claimed to have made a lifelong study of the Harrod family.
[9] Rachel Henton's Book; Draper Collection, Wisconsin Historical Society, Madison, 37J168-74.
[10] Records in private possession of Bernice L. Swainson of Piedmont, Calif.
[11] Swainson records.
[12] Rachel Henton's Book; Walter Harrod records.
[13] Draper Collection, 37J168-74.

Walkers, the Hites, and many other families who had known John and his brothers when they were living in New Jersey a few years after their arrival in America. The fine, level, fertile river valley was suited to their needs. Here wild grape and pea vines, hardwood forest, and rich, deep limestone soil seemed ready to serve their comfort. There were large patches of open land, too, where many years earlier the Indians had set fire to the trees and brush to make cornfields or provide large areas into which they could drive game from the mountains.[14]

This land, too, had been stained with blood. The Delawares, Catawbas, and other tribes had fought bitter struggles over it only to find that none was strong enough to stay unchallenged, and gradually they had moved on to other hills and valleys.

Only now and then was John Harrod aware of their existence. Sometimes he saw a hungry brave creeping inside his fence to kill a fat hog or a few cattle, then stealing away like a ghost; or, as he rode across the green valley levels through the shoulder-high grass, John would discover one of many old Indian wells, dug and walled in, filled with clear, sweet water for the cook kettle. Along the stream banks he stepped on an occasional tomahawk or clay pipe—even a human skull to remind him of past warfare. But from the North Mountain in the east, across the broad valley to the northwest, where a range of spurs was dimly visible through the fine blue haze, all was peaceful.[15]

Within a few years, as he told his sons, John Harrod had reason to fear the Indians; but by that time a greater challenge faced him.[16] Like most of the settlers along the South

[14] Samuel Kercheval, *A History of the Valley of Virginia* (4th ed.; Strasburg, Va., 1925), Chap. I, "The Settlement of the Valley."
[15] *Ibid.*
[16] Susan W. Atkins (comp.), *Hereward Records and Papers, 1620-1940* (Greenfield, Ind., 1940), 178 ff., discusses at length a tradition that John Harrod was the John Howard (Haward) of the Salee narrative, the man who made a journey with Salee, his son Josiah, and one Poteat in 1742 to New Orleans, where he was imprisoned, sent to France, and released. The Walter

Branch, John Harrod had not bothered to make the long trip to Williamsburg or to Orange, the county seat, to secure land titles before moving in; he had settled on the first vacant spot that looked good to him, and since there were only a few hundred people in the valley, with no official to challenge him, there had been no argument.

On one point John Harrod had miscalculated. He had gone along in this manner, building his stone house, walling in his pastures, raising his small crops of tobacco and corn, only vaguely aware that an English lord named Fairfax held title to this district. But in 1746, when his son James was an infant, Harrod learned of a disturbing announcement. It seemed that Lord Fairfax had determined by survey that the Valley was a part of his holdings and was about to open a land office here—not to issue titles in small parcels of a hundred acres or so for a few shillings each, but to establish a large manor on which the settlers could remain, provided they were willing to take leases.

Unwilling to meet these terms and eager to own land outright, large numbers of John's neighbors became panic-stricken and moved out, some of them taking stock and baggage all the way to the back country of North Carolina. But the Harrods with a few others crossed the Potomac and made their way along an old Indian trail through western Maryland, northward into a beautiful valley called the Little Cove, so named because of the steep mountain wall surrounding it.[17]

The only trouble with the Cove was that it too was in disputed territory. Originally a part of Virginia, it had been cut off when Pennsylvania and Maryland became colonies, but there had been no clear definition of boundaries between

---

Harrod records repeat this story in part, giving an earlier date, 1703-1704, and stating that it was James Harrod, father of John, who was a prisoner of France. The Swainson records show a mass of circumstantial evidence to support the Atkins theory, but no conclusive proof is given.

[17] Draper Collection, 12CC22-23, 37J168-74, 4NN2-3.

the two. Neither colony was ready to make an outright claim, preferring to wait until British authorities established the line without question. Nor was this uncertainty the only one facing the Harrods in the Cove. The Indians still claimed the land west of the Kittatinny range on the ground that Great Britain had not concluded a treaty purchase—a customary procedure used to quiet the Indians prior to attempts at settlement. At first this omission did not bother the Harrods; but after more settlers had joined them, they discovered that the Delaware tribesmen were becoming increasingly angry and threatening to attack centers farther east, places such as Lancaster, if the newcomers did not move quickly. News of this threat spread through the country like leaves in an autumn wind, until the Council of Pennsylvania felt obliged to send its rotund secretary, the Reverend Richard Peters, and several commissioners to straighten out matters.[18]

Peters was a fortunate choice for the task. Basically a kindly man, but capable of using strong and abusive language when he chose, he was also a good diplomat. Working his way south from the Juniata River, Peters and the other commissioners gingerly ousted a few settlers, warning others off the "Indian land" and here and there burning cabins, usually only the "meanest ones." In each case Peters was careful to have the furnishings removed first and to direct the owners toward land farther east, even advancing them money to start out anew. To the settlers it all looked like a joke, but for the present the Indians were satisfied.[19]

When the commissioners reached the border of the Little Cove they stopped, fearful lest they stir up the old boundary dispute with Maryland. Instead of being pleased by this turn of fortune, John Harrod and his neighbors were actually

---

[18] Hubertus M. Cummings, *Richard Peters, Provincial Secretary* (Philadelphia, 1944), 154-56; Samuel Hazard (ed.), *Minutes of the Provincial Council of Pennsylvania . . . March 10, 1683—September 27, 1775* (Philadelphia, 1851-1852), V, 440-49.

[19] Cummings, *Richard Peters*, 154-56; Hazard (ed.), *Minutes of the Provincial Council*, V, 440-49.

disappointed. At Peters' suggestion they drew up a petition to the governor of Pennsylvania, declaring their belief that the Cove was north of the temporary boundary line and expressing their desire to be recognized as citizens of Pennsylvania. Not that Harrod or any of the other signers had much love for Pennsylvania. All they wanted was protection from the Indians and secure land titles. Since Maryland would offer none, they were turning to their northern neighbor. Peters at first refused to accept the petition because he felt that there were too few signers, so Harrod and the other advocates hastened to remedy this situation. Their efforts were useless, for they never heard from their petition; it disappeared among the Council's ever increasing stack of papers on the boundary question.[20]

Meanwhile John became uneasy over Indian attacks which were more frequent and savage. To play safe he moved his family through the narrow pass to the area east of the range in the Conococheague Valley, where they would be closer to Pennsylvania's frontier territory.[21] However, when the excitement over legalities again subsided, and the Indian terror reached a lull, the Harrods moved west once more. They settled north of their old home, in the Great Cove that nestled between two high ranges, crosscut by many low ridges and abounding in well-stocked streams and fertile pasture land. But despite this sheltered location, the Harrods were even nearer the unfriendly Indians—an ominous consideration, since they could expect little sympathy from Pennsylvania authorities.

For ten years John had been trying to establish roots in Pennsylvania, and always it had been the same story as in Virginia—hazy land titles and Indians. In 1754 he died, leaving his wife and dozen children with his dream of a rich inheritance in land unrealized.

[20] *Ibid.* (entire note).
[21] For record of purchase of farm, see court records of Warren Township, Franklin County, Pa., March 18, 1755; Filson Club Collection, Louisville. John, Jr., died on this farm (Rachel Henton's Book).

Sarah, the widow, had no easy life, but she was luckier than many she could have named. Including her stepsons, Tom and John, who were coming from Baltimore to live with her, she had six healthy boys—tall, straight-made, olive skinned and dark-eyed—all of them excepting four-year-old Levi able to read and write,[22] thanks mostly to Sarah to whom this skill was a matter of pride and not to be neglected in any case. Her oldest boy, Sam, had recently joined the Maryland militia; William, who was sixteen, could handle a gun and a plow as well as anyone; ten-year-old James was already a skilled woodsman. She also had six girls, two of them almost grown. Nellie was engaged to marry a friend of her half-brother John, and Sarah was happy about this. They would live in the Connallways, a section along North Mountain in the western part of Maryland, and provide a home for John, Jr., and Samuel when they were not on militia duty.[23]

For all she knew, Sarah might have to bundle up her children and move to Maryland, herself. One by one the widow's neighbors were sifting across the mountains, looking for haven from hostile tribesmen. But Sarah was reluctant to leave the plantation she and John had established. Even the killing of her hogs and sheep could not frighten her.

Then one November morning, the year after John had

---

[22] Documents in the private collection of Howard L. Leckey, Waynesburg, Pa. James Harrod has often been termed illiterate. See Lewis and Richard H. Collins, *History of Kentucky* (Covington, Ky., 1878), II, 619. An example of his handwriting, in Draper Collection, 1M109 (attested to by his nephew, William Harrod) in Draper Collection, 37J168-74, is reproduced facing page 222.

[23] Swainson records. For birthdate of James, see the list of recruits under Captain Gavin Cochrane in Sylvester K. Stevens and Donald H. Kent (eds.), *The Papers of Col. Henry Bouquet* (mimeographed, Harrisburg, Pa., 1940———), VII (Northwestern Pennsylvania Historical Series 21645), 2. In January, 1760, James gave his age as sixteen, his height as five feet, two and one-half inches. His nephew, William Harrod, said that he was born in 1742 (Draper Collection, 37J168-74), while his wife told her son-in-law, John Fauntleroy, that he "was about ten years older" than she (Draper Collection, 12C23). There is reason to believe that James was born as late as 1745. See Capt. Cochrane to Col. Bouquet, in Stevens and Kent (eds.), *Bouquet Papers*, VII (N.W. Pa. Hist. Ser. 21645), 32-33.

died, Patrick Burns, who had been captured by the Indians, escaped and came running into the Great Cove, shouting that King Shingas, the great Delaware warrior whose hands had long been stained by white man's blood, was on his way to make ashes of the cabins and scalp every man, woman, and child he could find. Some of Sarah's neighbors refused to believe this rumor, but she knew the time had come. Without waiting to gather her pots and blankets together, she lifted young Levi, Elizabeth, and Jemima onto her one remaining horse; then, followed by the older children, she hurried toward the eastern sun.[24] A dozen other families straggled along up the steep wooded slope toward the river pass that led to the new Fort Littleton on the other side of the mountain. At the summit of the first foothill Sarah and her neighbors turned to have one last look at the valley. Before their eyes was an awesome spectacle of destruction. Their houses were in flames; Delawares were riding like wild men through the Great Cove; and even at this distance the refugees could hear "the last shrieks of their dying neighbors."[25]

Refugees crowded into the rectangular Fort Littleton, and by the following April the surrounding area was deserted. One report said that the people were "gathering in the greatest consternation." As added protection a garrison of seventy-five men was ordered to range the woods each day.[26]

It was during this year that Sarah's boys James and Will began their long military careers. They served first as guards at Fort Littleton, then as rangers and spies, and finally as commissioned officers. The boys vied with each other, testing their strength and skills. James was the marksman of the Harrod family and Will the strongest at hand-to-hand com-

[24] This material has been drawn from a biographical sketch of James Harrod by Reuben G. Thwaites (ed.), *Wither's Chronicles of Border Warfare* (Cincinnati, 1912), 190-91. The original sketch was based on the Draper Collection.
[25] Israel D. Rupp, *The History and Topography of . . . Cumberland, Bedford, Franklin . . . Counties* (Lancaster, Pa., 1848), 77-78, 89-94.
[26] For a description of this fort, see George D. Albert, *The Frontier Forts of Western Pennsylvania*, 2 vols. (Harrisburg, 1896), I, 555-56.

bat. In the stress of danger, alternating with humdrum confinement, there were frequent opportunities to display these skills.

One day, according to the story related by his eldest son, Will was hanging around the fort with little to do, talking and perhaps arguing with other teen-age boys, when one of them began to taunt him. Now the Harrods never carried chips, but neither would they receive a "contumelious insult" unchallenged. Will suggested they "have it out in a fisticuff fight." Spectators crowded round, eager to be in on the excitement; and when Harrod finally emerged disheveled but victorious, they all shouted, "Hurrah for the widow's sons!"[27]

This display of strength and the manifestation of other respected frontier talents must have enhanced Will's reputation, for soon after the encounter the eighteen-year-old youth received a sergeant's commission.[28]

By this time it was becoming evident even to the comparatively isolated Western settlers that the peace so necessary to the development of their plantations was not on the horizon. Even as Sarah moved back to her husband's old plantation on the Conococheague, her stepson John was already enlisted in a new campaign designed to drive the French from the upper Ohio Valley.[29]

The issue of who rightly owned this fertile area was a complicated one. Pennsylvania believed that by the terms of her charter it was hers, but Virginia refused to agree. Great Britain was not concerned with the merits of either case but looked on the French occupation as a serious threat to the very existence of her valuable Indian frontier trade and a menace to all her northern American colonies. "The first point we have laid down is, that the colonies must not be abandoned," wrote one member following resolutions adopted by the British Cabinet Council, "that our rights and possessions in North

---

[27] Draper Collection, 37J168-74.
[28] *Ibid.*
[29] See note 2 of this chapter.

America must be maintained and the French obliged to desist from their hostile attempts to dispossess us." [30]

It was with this larger view in mind that they appointed a British professional soldier, Major General Edward Braddock, as commander in chief of the forces in America. A man with forty-three years of experience in the Coldstream Guards and no newcomer to mountain tactics, Braddock, with two regiments of Irish troops as a backbone, could be expected to do a brilliant job of welding the raw, undisciplined colonial troops into an efficient fighting unit.

On this point the British miscalculated. The backwoods colonials, jealous of the professional soldier from overseas, were inclined to scoff at Braddock's rigid discipline and elaborate orders. He was haughty, he talked in strange terms of formations and of line, and he even forbade swearing and drinking. Furthermore, he used snuff.[31] The backwoodsmen watched glumly while the new commander gathered his forces at the new Fort Cumberland on Wills Creek. They gazed curiously at the brilliant red uniforms of the British regulars. What excellent targets for French bullets! Look at the rows of brass buttons as they catch the sunlight—whoever heard of fighting Indians in fancy dress! They looked down at their own greasy, frayed hunting shirts, their deerskin leggings, their motley array of firearms. The contrast was pathetic. But they had fought Indians before in this garb. It was well suited to mud and mire. The backwoodsmen neither knew nor cared that these brilliantly clad soldiers with their martinet commander looked on them as poor excuses for fighting men, undisciplined, untrained, and badly equipped.

Nor were they aware of the troubles that beset Braddock on every side—inadequate support from colonial governments, difficulties in obtaining wagons and horses for transport, poor

[30] Quoted in Gipson, *British Empire*, VI, 55.
[31] Draper Collection, 15E47.

roads connecting Fort Cumberland with the East, and failure of the promised Indian allies to put in an appearance.[32]

The one bright spot in the mind of John and Samuel Harrod was that Washington had joined Braddock's staff.

Early in June the four-mile-long caravan left Cumberland on its march to Fort Duquesne. It was an agonizingly slow journey through immense forests of white pine and northern cypress, and hardwoods with interlocking branches, and up steep precipices and down through swampy ravines crawling with snakes and wood ticks. Horses tumbled over rocky ledges, wagon axles broke, the men sickened on their salt-meat diet, and many of them, including Washington, became victims of the bloody flux.

At the Little Meadow, Braddock called a council. Washington urged "in the warmest terms" that they push on with only the barest essentials, leaving the bulk of the equipment to follow in slow stages.[33] Braddock heeded this advice. But the going was still slow because of the need for road clearing and bridge building. The horses sweated and galled as they dragged their dead weight of howitzers and cannon through the bogs, and the soldiers came to their aid with tackle and blocks.

While John and Sam Harrod were pushing wearily ahead with Washington and Braddock, their young brothers Jim and Will enrolled at Fort Littleton to help James Burd, a fiery Scotch immigrant who had been living at Shippensburg, to build a supply road to connect eastern Pennsylvania with the advancing British forces near the three forks of the Youghiogheny River (the location of the modern town of

---

[32] For a detailed description of this campaign, see Gipson, *British Empire*, VI, 62-98. An older study containing reproductions of related maps and documents is Winthrop Sargent, *The History of an Expedition Against Duquesne under ... Braddock* (Philadelphia, 1855). See also Stanley Pargellis, "Braddock's Defeat," in *American Historical Review* (New York), XLI (1935-1936), 253-69, and *The Olden Time ...* (Pittsburgh), I (1846), 89-91, for Franklin's estimate of Braddock.

[33] Gipson, *British Empire*, VI, 82.

Confluence).[34] Many delays and considerable bad feeling between Pennsylvania authorities and the British commanders hampered the progress of this vital connecting link. There was already a rough wagon trail as far as Chambersburg, near Sarah Harrod's plantation, but beyond, only a hunter's trace.

Burd called for more road builders, although he scarcely knew how he would be able to supply them with food, firearms, and digging tools. Still the frontiersmen pressed forward. News reached the half-starved men that the "French Indians" were waiting for them, that in fact a man had been scalped and a boy captured in the mountains ahead.

A company was sent out to cover their operations. The men "cut away sturdy timber," broke up "the hard rock without the aid of dynamite, found a suitable grade over such mountainous heights as Sideling Hill," and made a good wagon road through sixty-five miles of wilderness to a point a few miles west of Raystown (Bedford).[35]

But the road was not used to supply Braddock as intended, for word reached the road builders that Braddock had been defeated soon after he crossed the Monongahela. Indians had ambushed the main force, scattering them in confusion. The backwoodsmen took to trees and rocks to fight the Indians in their own way, while Braddock tried heroically to realign his army. In the end, after five horses had been shot from under him, the commander was fatally wounded. Washington narrowly missed being killed, and John Harrod received a serious injury for which the Virginia House of Burgesses later granted him a pension.[36] Samuel was unhurt.

In spite of the gloom that spread like mountain haze over Pennsylvania, Maryland, and Virginia, the disaster had not been without a brighter side. The Harrods and their friends undoubtedly blamed their defeat on Braddock, whose in-

---

[34] Lily Lee Nixon, *James Burd, Frontier Defender* (Philadelphia, 1941), 21-34.
[35] *Ibid.*
[36] See note 2 of this chapter.

experience in wilderness travel and ignorance of Indian methods of warfare were to them convenient excuses for the failure of the expedition. They would have been the last to admit it, but the frontiersmen owed a great debt to this brave commander. His army had demonstrated for the first time that it was possible to carry great loads of equipment across the mountains, a feat unparalleled in the military annals of this country.[37]

John and Sam Harrod had been the first of the Harrods to see the Ohio Valley, but Sam, Jim, and Will would be the first of the family to live there. The road they had made was pointing the way which the pioneers would travel twelve years later to settle the upper Ohio Valley.

[37] Solon J. and Elizabeth H. Buck, *The Planting of Civilization in Western Pennsylvania* (Pittsburgh, 1939), 82; Gipson, *British Empire*, VI, 78. For documents covering the broader significance of Braddock's appointment, see Clarence E. Carter (ed.), *The Correspondence of General Thomas Gage, with the Secretaries of State, 1763-1775* (New Haven, 1931-1933).

Chapter II
THE ROAD BUILDERS
(1756-1767)

... he brought to a happy issue a most extraordinary campaign, and made a willing sacrifice of his own life to what he valued more, the interest of his King and Country.[1]

THE GLOOM displayed in England and along the American seaboard as the result of Braddock's defeat was even more keenly felt on the frontier. With aid from the French the Indians renewed their raids, and as a result the colonials had more men killed and captured during the three years that followed than in the preceding battles.

The Harrods were forced to lay aside their ploughs to join in the defense. Sam and Tom, newly arrived from Baltimore, joined Alexander Beall's company at Fort Frederick; and Will soon followed, although he also enlisted for a short term as commissary at Fort Littleton.[2]

One day while Will was stationed at Fort Littleton, a party of Indians made a sudden stab at the fort, killing a few men. Those who managed to escape reported that the attackers numbered as many as fifty. A party of this size roaming the country was a real danger, and Will Harrod, never one to

---

[1] Obituary of Gen. John Forbes from the Philadelphia *Pennsylvania Gazette*, March 15, 1759, as printed in Alfred P. James (ed.), *The Writings of General John Forbes* (Menasha, Wis., 1938), 301-302.

[2] Draper Collection, 11DD1-2, 11DD27, 1JJ20-21. See Draper's Index to Volume JJ. See also note 2, Chap. I of this study.

hold back, raised a company of thirty-five men from Juniata and a neighboring fort to track down the attackers. Following the signs left by the Indians in their hurried retreat, Will's men caught sight of their enemies shortly after dark. Since the Indian party was large and the volunteers' only hope would be to take them off guard, Will made camp at the head of a hollow in order to start an early-morning attack. At dawn, but before the Indians had a chance to grab their rifles, he gave the signal to shoot.

The men fired from two or three directions at once. At the first crack several tribesmen fell; the others fled in panic without firing a shot, leaving their firearms on the ground along with blankets and various kinds of plunder. With this booty Will and his men returned in triumph to the fort.[3]

Numerous Indian attacks demoralized the inhabitants of frontier Pennsylvania. The residents of Cumberland sent hysterical petitions to Philadelphia, pleading for aid, describing incursions into the county, and pointing out that they were incapable of defending themselves. To the Reverend Richard Peters they wrote: "May it please all to whom this shall come, to consider what an evil case we will be exposed to, in leaving our places, grain and cattle; for we are not able to buy provisions for our families, much less for our cattle. And to live here we cannot. . . . Begging for God's sake, you may take pity upon our families. . . ."[4]

In spite of the general hysteria the Widow Harrod would not budge, probably because of news which arrived unexpectedly from Philadelphia. The peace-loving Assembly had finally aroused itself, contributing £60,000 to the defense of the colony and passing a militia act. Provisions were also made for the construction of new forts along the Blue Mountains. After Colonel John Armstrong's victory over the Delawares at Kittanning (where he lost almost as many men as the Indians), the settlers began to take heart, realizing that the fa-

---

[3] Draper Collection, 37J168-74.
[4] Rupp, *History and Topography*, 119-21.

vorite rendezvous for expeditions against them had been destroyed.[5]

The Quakers refused to put their faith in declarations of war against the Shawnee and Delawares, however, and continued their efforts to win over the Indians by diplomatic action.[6] These efforts began to take root, partly because of events abroad. The conflict that had begun with Washington's expedition to the Ohio had now developed into a world war, and the French found themselves unable to supply their Canadian and Ohio Valley forces. The Allegheny, named by the Indians the River of Blood, had up to now been their chief northern artery. Fewer and fewer boatloads of food, ammunition, and expensive Indian presents came down its beautiful course, a fact that was not lost on the tribal allies.[7]

In 1758 Great Britain launched plans for a three-pronged campaign against the French: an attack on Canada by way of Lake Champlain, a naval assault on Louisburg, and, what was most important to the Harrods, an advance on Fort Duquesne. Brigadier General John Forbes, a handsome, mild-mannered soldier experienced in European warfare, was made commander of the forces against the Forks of the Ohio. For ten weeks, beginning in April, he remained in Philadelphia assembling his expedition.[8] Whereas speed had been essential in 1755, the declining French fortunes were now working in favor of the American and British.

During these hard weeks, harassed by difficulties with colonial legislatures from whom he laboriously pried troops and supplies, General Forbes never lost sight of the problems which had contributed to Braddock's defeat. "It is needless to sett forth the necessity that there is, to examine the Strength, nature, and Genius of any people, that you wage warr with," he declared soon after his arrival in America, "but

[5] Buck, *Planting of Civilization*, 85.
[6] *Ibid.*
[7] *Ibid.*, 82-86; Draper Collection, 13E1.
[8] For contemporary documents on this campaign, see James (ed.), *Writings of Forbes.*

it is absolutely necessary for a Commander in Chief, to have a perfect knowledge of that country where the warr is most likely to be carryed on. . . ."[9] Furthermore, from the first he studied carefully the problem of supplying his troops on the march and made continuous effort to enlist Indian allies.

Tom, Will, and Sam Harrod witnessed a part of these negotiations while they were serving with Evan Shelby at the new Fort Frederick, near North Mountain in Maryland, during 1757 and 1758. Word had reached the Cherokee and Catawbas that Pennsylvania was making peace with their tribal enemies, the Shawnee and Delawares, and a party of them came to Frederick "desirous of smoking a pipe" and expressing their disapproval of these tactics. Alexander Beall, who was in command of the Maryland forces stationed there, tried to placate the Indians, inviting the principal warriors to dine with him and the garrison, meanwhile sending out a hurry call for presents. On the evening of the dinner, Beall laid the gifts in two parcels on a table, and when the Indians had assembled he presented them and formed a "League of Friendship" wherein he agreed to treat with the Indians at all times.[10]

The Marylanders and Virginians managed to collect six hundred Cherokee and Catawbas at Winchester, but delays in launching Forbes's expedition, the late arrival of presents and food supplies, coupled with the Indians' impatience caused most of them to drift south to their home territory. Their presence had had a beneficial effect during the long months prior to the campaign, however; frequent forays against their Northern enemies kept the frontiers quiet, allowing the militia a breathing spell in which to recruit men and build roads.

The problem of which road he would take toward Duquesne caused General Forbes much trouble. At first it ap-

---

[9] *Ibid.*, 33.
[10] William H. Browne (ed.), *Archives of Maryland* (Baltimore, 1883-1912), VI, 557-59.

peared that it would be best to go as far as Raystown (Bedford), thence to the new Fort Cumberland, and then by way of Braddock's old trail to the Monongahela. But this idea was abandoned in favor of the more direct route across Pennsylvania.[11] The Harrods found themselves aligned on both sides of this argument, one in which their friend Evan Shelby took a prominent role.

The Harrods had known Evan Shelby since their early days at the Great Cove.[12] The son of Welsh immigrants, he had developed into a highly respected leader among frontiersmen. Strong-minded, with boundless energy and strength, he was also moderate in speech and habit, well disciplined, and intelligent. Shelby had been a friend of John Harrod, Sr., and he took a kindly interest in Harrod's boys. His sons and nephews, too, were to be associated with the Harrods for many years to come—Isaac as the first governor of Kentucky, and Evan, son of Evan Shelby's brother Rees, as the husband of the Harrods' sister Mary. Tom and Sam helped Shelby blaze and construct a new road between Fort Frederick and Cumberland;[13] and when after a long argument the Marylanders and Virginians finally gave up hope of routing Forbes through their provinces instead of across Pennsylvania, the older Harrod brothers followed Shelby to Shippensburg to enlist in Forbes's campaign under Colonel Henry Bouquet, the deputy commander.[14] The problem of rival colonial land and trade interests, which was the crux of the argument, could hardly have concerned these woodsmen. They arrived well equipped with blankets, moccasins, and camp kettles, supplied by Governor Horatio Sharpe, who also sent to Forbes a letter recommending Shelby and his men.[15]

[11] Buck, *Planting of Civilization*, 90.
[12] Draper Collection, 11DD6; Browne (ed.), *Archives of Maryland*, IX, 164-65; Swainson records.
[13] Company rolls of Beall and Shelby, Draper Collection, 11DD2, 11DD27; records in the possession of Cass K. Shelby, Hollidaysburg, Pa.
[14] Stevens and Kent (eds.), *Bouquet Papers*, V (N.W. Pa. Hist. Ser. 21643), 154; Browne (ed.), *Archives of Maryland*, IX, 164-65, 237.
[15] Browne (ed.), *Archives of Maryland*, IX, 237-38.

Jim Harrod, who was again serving under Colonel James Burd, was helping build a fort at the end of the road to Raystown. Although the dispute over the route was still in progress, Shelby's company joined Burd in the slow arduous task of carrying the trail across the mountains from Raystown to Loyalhanna on the west side of Laurel Hill, ". . . hewing, digging, blasting, laying fascines and gabions . . . along the sides of deep declivities, or worming their way like moles through the jungle of swamp and forest."[16]

Forbes, suffering from a complication of serious illnesses, directed the operations from his bed at Carlisle, reporting his delight that the enemy was apparently under the impression that the forces would advance over Braddock's road. Under these orders Shelby and his men made a scouting tour to the vicinity of Fort Duquesne to find out, if possible, how strong the garrison was there. To spur them in their efforts, Forbes told Bouquet to allot the men a "Gill of Spirits" each day.[17]

In spite of this "fortification" they were unable to learn anything of note concerning the French garrison, but a week later, under Major James Grant, they paid heavily for the desired information. Grant, apparently overconfident, attacked an encampment at Duquesne, whereupon the French poured out of the fort in large numbers, outflanked the provincials, and inflicted a stunning defeat.

The 540 remaining of the original force of 800, minus Grant, who had been taken prisoner, stumbled back to Loyalhanna. Shelby and the Harrods escaped injury. The one consolation for the English was that the northern and western Indians decided to return home from Duquesne to celebrate the victory and divide the booty.[18]

Soon after the return of Grant's force, Colonel Burd, who was now in command, received orders to build a fort enclosing the storehouses at Loyalhanna and to proceed with the road building toward the French fort. The Harrods along

[16] James (ed.), *Writings of Forbes*, 173; Albert, *Frontier Forts*, II, 196.
[17] James (ed.), *Writings of Forbes*, 173-95.
[18] Buck, *Planting of Civilization*, 92.

with 550 others set to work with Shelby in charge.[19] One morning they were alarmed by the sound of firing and Indian halloos a mile distant. Running up to meet the attack, the Marylanders encountered a brisk fire which sent them reeling back toward the fort. Burd sent out reinforcements to assist the encircled troops, but since it now became apparent that the French had a considerable force, a third battalion was sent forward. In about an hour the men, followed by the enemy, had backed to the palisade. Burd fired on the French with all the cannon at his command, and after several hours they retired. Although momentarily happy over their success, the English were soon demoralized by the assertion of an enemy prisoner that Fort Duquesne had been greatly reinforced with men and provisions, sufficient to withstand a siege. Forbes was in despair over the possible failure of the entire expedition.[20]

A month later when the commander—carried in a sling between two horses and unable to stand without assistance—arrived at Loyalhanna, an Englishman who had escaped from the French told him the truth about Fort Duquesne. The supply of provisions there was now so low that all but two hundred troops had been sent to Detroit and other French garrisons. Forbes and his men, heartened by this news, gave up the plan for wintering at the fort and made immediate preparations for advancing to the Forks.[21]

The road beyond Loyalhanna was unfinished, but Forbes, his spirits high, moved with dispatch toward his destination, leaving wagons and heavy artillery behind.

William Harrod must have been chagrined, as was Colonel Burd, when he was assigned to help care for the stores. But his brothers went on with Forbes and a week later arrived at Duquesne. As they approached the fort they saw a cloud of smoke. At six that night they found that the French had al-

[19] Stevens and Kent (eds.), *Bouquet Papers*, V (N.W. Pa. Hist. Ser. 21643), 184.
[20] James, (ed.), *Writings of Forbes*, 234-40.
[21] Buck, *Planting of Civilization*, 94.

most destroyed the installment. Rummaging around in the ruins the men salvaged sixteen barrels of ammunition, a large quantity of old carriage iron, barrels of guns, and a cartload of scalping knives.[22]

The mortally ill Forbes wrote a triumphant letter to William Pitt, telling him of the success of "His Majesty's arms" and of the enemy's retreat by boat down the Ohio. "So give me leave to congratulate you upon this great Event, of having totally expelled the French from this prodigious tract of Country, and of having reconciled the various tribes of Indians inhabiting it to His Majesty's Government. . . . I have used the freedom of giving your name to Fort DuQuesne, as I hope it was in some measure the being actuated by your spirits that now makes us Masters of the place. . . ."[23]

Leaving several hundred men to erect the new Fort Pitt amid the ruins, Forbes declared the campaign at an end and sent the troops back to their homes.

To the Harrods and thousands of other provincials the close of the campaign was not the end. They had stood on the angular piece of ground above the junction of the swift waters of the Allegheny and the more sluggish Monongahela, watching the conflicting currents as they merged to form the Ohio —the gateway to a new frontier. Only a month later one of these men penned a rapturous description of the country. He envisioned a new colony which would be impervious to French interference. "The importance of such a colony to Britain would be vastly great," he wrote, "since the climate, and its remoteness from the sea, would turn it immediately to raising raw silk, an article of vast expence to our nation, which we are at continual difficulties and disappointments in procuring. . . . The Ohio is naturally furnished with salt, coal, limestone, grindstone, millstone, clay for glass-houses and pottery. . . ."[24]

But there was more work and fighting ahead before the

[22] Draper Collection, 7J84-100; Swainson records.
[23] James (ed.), *Writings of Forbes*, 267-69.
[24] Draper Collection, 1JJ142.

Harrods could settle in this new land. The road at the Forks of the Ohio had to be improved, storehouses and forts erected, and provisions carried to the new garrison.[25] Jim, Tom, and Will Harrod had little time to spend at home, nor had Sam, either, for he and Jim went out to the Illinois country, probably with troops sent to garrison the new British military establishment there.[26] But Sarah was not lonely; for John, still not recovered from his wounds, had recently married Rachel Shepherd and brought her home to live with them.

The cost of maintaining the small fort at Pittsburgh was high because of the great distance and the constant need for supplying the Indians with food and presents to keep them in a good humor. The British grew tired of the continual outlay and began to complain that it was unnecessary.

This brought on discontent among the tribesmen, who could not understand why the English, now that they had defeated the French, did not retire to their homes and leave the country to its rightful owners.[27] Attacks on parties of road makers forced the Harrods to take up their rifles again. Rumors of grumbling came from the Delawares, the Shawnee, the Mingos and the Seneca; but a full-scale rebellion such as developed was not anticipated, for the frontiersmen well knew that tribes seldom co-operated in attacking white settlements.

When the Pennsylvania and Lake Erie tribes discovered that they had been handed over to the English by the French at the close of the Seven Years' War in 1763, they at last banded together under the Ottawa chieftain Pontiac.[28] Long resentful of their vassalage under the powerful Six Nations, they despised even more this highhanded method of placing them "under the protection" of the white men. One by one the settlers who had pushed westward along Forbes's road were

[25] Stevens and Kent (eds.), *Bouquet Papers*, VI (N.W. Pa. Hist. Ser. 21644), Foreword and p. 98.
[26] Draper Collection, 12CC97.
[27] Buck, *Planting of Civilization*, 100.
[28] For a detailed study of this warfare, see Howard H. Peckham, *Pontiac and the Indian Uprising* (Princeton, 1947).

wiped out, captured, or forced to flee to Fort Littleton for safety, while the new Western forts erected in the flush of victory were besieged and many of them captured.

Finally Bouquet received orders to march to the beleaguered Fort Pitt. He set up headquarters at Carlisle, and once more the Harrods volunteered, Will as orderly sergeant, and Jim as ranger in Captain John Piper's company. Bouquet, with his force of five hundred men started west in July, 1763.

A month later near Bushy Run, only fifteen miles from Pittsburgh, the advance guard was attacked. Trying to confuse the Pennsylvanians with tactics similar to those which had won the spectacular victory over Braddock, the Indians spread out through the forest. Although the British troops incurred heavy losses, they managed to outwit their foe by a mock retreat. When the Indians left cover, they attacked them from the sides and dispersed them after heavy hand-to-hand fighting. Discouraged by the defeat, the tribesmen returned to their villages beyond Fort Pitt, restoring for the time being the British supremacy in the upper Ohio Valley. Apparently the dreary Indian war was coming to an end.

The lull that followed was brief, and the northern Pennsylvania tribes again took up the fight, causing wide damage in the province. The next year Jim and Will marched again under Bouquet to Fort Pitt, where preparations for an expedition to the heart of the Indian trouble got under way. Awaiting reinforcements from Virginia, the men drilled and organized their force. Jim Harrod came in fourth at a shooting match in which both the First and Second Pennsylvania battalions participated. Will made several journeys eastward in a difficult search for wagons and horses. Some of the animals were so poor they died on the road, while the twenty he brought in to headquarters on one occasion were "unfitt for any Bussiness."[29]

Meanwhile Sir William Johnson, British Indian agent in

---

[29] Stevens and Kent (eds.), *Bouquet Papers*, III (N.W. Pa. Hist. Ser. 21653), 321; *ibid.*, IV (N.W. Pa. Hist. Ser. 21654), 23, 69-70.

The Indians delivering up the English Captives to Colonel Bouquet, near his Camp at the Forks of Muskingum in North America in Nov.R 1764. *Library of Congress, Prints and Photographs Division.*

the Northern Department, invited the Seneca to a conference and persuaded them to withdraw from the war. Also, a northern expedition under Colonel John Bradstreet made a preliminary treaty with the Delawares and Shawnee; so that by the time Bouquet's army reached the Muskingum, the remaining tribesmen were ready to give up the struggle.

At the mouth of Whiteman Creek the commander made camp and awaited the surrender of the colonials whom the Indians had been holding as hostages. A contemporary newspaper clipping gives a colorful account of the proceedings. Here in early November the Seneca, Delawares, and Shawnee, according to agreement, delivered their 206 prisoners and promised to bring in 100 more in the spring. Fathers recognized lost children; husbands found their wives. The Indians "delivered up their beloved captives with the utmost reluctance—shed torrents of tears over them—recommending them to the care and protection of the commanding officer. Their regard to them continued all the while they remained in camp. They visited them from day to day, brought them what corn, skins, horses, and other matters had been bestowed upon them while in their families .... Nay ... when the army marched, some of the Indians solicited and obtained permission to accompany their former captives to Fort Pitt and employed themselves in hunting and bringing provisions for them on the way...."[30] One young Mingo persisted in following "his wife" at the risk of his own scalp. During the following weeks and months many who had been released found themselves unable to adjust to civilization and returned to the Indians.[31]

Nor were all the soldiers under Bouquet eager to return to "civilization." Will returned home and the next year married Amelia Stevens, but he could not forget the Monongahela country. He had seen the gentle, rolling hills along the tributary of Ten Mile Creek, a few miles below Redstone,

[30] Draper Collection, 26CC3.
[31] *Ibid.*

and noted that it was fertile and easy to cultivate—an ideal place for settlement. Indeed, many families were already bringing their ploughs and axes to the region, in spite of a British proclamation, issued in the fall of 1763, prohibiting "for the present" any settlement or purchases of Indian land west of the Allegheny watershed. However, few of the backwoodsmen looked on this proclamation as more than a temporary expedient to quiet the Indians.[32] When Thomas Gist, son of the trader Christopher Gist, who had already made a settlement east of the Monongahela, offered to get them title to the Ten Mile Tract, Jim rushed back to the Conococheague, after his service in the Illinois country, to tell his brothers and mother the good news. Will, living on his father's old claim in the Little Cove, was enthusiastic; but John preferred to remain on the Conococheague plantation. Sarah began packing at once, and the Hughes, the Swanns, the Vanmetres, and others did too. When all were ready they started from Fort Cumberland on Wills Creek for Ten Mile Creek, along Braddock's old trail.[33]

Sarah must have had a difficult time trying to decide what to take along, for only the mere essentials—clothing, feather beds, a few cooking utensils, and seeds—could be packed into the two or three wagons that must serve the company. But Jim no doubt assured her that they would not lack for food. Deer, turkey, and bear were plentiful in the Ten Mile country, and the creek itself was well stocked with bass and catfish. Pumpkin and corn would add variety to their meals by dint of their own industry, and wild berries and greens had only to be gathered.[34]

The immigrants left Braddock's road six miles east of the present city of Uniontown and pushed on to Redstone, setting up camp on the west side of the river near the mouth of

---

[32] James Veech, *The Monongahela of Old* . . . (Pittsburgh, 1858-1892), 84; Buck, *Planting of Civilization*, 111-13; John C. Fitzpatrick (ed.), *The Writings of Washington* . . . , 39 vols. (Washington, 1931-1944), II, 468-69.
[33] Collection of H. L. Leckey.
[34] Draper Collection, 23CC1 and 11E14-16.

Ten Mile Creek. George Hupp and his family were living in a near-by cabin. His wife, who had been the only white woman there, cooked tasty meals for the families, as she had for lonely hunters and land seekers since her arrival. There is a tradition that the men used to gather at the Hupp cabin on Sundays just to have a taste of home cooking and a look at a white woman.[35]

Jim and Will, with Gist and the other men, followed the course of Ten Mile Creek, from its steep banks at the mouth, along its gently winding course to the south fork, through a forest of hickory, sugar maple and locust. Soon after the Harrods and their neighbors had marked off their clearings and set fire to the trees, great volumes of smoke filled the air, and the sky was brightened by the flames that served as beacons to other immigrants pouring into the fertile valley.

After burning and chopping down most of the trees, Jim and Will girdled those remaining to kill the foliage. For years thereafter these gaunt testimonials to advancing civilization dropped their dead twigs and branches to renew the deep rich soil.

The Harrods had only to walk to the edge of their new clearings to find virgin chestnut trees, ideal for split-rail fencing. Black walnut and oak formed the walls of their cabins, and tall straight pines from the creek bottom served as ridgepoles. Maples, tapped by a slash of the ax, furnished sugar. The women could roam the woods gathering wild orchids, lady's slippers, and golden seal to brighten their crude slab tables.[36]

The Widow Sarah, surrounded by children and friends, was snug and comfortable in her new home. This was the good life her sons had been fighting for, and she was content.

---

[35] Andrew J. Waycoff, *Local History* (Waynesburg, Pa., n.d.), No. 145, published by the Waynesburg *Democrat Messenger*.
[36] Collection of H. L. Leckey.

Chapter III

THE WESTERN FEVER
(1767-1773)

"Any person therefore who neglects the present oppertunity of hunting out good Lands . . . will never regain it. . . ."[1]

JIM HARROD scarcely had time to settle his mother in her new cabin when he again went out to the Illinois country. Sam, his period of enlistment in the Illinois troops finished, had turned to fur trading, and Jim wanted to join him.[2] Since individual Englishmen, working alone, were having difficulty competing with the more adroit French traders, Sam had moved to Kaskaskia; there he soon learned to speak French and won friends among the traders, with whom he worked in partnership. Jim found this life much more exciting than the more prosaic one of farming. Besides it was difficult for a young man who had been in military service since boyhood to settle down. He and Sam got on well with the lighthearted Frenchmen, and it was not long before they had built up a lucrative business in furs, traveling with their

[1] George Washington to William Crawford, September 21, 1767, in Fitzpatrick (ed.), *Writings of Washington*, II, 469.

[2] Draper Collection, 12CC97-98. While there is no direct evidence to prove that Sam and Jim were among the troops sent to the Illinois country, it is presumed from this Draper manuscript and from the fact that Jim Harrod was serving in Piper's and Cochrane's companies at Fort Pitt during these years, that they were in military service in the Illinois country also. Neither appears in Pennsylvania records at that time. In 1772 James was listed in tax assessments of Bedford County as head of a family. While this might indicate that he was married, it is more likely that he headed his mother's household. Two of her grandchildren were living with her. Collection of H. L. Leckey; Swainson records.

cargoes down the Mississippi to New Orleans in violation of British orders to take the peltry to Fort Pitt. Since the prices at the Gulf port were higher, why make the tedious journey to the Forks of the Ohio?[3]

In the course of their fur-trapping and hunting activities, the Harrods traveled far into territory east of the Mississippi, into Tennessee and Kentucky. On one of these journeys Jim and Sam met their old friends of Indian war days, Michael Stoner and Daniel Boone.[4] Stoner's real name was George Michael Holsteiner, which had been shortened to suit the convenience of clerks and record keepers. Although of massive, powerful build, Stoner was famous for his remarkable agility; while his lovable ways, his kind heart, and his amusing gutteral accent endeared him to friends as much as did his skill in woodcraft and hunting.

The two parties met by accident up the Tennessee River at the site of the present city of Nashville, where deer, bear, buffalo, and otter were abundant. They must have had a good time talking over their exciting years in the campaigns of Forbes and Braddock, but it was talk of the future that absorbed most of their interest. Boone, who had settled in the back country of North Carolina, had like the Harrods contracted the "western fever" and had traveled around the forest lands marking trees and stumps with his initials, with a view toward possible settlement.

On his return trip to Ten Mile to visit his mother, Jim followed the north bank of the Ohio, making friends with the Indians, even sharing their huts and food and accompanying them on hunting trips into Kentucky.[5] He found the

---

[3] Clarence W. Alvord, *The Mississippi Valley in British Politics* (Cleveland, 1917), I, 303.

[4] Draper Collection, 37J168-74, 12CC97-98; Collins, *Kentucky*, II, 417; Theodore Roosevelt, *The Winning of the West*, 7 vols. (New York, 1906), I, 185. John Haywood, *The Civil and Political History of . . . Tennessee . . .* (Knoxville, 1823), 75, does not give the name of James or Sam, but merely leaves a blank space in front of the name Harrod. Other historians mention either Jim or Sam; it seems most likely that both were there.

[5] Draper Collection, 12CC97.

Delawares so congenial that he frequently tarried for several months in their towns. The Indians liked this slim, erect, bronze-skinned frontiersman with his prominent nose and long black beard.

Between visits with the Delawares Jim often journeyed along the ridge of the Alleghenies, stopping to visit friends along the Greenbriar, Holston, and Clinch rivers. In 1771 he discovered that his Maryland commander, Evan Shelby, had opened a store on the Holston and was trying to induce his sons Isaac and Evan to join him. In North Carolina Jim found other friends, the Walkers, Coburns, and McGarys, living on the Yadkin and Catawba rivers. Jim's half brother, Tom, was already building a cabin near Boone's for his wife, Hannah. This gave Jim an added excuse for visiting North Carolina, although it grieved him to see his brothers so widely separated. Jim looked forward to the time when the entire Harrod family might be reunited—a foolish dream indeed, since his sisters and brothers were forming new ties and associations. When, several years later, this dream began to look impractical even to Jim, he concentrated on his nieces and nephews.

Up and down the Alleghenies, wherever Jim went in 1772, he found other eager, land-hungry young men who were thinking and dreaming of a new frontier in the rich, unclaimed country below the Ohio.[6] Jim heard of plans for establishing new colonies, of proposed grants to companies on a large scale. Apparently few Westerners were likely to be dissuaded by the Royal Proclamation of 1763 or by warnings from colonial governments.

Within a few years Great Britain had supplemented the Proclamation by three treaties—one at Fort Stanwix in 1768, in which the Iroquois had relinquished their claims to lands south and east of the Ohio, and two with the Cherokee, who

[6] Clarence W. Alvord, "The Daniel Boone Myth," in *Journal of the Illinois Historical Society* (Springfield), XIX (1926), 16-29; Max Savelle, *George Morgan, Colony Builder* (New York, 1932); Albert T. Volwiler, *George Croghan and the Westward Movement, 1741-1782* (Cleveland, 1926).

THE WESTERN FEVER

had not participated in the Fort Stanwix negotiations. John Stuart, the Indian Commissioner in the South, negotiated these two treaties with the Cherokee. The first was the Treaty of Hard Labour (1768), wherein the Southern Indians yielded their claims east of the Great Kanawha. The second was the Treaty of Lochaber in 1770, which yielded claims to a triangular piece of land beginning where the thirty-fifth degree of latitude crossed the Hard Labour line on the west, thence west 76 miles, and due north to the Great Kanawha.[7]

Veterans of regular colonial forces had received promises of pay in Western land; even the 1763 Proclamation against settlement had confirmed this. While the Harrods had served only as volunteers, they and everyone they knew expected the bounty ruling to be broadened to include them as well.[8] If not, then they still had a chance to buy another soldier's claim, for many veterans had no desire to risk their lives in a distant wilderness. Speculators like George Washington were already buying their rights like corncakes.[9]

But few of the landless younger men who could be counted upon to favor settlement in the wilds of Kentucky had money to buy claims of any kind. Most of them were destitute of resources, partly because of the inflation that had struck the continent after the French and Indian War. If they took their chances they had little to lose. Virginia had long ago tried to encourage settlement on Western waters. It would be only a matter of time before their claims would be recognized.[10]

From the looks of things the sooner they moved west the better, because in a year or two, hundreds would be going

[7] For a discussion of the various companies interested in obtaining land, see Thomas P. Abernethy, *Western Lands and the American Revolution* (New York, 1937), 1-90; also Alvord, *Mississippi Valley*, Index.

[8] Abernethy, *Western Lands*, 105 and Index. Their confidence in Dunmore was well justified in regard to the bounty ruling.

[9] Buck, *Planting of Civilization*, 143.

[10] Abernethy, *Western Lands*, 105. The records of Dr. O. M. Strickler, Louisville, show that James Moore, father of Sarah Moore, and possibly his father (James) had been interested in land near the Mississippi at least twenty years earlier. The Swainson records indicate that Sarah was a descendant of Governor James Moore of South Carolina. Research on this subject is incomplete.

west. Certainly they would be taking no greater risk than their families were facing that very minute on Ten Mile. The rival claims of Virginia and Pennsylvania to the territory west of the Monongahela had them all worried lest their hard work go for nothing.

To help in the struggle the Virginia settlers had a new champion in Dr. John Connolly, an Irish physician and a personal representative of Lord Dunmore, the newly appointed governor of Virginia who was himself interested in Western lands. Connolly was a fighter and, as it soon developed, had frequent occasion to prove his ability. For instance, when rumors reached Ten Mile that the region had been included in Pennsylvania's Westmoreland County and that the next court would be held at Pittsburgh, the Virginia settlers complained to Connolly. The irate doctor used some choice "swear words" and promptly sent for reinforcements to back up his colony's authority, whereupon the Pennsylvanians threw Connolly into jail. Somehow he managed to get released on the solemn promise that he would appear in court to answer the charges. Two of Will Harrod's neighbors then organized a noisy celebration at Fort Pitt. On the day appointed for the trial they all appeared at the Westmoreland courthouse in Hannastown—182 of them. When the court adjourned for dinner, they placed sentinels at the door to prevent the afternoon session. Then Connolly read a proclamation from Dunmore, reiterating Virginia's stand that the territory belonged to her.[11]

Although the Harrods had lived most of their lives in central Pennsylvania, they preferred at this time to consider themselves Virginians, since they had taken up their Ten Mile tracts in expectation of title under Virginia's favorable settlement law. Actually it made little difference to any of them to which colony Ten Mile belonged—as long as they could keep

[11] These facts are taken from Percy B. Caley, "The Life Adventures of Lieutenant-Colonel John Connolly," in *Western Pennsylvania Historical Magazine* (Pittsburgh), II (1919), 10, *passim*.

their land. Will had only recently accepted a captain's commission from Lord Dunmore. The Harrods had seen service in the Maryland, Virginia, and Pennsylvania militias. The goal of any expedition had always interested them more than its origin. Since Virginia had been granting patents along the Monongahela for years and had taken the leadership in defending the territory, it was only natural that they looked to her for authority. But the Connolly affair was a different matter. Will refused to join in an open revolt against Pennsylvania. His was a wait-and-see attitude, and many of his neighbors thought he was acting wisely.[12]

Jim had no intention of getting mixed up in the intercolonial rivalry either.[13] Consequently, when Captain Thomas Bullitt, whom the Harrods had known in Indian war service, called for volunteers to survey land at the Falls of the Ohio (the location of the modern town of Louisville), Jim signed the roll.

According to regular procedure Colonel William Preston, the official surveyor for Fincastle County, which at that time included Kentucky, would have named his own deputy to do the work. But Connolly, who had received a patent for this land from Governor Dunmore, had chosen the cocksure, aggressive Bullitt. The captain also displayed a license from the College of William and Mary, which everyone knew had the authority to grant one. Furthermore, gossip had it that Dunmore was Bullitt's sponsor;[14] Jim was sure this was right when an advertisement appeared in the *Virginia Gazette,* calling on all those interested in Western surveys for military warrants to meet at the mouth of New River or at the Great Kanawha on Thursday, April 14, and to bring chain carriers and "other necessaries."[15]

[12] Collection of H. L. Leckey.
[13] *Ibid.*
[14] Dunmore ignored the new (1773) British ruling against Western land grants. See St. George L. Sioussat, "The Breakdown of the Royal Management of Lands in the Southern Provinces, 1773-1775," in *Agricultural History* (Chicago), III (1929), 68-98.
[15] Williamsburg *Virginia Gazette,* December 3-17, 1772.

Will remained on militia duty, but James Harrod enrolled immediately. It is not clear that Jim was a deputy to Bullitt, but he probably was, since as a veteran of the French and Indian War he would be eligible for bounty land as soon as the ruling was broadened to include militia volunteers.

Jim and the other men spent several weeks at Fort Pitt, burning and hollowing out logs to make pirogues, talking over plans for their trip, and laying in supplies, a matter requiring careful consideration. Once they passed the upper reaches of the Ohio there would be no forts where they could buy new equipment. The party must take plenty of axes, butcher knives, blankets, extra moccasins, and hunting shirts, as well as a good supply of fishing tackle, bullets, and powder —all in addition to their meager surveyors' equipment which included a rod, chain, and compass.

Perhaps the most important article that Jim Harrod took along was his long rifle. It had cost him more than anything he owned, probably as much as seven pounds. Kentuckians used to claim that Jim's rifle was among the longest, the straightest, and the truest in the wilderness. It was tailor-made, like all others manufactured by the old Pennsylvania Dutch in that day, and was long enough to shoot far into a herd of buffalo, but not too long to keep a six-footer like Jim from blowing down the barrel and watching for Indians at the same time.

Although nearly all the best rifles had been developed in Pennsylvania, they were usually termed "Kentucky rifles" because they were made to fill the needs of hunters in the western country. The old short-muzzle, large-bore European weapon would not do, for it lacked the precision and range to perform such necessary feats as downing a buffalo at two hundred yards. A man going out on a three months' hunt must be sparing with his lead and powder, making every shot count, and Harrod's graceful, deadly, precise weapon measured with the best of them. No rifle would work if not cared for properly. The locks had to be well oiled so that the hammer would fall quickly and effortlessly, and unless the flints were picked sharp the rifle might miss fire. The bullets had to be filed to paper smoothness, and deerskin or linsey patches for wrapping them needed to be oiled with great care to keep the bullets from sticking in the barrel.[16]

All these detailed jobs received more than usual care as the men sat around the evening campfires, eagerly listening to Jim and the other wise ones who had been "out to Kentuck," shaking their heads at the stories of fabulous amounts of game, of great meadows ready for the plough. And when the first spring freshets brought a rise in the river, Bullitt, Jim Harrod, and Hancock Taylor were eager to shove off, as was every chain carrier, oarsman, and would-be farmer.

Meanwhile, although neither Harrod nor any of his companions were aware of it, another party led by the McAfee brothers from Botetourt County, Virginia, was also making plans for surveying bounty lands in Kentucky.[17] At about the same time that Bullitt's party started, the McAfees struck across country, reaching the mouth of the Kanawha shortly before the Monongahelans' arrival. The meeting was entirely unexpected, but the two parties at once went ashore to hold a conference. They joined forces and chose Bullitt as their commander.[18]

The leader first proposed that he make a trip to the Shawnee country in Ohio, to sound out the Indians at the Chillicothe towns and perhaps win their friendship. Jim Harrod and the others at first thought this idea a little wild, but after considerable discussion they agreed that it was worth the risk. Three of the men volunteered to go along with Bullitt, and two Delaware Indians who happened to pass by on their return from a few months' hunt in Kentucky offered

[16] Facts taken from John G. W. Dillon, *The Kentucky Rifle* (Washington, 1924).
[17] Thomas Hanson Journal, Draper Collection, 14J58-84.
[18] Robert B. McAfee, "The Life and Times of Robert B. McAfee," in *Register of the Kentucky State Historical Society* (Frankfort), XXV (1927), 5, *passim*.

their services as pilot and guard. Jim was to go on down the Ohio with the others as far as the mouth of the Scioto.[19]

A risk it certainly proved to be, as Bullitt reported later to Jim and the McAfees. When he suddenly appeared among the Shawnee, unheralded by the usual advance runner, the Indians were so surprised and bewildered that they locked up the party for the night in order to give themselves a chance to talk over this strange happening. In the morning an impressive array of one hundred painted tribesmen, yelling and brandishing tomahawks, approached the jail. Bullitt, believing that they were about to take his scalp, reluctantly followed them into the council house, where to his astonishment he received orders to make a speech.

As soon as he could recover from his surprise, Bullitt explained that he and his people intended "to settle the country on the Ohio as low as the Falls," adding hastily that of course he and his men intended to live in friendship with all the Indians and hoped that the tribesmen "would take the same view." To offset any possible fear that the Shawnee might consider settlement as a threat to Indian hunting in Kentucky, he said that the whites would not interfere there, as "we shall expect you will live with us as brothers and friends."[20]

It is doubtful that Bullitt believed his own words. Certainly Chief Cornstalk must have realized that these were empty professions, for he and his fellows had watched the white men pushing game westward across the Alleghenies and ploughing up the Indian hunting grounds; nevertheless, he promised to take the proposal under advisement until the next morning, when the council would again assemble. At that time Cornstalk opened the discussion, assuring Bullitt that he was now standing among his brothers, "who think well of you and what you have said to us." But he concluded his speech with a veiled warning: "This spring we saw some

---

[19] *Ibid.*
[20] These and subsequent quotations are from *ibid.*, 14-19.

THE WESTERN FEVER 39

wrong by our young men in disturbing your people by taking their horses, but we have advised them to the contrary . . . and expect it will be harkened to by them."

While the second council was in progress, Harrod and his fellow surveyors stood at the mouth of the Scioto, watching in suspicious quiet as four young Indians, leading seven saddled and packed horses, swam from the Kentucky shore. The land seekers knew without asking that the horses had recently belonged to white men.[21]

When the emissaries arrived at the Scioto, Harrod and the McAfees joined them, proceeding slowly down the Ohio to allow their hunters time for procuring meat along the way. All went well until Bullitt's surveyors announced that they planned to lay out their plots in squares, leaving no patches in between. An argument arose. "Why not take in only good land and let the rest go?" the McAfees asked. They had no interest in the Ohio bottom land; they wanted to locate on small streams with good springs near by, where they could put up mills.

Bullitt did not agree, but he again directed Jim and his other surveyors to continue with his original plan. The McAfees remained quiet on the subject, and the surveying continued.

One hot day in early July the party found the Big Bone Lick. Harrod, Bullitt, and Taylor, who had all been there before, suggested this as a good place to camp. When they reached the spot the others expressed amazement. In a depression of ten acres, as bare as a sand bar, were quantities of large mastodon bones scattered around or sticking out of the marshy ground surrounding the salty lick. One of the McAfees recorded in his journal that teeth of these huge animals must have weighed nearly ten pounds each, while

[21] "Journal of James McAfee," in Neander M. Woods, *The Woods-McAfee Memorial* (Louisville, 1905), Appendix A.

the thigh bones were fully four or five feet long, and the ribs between three and four inches wide. The origin and fate of these animals mystified all of the surveyors, one of them speculating on what sort of elephant they could have been. Or were they, perhaps, a kind of buffalo? An aged Delaware Indian, out on an early summer hunt, appeared as the men puzzled over their finds. Did he know anything about them? Well, when he was a boy, the Delaware replied, the bones were just as they now saw them.[22]

After a few days at Big Bone Lick the party broke up, Hancock Taylor going up the Kentucky in search of good farm land, while Harrod stayed with Bullitt to lay off a town at the Falls, where the city of Louisville now stands. The McAfees left the others to follow a small buffalo road that struck the Kentucky at a ripple below the present town of Frankfort. Here they left a tomahawk and fish gig in a deep spring and marked a gum sapling. Not satisfied with this site for a permanent settlement, however, they traveled along the buffalo roads that led to the numerous salt licks dotting the country. Finally they reached the banks of Salt River, which one of Jim Harrod's men later described as so crooked a fish could not swim upstream without scraping his fins. Here the McAfees made more extensive surveys—this time with a view toward settlement.

Late in the summer Will Harrod went down the Ohio to see how the surveyors were getting along and to do a little scouting with his brother Jim, who was planning to start his settlement on what he considered the best piece of land in Kentucky.[23] It was far from the Ohio and not as well timbered as wilderness country was expected to be. The Indians called it the "Great Meadow," because of the tall grass and the thick cane that grew there. The location was high, well drained, and away from the swampy mists that hung along the river

---

[22] Collins, *Kentucky*, II, 51-52, 55.
[23] Reuben G. Thwaites and Louise P. Kellogg (eds.), *A Documentary History of Dunmore's War, 1774* (Madison, 1905), 68.

bottoms and made men sick; and, most important to Jim, it afforded a natural protection from possible Indian attack.

Strangely, neither the Harrods nor the McAfees knew at that time that they had chosen almost identical locations for settlement.

Finished with their preliminary scouting, Jim and Will went back to the settlements alone, across the Cumberlands to the Greenbriar and on down to North Carolina, to talk over plans for settlement with their oldest brother Tom, who also had the "Kentucky fever." In the back country of Virginia and North Carolina, people were talking of nothing but Kentucky, and the settlements were buzzing with plans for removal to this paradise, where the buffalo were too fat and lazy to run from the rifleshot, and the thick rich cane offered perfect winter pasture for horses and cattle.

As Jim and Will rode up the Allegheny ridge toward Ten Mile, they met other men as enthusiastic as they—young fellows who wanted to talk with their families and perhaps meet Jim Harrod at Wheeling fort the next spring to go down the stream with the first spring rain and make a settlement in Kentucky.

Chapter IV
THE FIRST KENTUCKY SETTLEMENT
(1774)

"I have been amused at the efforts made by some in these latter days, to get up some one individual as the hero of the settlement of Kentucky, to whom all looked as a leader, when in fact nothing is more fallacious."[1]

A LONG series of Indian attacks almost killed the interest in Kentucky which Jim and Will Harrod had found so widespread along the Allegheny frontier in the late summer of 1773. Chief Cornstalk, whose protestations of friendship had allayed Bullitt's fears, directed a massacre of the unsuspecting families on the Greenbriar, and other tribesmen attacked outlying stations. They fired on a small band of settlers led by Daniel Boone and Captain Billy Russell as they set out for Kentucky, killing sons of the leaders and forcing the remainder of the party to seek shelter at Russell's Clinch River station.[2] Only the arrival of cold weather brought a lull in the terror.

Talk around the fireplaces changed from the wonders of the new West to measures of defense against the dangers of springtime, when snow and ice would melt, leaving streams and valleys passable for even more extensive and savage forays. Indeed, a rumor made the rounds that all the Holston and Clinch river settlements—the farthest Western penetra-

[1] Gen. R. B. McAfee, Sketches of the First Settlements in Kentucky, No. 2, Draper Collection, 4CC89.
[2] Thwaites and Kellogg (eds.), *Dunmore's War*, 2 (note 1) and 432.

THE FIRST SETTLEMENT

tions—would break up completely.³ Every day saw great numbers moving back to the Valley of Virginia or across the mountains to Lancaster, leaving behind precious spinning wheels, feather beds, and brass kettles in their dash for safety. A report reached Williamsburg that as many as a thousand people a day were crossing the Monongahela on the narrow, hilly road to the eastern settlements.⁴

Jim Harrod went right on with his plans for returning to Kentucky. Indian scares, however, were not the only obstacles he faced. There were complications of an official nature, too. Colonel William Preston, surveyor of Fincastle County, absolutely refused to enter any of Bullitt's surveys, sending word that they would have to be done all over again, this time under his official supervision.⁵ Preston also expressed doubt that the men had a legal right to survey below the Kentucky River.⁶ But these warnings bothered Jim not at all. Like most Virginians, he continued to put great stress on the Fort Stanwix treaty as well as on Virginia's charter claims, and he proceeded with his plans for settling in Kentucky.⁷ Jim expected to go out under ordinary settlement rights and wait for Virginia to validate them—as most people thought she was bound to do. To his way of thinking, it was her land to grant as she pleased, so who cared what unknown, faraway British officials had to say? Harrod had more immediate problems to worry him.

The difficulty of making a settlement several hundred miles from old friends and neighbors was all too apparent, and Jim had to make careful preparations if he hoped to accomplish anything permanent. After scouting all winter for men of

³ *Ibid.*, xii.
⁴ *Ibid.*, xiii.
⁵ W. P. Palmer and others (arrs.), *Calendar of Virginia State Papers* (Richmond, 1875), I, 262; Abernethy, *Western Lands*, 102-103. See notice in the Williamsburg *Virginia Gazette*, February 24, 1774.
⁶ For details, see Abernethy, *Western Lands*, 98-112.
⁷ *Ibid.*, 105. The boundary line was drawn by John Donelson. The identity of the "Louisa" River, which formed the northern boundary, is still in dispute. See John R. Alden, *John Stuart and the Southern Colonial Frontier* (Ann Arbor, 1944), Appendix B, 344-50.

various talents, he had assembled a well-balanced expedition: there was an amateur doctor; there were several surveyors, a metalworker, a number of good farmers, and some textile workers—men who knew how to use native products like nettles and buffalo wool; he had carpenters, an expert stonecutter, and a man who could fashion broad-brimmed hats from buffalo skins.[8] Such hats were important articles in Kentucky, where the mild climate made the tight-fitting coonskin caps of western Pennsylvania too hot and "itchy" for general wear.

The forty-eight or more adventurers who signed Harrod's company book or gave oral consent gathered at Grave Creek about the first of March. They were from several parts of the Virginia frontier—the Monongahela country, and the Roanoke, the Clinch, and the Holston settlements—and several of them were Jim's relatives by blood or marriage, cousins, near and distant, young and adventuresome, and all eager to make their fortunes in Kentucky land.[9] Levi, Jim's youngest brother, was probably the only member of his immediate family to go along,[10] although Tom met them in Kentucky.

Among the enrollees who were not related to Jim was Abraham Chapline, a young man who had come out from Frederick County, Virginia, to seek his fortune.[11] An old friend of the Harrods, he was one of those younger sons who had inherited only a pittance from his father's estate. Rather than live on his eldest brother's hospitality, he had moved to the frontier and built an isolated cabin—only two neighbors were within a twenty-mile radius of his newly cleared plantation. When he heard of Jim's plan for settlement he hid his plowshares, took his ax and rifle, and started for the place of rendezvous.

[8] Major George Chinn (USMC), of Harrodsburg, Ky., quoting Mercer County (Ky.) Records in conversation with the author, 1946.
[9] Draper Collection, 4CC33-36, 12C24, 48J10-11; Swainson records.
[10] Draper Collection, 18J47-48.
[11] Abraham Chapline's narrative, written in later years, is used for factual data in the account of the journey. Draper Collection, 4CC33-36. Several of the Harrods had served under his father in the Maryland militia.

THE FIRST SETTLEMENT 45

Jim, waiting at Grave Creek, greeted this surprise addition to his company enthusiastically. Every new gun lent a feeling of greater security to an expedition which to many frontiersmen must have appeared hazardous in the extreme. After a few more days had passed and no additional recruits had arrived, Harrod called an election to choose a captain for the expedition. Although Jim was the natural choice and the occasion obviously superfluous, it is unlikely that anyone pointed to this fact, for such elections were customary procedures on the frontier. Bullitt had held an election in 1773. The backwoodsmen accepted the formality without comment, for in peaceful activity as well as in warfare they served willingly only under captains chosen by themselves.

As soon as the election was over Harrod ordered his men to load the dugouts and make ready to leave. The water was high, the current strong, the weather ideal for their expedition as the men left Grave Creek, joking and chatting about the fortunes that awaited them in Kentucky. When they reached the mouth of the Great Kanawha, Captain Jim noticed a party of white men laboriously rowing upstream.

After friendly halloos from both sides, Jim and the leader of the other party agreed to go ashore in order to make camp for the night and exchange news. During the two days that followed, the companies remained at this spot, as each leader tried to persuade the other to join forces with him. But Harrod learned that he could not induce the other group to change its course. On their way to survey they had found hostile red men along the shore, and it had been evident, according to their view, that Kentucky was no place for a white man. Since nothing Harrod could do or say would induce them to go back and he realized that this group of discouraged surveyors might influence his own men, Jim said good-by, gathered his company together, and left without further argument.

They proceeded downstream as quietly as possible, with Jim more acutely aware of the danger they faced from stray

Indian bands, who, if the other party was right, were in the neighborhood ready to attack any settlers on the way to the Kentucky country.

When night came Harrod directed the men to pull ashore in order to make camp. One of them jumped out of his canoe ahead of the others, announcing emphatically that he would go no farther, that Indians would surely kill anyone foolish enough to do so. In dread of a general clamor after this challenge, Captain Jim ordered them to push off at once, and to stay afloat all night. It was as plain as war paint that several others in the company wished they had joined the party returning to the settlements.

From then on, strangely enough, the men were amenable and good-natured and said nothing more about going home. Before they reached the mouth of Deer Creek, where the city of Cincinnati is now located, they had either lost their fear of the wilderness or decided that they would be safer with a large party than wandering aimlessly and alone through the woods. In order to establish a kind of discovery claim they cut a tree near Deer Creek but made no improvements there. Rowing on instead to the Kentucky River, they went upstream to a point later known as Harrod's Landing and cut across the gently up-tilted country along an old buffalo road.[12]

The land was "delightful beyond conception," one of the pioneers recalled, nearly half of it being covered with cane and interspersed with open spaces ready-made for fields. The ground appeared to be extremely fertile, producing amazing quantities of weeds of various kinds, including grass, wild rye, and clover. "The dews were very heavy" and "the nights in the heat of summer cool," one of the men wrote.[13] The land appeared more level than it really was because of the thickness of growth which hid the small ravines and masked the gentle slopes.

[12] *The Cincinnati Miscellany* . . . (Cincinnati), II (1846), 137-39.
[13] Draper Collection, 48J10-11.

THE FIRST SETTLEMENT 47

With pride Harrod showed his men the site he had chosen for the town. The big spring, gushing and overflowing with great quantities of clear water, the fine meadowland, the high location overlooking the surrounding country were matchless. There was no sign of either Indian or white stranger; the silent woods dotting the landscape seemed friendly; and as far as a man could see there was untilled soil, theirs for the marking.

Jim called a meeting to talk over their first day's activities.[14] The men agreed to go out in small parties to locate springs and desirable acreages for individual plantations. Each evening they were to hold councils on their findings. At one of these meetings Abraham Chapline reported the discovery of another fork of the Salt River that flowed a few miles from their camp. This branch retained the name the surveyors gave it the day of its discovery—Chapline's Fork.[15] Since the party was unanimous in praising the country, Harrod suggested that before they made further surveys it might be well to draw up an agreement including plans for a town. This seemed to appeal to the men as a sensible proposal which would give an air of permanence to their activities; however, before the lots were even surveyed, they gave the first Kentucky settlement a name—Harrodstown, in honor of the company leader.[16] Then they drew up their agreement:

". . . that a Cabbin should be built each person contiguous to each other, or as much so as the situation of the country would admit. That after the cabbins were built, they should be numbered and each person to draw his lott and to possess that cabbin on which the number stood, and that the dividing line should be half way between each cabbin. . . ."[17]

They put up a number of cabins in this town area, all of them south of the branch that had its headwaters in the big

---
[14] Collins, *Kentucky*, II, 605.
[15] See Filson's map of Kentucky, facing page 208.
[16] Draper Collection, 12CC45, 4CC33-36.
[17] Deposition of James Brown, quoted in William S. Lester, *The Transylvania Colony* (Spencer, Ind., 1935), 55.

spring by which they were camped.[18] They built thirty or more houses that summer, counting the town and plantation buildings in the surrounding territory.[19] Frequently they placed them in small clearings or meadows, near the brow of a hill or by the creek bank; but in Harrodstown proper they set out their houses in neat rows, with only an occasional cabin off by itself in silent witness to a pioneer's individual taste or craving for privacy. They were crude but typical pioneer homes, not "pigpens" nor makeshifts put up merely to comply with settlement laws.[20] Most cabins were twenty by thirty feet and a story and a half high. The chimneys were of mud and sticks, the roofs covered with split staves, about four feet long and five inches wide, of oak or ash. Usually a fireplace occupied one end of the room, but probably there were no windows in these first buildings, and the only light came from the fireplace or open doorway. Certainly the men did not take time to chink the logs or to put in puncheon floors. The doors were roughhewn slabs which could be barred at night by rolling logs against them or by letting down heavy crossbars. Owners added many refinements during the years that followed, but in 1774 the main thought was for protection rather than for comfort. As soon as the houses were completed Harrod held a lottery to decide their ownership.[21]

Later he and Chapline built a cabin for Harrod's brother Levi, who had returned to the settlements before time for the lottery.[22] For his own home Jim selected what proved to be one of the most fertile pieces of land in Kentucky, located about six miles south of the camp.[23] Here he cut brush and marked a cabin site, calling it the Boiling Spring settlement because of its large pool fed by an undersurface spring.

[18] Depositions quoted in Max Charleston, *The Oldest Town in Kentucky* (Harrodsburg, 1929), 6-9.
[19] *Ibid.*
[20] A. G. Bradley (ed.), *The Journal of Nicholas Cresswell* (New York, 1928), 82.
[21] Charleston, *Oldest Town*, 6-9.
[22] Draper Collection, 18J47-48.
[23] *Ibid.*, 12C23, 12C24, 12CC45.

THE FIRST SETTLEMENT 49

The other men scattered around the country,[24] staking boundaries for later clearings or wandering from place to place, looking things over for the sheer fun of discovery. On one of these trips a small party found the Blue Licks northeast of Harrodstown—a site that became famous for a disastrous battle during the Revolution. They were astonished over what they found there. From the top of a ridge overlooking the lick basin they saw "ten thousand or more buffaloes" and perhaps as many "other animals of every species known in the western wilds," including bears, wolves, panthers, foxes, wildcats, deer, and elk, "all moving about in one vast throng, rubbing against each other, the stronger frequently preying upon the weaker. The ground about for miles was a perfect barren waste, worn out and torn up by the stamping and pawing of the animals."[25]

There was little more Harrod or his men could ask of a country.[26] The soil was the most fertile they had ever seen; there were abundant clear springs; game was plentiful; all agreed that brides would be easy to find once the news of Harrodstown reached the Holston and Monongahela country.

Jim's party was not the only one in the Kentucky country that summer. Two other groups arrived, one under Isaac Hite, grandson of Jost Hite, pioneer of the Shenandoah Valley. He helped lay off Harrodstown.[27] The other was led by John Floyd and included a few of Preston's surveyors who had been marking off land along the Ohio for prominent Virginians, including George Washington, Patrick Henry, and Dr. Connolly. Floyd's men used Harrod's cabin as their headquarters.

Few surveyors knew how to figure measurements in terms of degrees. Their instruments were simple—a plain compass

[24] Collins, *Kentucky*, II, 605.
[25] Draper Collection, 4CC113-14. According to the United States Biological Survey, early American buffalo herds numbered as many as four million. In 1871 a representative of the National Museum saw 480,000 in one day on the Western plains (written communication, January, 1946).
[26] See page 243 for a list of Harrod's company.
[27] Draper Collection, 14J58-84, 4CC69-71.

and measuring chain and rod. Floyd was handicapped by such scanty equipment, but he managed to lay off his plots with a fair degree of accuracy. James Harrod was also a better than average surveyor, having gained experience when commissioned by friends in Old Virginia to mark western land. Although he did not always locate acreage up to the ample standard some of his customers expected, he was associated as deputy with the best surveyors in the west.[28]

Two other prominent frontiersmen were in Kentucky that summer: James Knox, leader of the Long Hunters of Tennessee, deserted Floyd's company early in the season to join Harrod's men; and Simon Kenton, hiding behind the name of Butler because of the mistaken belief that he had killed a love rival, had fled to the wilderness to escape punishment. An old trader had told him about the Kentucky country, and after his first visit Kenton had vowed never to return to his old home. In 1773 he had piloted surveyors returning to the Greenbriar; now he was back in the New West, without party or official tie but as enthusiastic as before over the future. George Rogers Clark from the Virginia Piedmont was there too. He had made his first journey to the West in 1771, and had roamed the Monongahela, talking with Indians, visiting frontiersmen on Ten Mile, and making keen-eyed observations on land for himself and his family.[29] But neither Jim Harrod nor any of these men expressed any immediate concern over Indian hostility. They heard rumors, but so far all had been peaceful in Kentucky.[30]

Back in Fincastle the danger was more apparent. Reports were arriving daily of numerous attacks along the Ohio and Monongahela; and Colonel Preston, who declared frankly

---

[28] Bolling Stark stated in his will that Harrod had located five thousand acres for him on the Ohio River. *William and Mary Quarterly* (Williamsburg), XXI (1913), 205. See James Nourse, "Journey to Kentucky in 1775," in *Journal of American History* (New York), XIX (1925), 121, *passim*.

[29] *Cincinnati Miscellany*, II (1846), 244, 252, 254. Clark had made a clearing on Fish Creek, west of the Monongahela.

[30] Draper Collection, 4CC33-36.

THE FIRST SETTLEMENT

that he was worried over the increasing number of Indian attacks,[31] wrote Captain Billy Russell on the Clinch asking him to suggest scouts to notify the surveyors in Kentucky of the danger.[32] Russell chose his old friends and new neighbors from North Carolina, Daniel Boone and Michael Stoner, both men of long experience in the wilderness.[33]

He gave the scouts instructions to hurry as much as possible—which they did, arriving in Harrodstown only ten days later. Whether they warned the official surveyors on the way is not known, but when they saw the activity in Jim Harrod's settlement, they appeared to forget about Indian dangers. In his enthusiasm Boone told Jim that he wanted to lay off a lot for himself and put up a cabin; and with the help of his neighbor, Evan Hinton, he erected a double dwelling on the dividing line of their holdings, not far from the town spring.[34]

This infectious enthusiasm received a severe jolt, however, when Indians fired on a group of men who were working near a large spring. The attack came unexpectedly as the men were preparing for the day's work, cooking their breakfast of corn porridge and fish. One sleepyhead, a man named Poague, was still rolled up in his blanket; and, as the other men later told Jim, he was kicking and mumbling in his sleep. When Poague awoke he told the men about his dream that a large number of guns were pointing at him in front while the campfire was about to burn his "britches" in the rear.

As Poague was talking, another man standing in front of the fire, drying his notes and surveyor's papers which had been soaked in a downpour the night before, was killed by Indians hiding in the brush. The rest of the party hastily grabbed their rifles and tumbled over one another in their haste to get back to town.

The dreamer jumped to his feet and ran also, one of the Indians close on his heels as he dodged in and out of the cane-

[31] *Ibid.*, 3QQ42-47; Thwaites and Kellogg (eds.), *Dunmore's War*, xiii, xvi.
[32] Draper Collection, 3QQ46.
[33] *Ibid.;* Thwaites and Kellogg (eds.), *Dunmore's War*, xvi.
[34] John Bakeless, *Daniel Boone* (New York, 1939), 78-79.

brake in a futile attempt to gain ground. Finally, he threw his rifle across a creek in an attempt to distract the Indians' attention. The scheme worked. His pursuers quarreled over the weapon, and he had a chance to gain distance and make his way in safety to Harrodstown.

Now thoroughly alarmed, Captain Jim sent orders to the scattered surveyors to return at once and prepare for a stand against mass attack. Meanwhile the men at hand grabbed their supplies, filled their kettles with water, and dashed into the houses. Several days passed while the party, barricaded and huddled in the new cabins, waited for the red men to arrive. Finally, when it appeared certain that the tribesmen had left the vicinity, Harrod led a party to the scene of the early morning attack. There they buried the dead; then, gathering what was left of the scattered papers, they returned to the town.[35]

There was no longer any doubt in Harrod's mind. Trouble was ahead. He must stop the surveying and cabin building to prepare for an immediate return to the settlements, for there could be no peace until the white men put a stop to these attacks once and for all.

[35] Reminiscences of John Poague (the son of the dreamer), Draper Collection, 4CC113-114. See also *ibid.*, 4CC33-36.

Chapter V
VIRGINIA'S PRIVATE WAR
(1774)

Ye daughters and sons of Virginia incline
Your ears to a story of woe;
I sing of a time when your fathers and mine
Fought for us on the Ohio.[1]

WHILE James Harrod was directing work at his new Kentucky settlement his brother Will was engaged in activity of an entirely different character.[2] Since early spring parties of marauding Indians had been pestering land seekers and hunters in the Monongahela region with sharp attacks which brought fear of an even greater hostility in the months to come. The recruiting center in the Ten Mile area was Richard Jackson's fort, Waynesburg, and it was here that Will and the other captains organized their companies. They did not have much difficulty in finding men, for the settlers were all too aware of the danger. If a man was forced to stay at home to tend his stock or crops there was always a son or brother willing to do the service for him.

Although at first he did only routine scouting with his company, Captain Will Harrod soon discovered that he was in constant demand as a purchaser of fort supplies in preparation for an Indian war which Connolly considered inevitable.[3] This meant that Will had to make numerous extended journeys through the country, leaving Amelia and the children

---

[1] Draper Collection, 8ZZ18.
[2] *Ibid.*, 4NN5, 3QQ15.
[3] Thwaites and Kellogg (eds.), *Dunmore's War*, xiii.

54 JAMES HARROD OF KENTUCKY

as well as his mother without adequate protection;[4] so he moved them to Ross's fort, ten miles distant, where he was in command. At the same time Levi, the youngest of the widow's sons, left his wife and baby at Ross's while he went out on short scouting tours.[5]

Although most of Will's men were similarly engaged, a few of them had to stay around the forts in order to guard the families. Time passed slowly, for everyone was eager to return home, where crops grew untended and insecurely barred cabins served as invitations to stray Indian bands who were in a mood for pillaging. Whenever possible the men returned to their clearings to make sure that all was well, and frequently, if several neighbors worked together, they were able to harvest a few vegetables or bring in newly ripened grain. This involved great risks, however, and many pioneers were killed by eager red men crouching in the tall grass at the edge of the clearings, waiting for just such a chance to take a white man's scalp.

Will's neighbors were not so eager to risk more distant adventures. When Colonel Angus McDonald, a Scotch Highlander who had been living near Winchester in recent years, tried to enlist recruits for an expedition to the Ohio country, they held back on the excuse that it would not be safe to strike off into the midst of the hostile tribes on a foolhardy expedition, leaving their wives and children to be killed by Indians during their absence.[6]

The frontiersmen had other equally strong reasons for opposing McDonald. The colonel was a man of strong personality with a reputation for maintaining rigid discipline among his men, and those who knew him claimed that he was snobbish, that in fact he was a typical British regular.[7] The older men recalled their experience under Braddock and shook their heads. No, McDonald's plan was not for them.

[4] *Ibid.*, xv.
[5] Draper Collection, 37J168-74; collection of H. L. Leckey.
[6] Draper Collection, 3QQ62, 3QQ64.
[7] Thwaites and Kellogg (eds.), *Dunmore's War*, 152.

When Will Harrod returned from the mouth of the Wheeling River with a "parcel of cattle" he had purchased there, he listened with a great deal of interest to the talk around the forts, but he did not agree with his neighbors.[8] He thought it was possible that a quick raid might put the fear of the Lord into the redskins and ward off trouble—for a while, at least.

George Rogers Clark, who had been visiting the various forts, agreed with Harrod and joined him, Michael Cresap, and others in making a general appeal, one that Harrod knew from experience would carry much weight with backwoodsmen. The leaders wandered through the fort enclosures, talking freely about large amounts of grain, gunpowder, blankets, and salt which the expedition was sure to win in a smashing victory, at the same time praising McDonald for his enterprise and declaring their own willingness to go out under him. These tactics worked well, and from then on Will, Cresap, and Clark won recruits in large numbers.[9]

Late in July, McDonald's expedition left the newly constructed Fort Wheeling and marched into the Ohio country toward the towns on the Scioto where the federated tribes had their headquarters.[10] But in spite of their success in talking men into enlisting, Will could see that he and Clark and the others had not convinced them of the merits of the leader. They apparently disliked him as much as before. From the start they gave the commander a rough time of it, heckling and arguing at every turn. And when McDonald ordered the men to halt for three days while he sent scouts ahead, grumbling began in earnest.[11] McDonald had told the men to bring only seven days' supply of corn and jerked meat in their knapsacks, and with this kind of dillydallying, they complained, they were bound to run short. To add to their woes, a violent storm came up on the third night and wet their

[8] Draper Collection, 4NN8.
[9] Abraham Thomas Recollections, *ibid.*, 27CC32-33.
[10] Thwaites and Kellogg (eds.), *Dunmore's War*, 151-54.
[11] Details of this march are from Draper Collection, 27CC32-33.

arms and blankets. In the morning McDonald ordered the men to clear their rifle barrels by firing into a hollow stump as a precaution against noise which might attract stray bands of red men.

One eighteen-year-old boy, who had run away from home in order to join the expedition, found that his gun would not go off. As he was beating it with his tomahawk, the commander marched over to him and, with his cane held high above his head as if to strike the boy for making so much noise, glowered at him. The young warrior clambered to his feet, clutching his rifle barrel in both hands as he faced McDonald defiantly, and declared that he had been insulted. He would take that kind of treatment from no one, much less from a haughty Scotchman.

The two soldiers stood eye to eye for some time, as Will and the others crowded round to see the outcome of the incident. Presently the colonel lowered his cane and, without saying a word, slowly walked away.

The troops broke into a hearty shout, crying in derision, "A boy has scared the Colonel! A BOY has scared the Colonel!"[12]

Incidents of insubordination such as this were common wherever the backwoodsman found himself under strong discipline—so foreign to the carefree, individualistic life of the frontier. Fortunately there were backwoods leaders on the frontier who recognized the merit of highly trained Britishers and were willing to obey their commands and to induce others to follow them. Will Harrod, for example, overlooked McDonald's haughty bearing for the sake of the expedition, with the result that he and others like him received their reward in added authority and trust. They alone formed the basis for what law and order there was during the precarious years of transition from war to peace, from scattered settlement to statehood. But they never attempted to imitate the British commanders; instead of strict order and discipline,

[12] *Ibid.*

these backwoods soldiers depended on the example set by their own actions and on the force of personality, to keep their men in line. It was a most difficult and hazardous military method, but at that time it was the only one that worked consistently.

In spite of all the preliminary attempts at secrecy, McDonald's followers discovered that most of the Shawnee warriors had retreated in expectation of the attack. The Virginians had only a few minor skirmishes with the Indians who had stayed behind to guard the towns, and they found but a small amount of grain in the cribs.[13] The new corn, not ripe in the fields, they cut down but could not use.

Chagrined and disgusted, the men returned to their homes. The young runaway who had "stood up" so impudently against the Colonel arrived after a difficult march only to face "a little domestic storming" and to join a larger expedition when it passed his way a few weeks later.[14]

Reports to the Virginia Assembly, as well as published accounts of the skirmishes, expressed the hope that this campaign had succeeded in frightening the northern Indians into submission, but the actual result was entirely different.[15] The northern tribesmen became more than ever aware of the aggressive menace which this white invasion of their country presented. McDonald's campaign had actually united tribes that had previously been unwilling to take desperate measures against the white men.[16]

Governor Dunmore, who had anticipated this outcome, had sent word ahead to the southwestern-county lieutenants, ordering them to enlist men for a regiment to be commanded by Colonel Andrew Lewis.[17] Meanwhile, Dunmore planned to make up another regiment on his way from Williamsburg through the northern counties and to assemble it at Fort

[13] Thwaites and Kellogg (eds.), *Dunmore's War*, 151-55.
[14] Draper Collection, 27CC32-33.
[15] Baltimore *Maryland Journal*, September 7, 1774.
[16] Thwaites and Kellogg (eds.), *Dunmore's War*, xvii.
[17] Draper Collection, 46J7.

Pitt, from where they would march to the mouth of the Great Kanawha, or Point Pleasant, as it was called, to join forces with Colonel Lewis.

When the governor arrived at the Monongahela, Will Harrod and most of McDonald's men declared themselves eager to join his force. Actually, because of their recent experience and greater cohesion, they formed the core of 1,200 soldiers in the northern regiment.[18] Dunmore separated them into two divisions, one to go by land and the other by water to the Hockhocking, where they were to make joint camp. Most of the militiamen and volunteers expected to march on to the Point, as had been previously announced, and they were greatly disappointed when Dunmore sent word that Lewis would meet them at the Hockhocking rather than at the Kanawha.[19] This left them with nothing to do but wait— the most unpleasant assignment any frontiersman could imagine.[20]

When James Harrod and his men arrived at the Holston settlements after their hurried journey from Kentucky, they found preparations for the governor's expedition well under way, with recruitment and fort-building activities at a high pitch.[21] Although Jim lost no time in persuading most of his followers to enlist in the Fincastle County regiment—which was to march as soon as the requisite number of men could be enlisted[22]—he was handicapped by the uncertainty of his own status, since owing to his late arrival he had no commission.[23]

In the colonial military setup a captain such as Jim acted as the pivot of operation, the go-between for the county

---

[18] Thwaites and Kellogg (eds.), *Dunmore's War*, xix.
[19] Draper Collection, 27CC32-33, 15J4-48. Dunmore's account of the march has been printed in Thwaites and Kellogg (eds.), *Dunmore's War*, 368-95.
[20] Draper Collection, 27CC32-33.
[21] Thwaites and Kellogg (eds.), *Dunmore's War*, xviii.
[22] *Ibid.*, 108; Draper Collection, 4CC34-36.
[23] *Ibid.*, 3QQ70.

lieutenants who regularly ranked as colonels in actual warfare as well as in volunteer militia service. He alone possessed the necessary leadership to line up his highly individualistic followers. Discipline was spotty at best and greatly affected by domestic considerations of health and season. Men would volunteer for spy and guard duty or be drafted, if necessary, usually for no longer than three consecutive months. This meant that when a major expedition was planned the government had to commission additional captains, since few backwoodsmen would volunteer for these occasions unless they approved of the men in direct command of their particular companies.

Previous disastrous experiences, such as those under Braddock many years earlier, had taught the frontiersmen a never to be forgotten lesson: they could put no dependence on military glamour or on traditional army experience. (Their own failures, due to lack of training or refusal to obey orders, they carefully ignored.) To Jim's men, a different kind of experience was important—the experience which gave soldiers a chance to prove themselves in isolated, hand-to-hand Indian combat, in woodcraft, and in ability to inspire others. Out of these limited ranks they chose their natural leaders.

Knowing all this, Jim Harrod was careful to ask that he become the chief officer for his men.[24] Although the major in charge of recruitment sent him to Colonel Preston with a recommendation that he grant the request, it was some time before the actual commission arrived. Meanwhile a number of men on whom Jim could have depended to join his company had enlisted under other well-known leaders whose status was assured. But Harrod stood firm in his resolve to go on the expedition, and twenty-two of his party stayed with him.[25]

In reporting to the county lieutenant the major remarked that it might be well to encourage such a man as Captain

[24] *Ibid.*
[25] Thwaites and Kellogg (eds.), *Dunmore's War*, 420-21.

Harrod, "as he seems very forward to go against the Enemy."[26] A short time later the commission arrived, and Harrod notified his own lieutenant to rendezvous at the major's house on the Holston.

Companies were assembling at various other points on the Virginia frontier. Every man and boy who could "tote a gun" was eager to join. The commanders discovered that there were veterans who had fought with Forbes and Braddock, and who had been in Bouquet's more recent expedition—the finest men the frontier could muster. In one company alone every soldier measured more than six feet in his moccasins. They arrived from many parts of the western country, outfitted according to their individual tastes or resources. While a few of the men on regular colonial establishment had the usual military uniform with its buttoned jacket and long waistcoat, knee breeches and three-cornered hat, the greater number wore border clothing—caps from buffalo skins or knit from wool, hunting shirts, homemade breeches of linsey, and leather leggings. But equipment was more important. Every man had either a long flintlock rifle or an English musket, a bullet pouch and powder horn, tomahawk and butcher knife—indispensable aids in cutting trails or fighting Indians.[27]

The delay in marching orders occasioned by the commissioning of new officers, the friction due to jealousy between the captains, many of whom accused others of stealing men promised to their own companies, and the difficulty of obtaining supplies for a large undertaking caused uneasiness among the colonels. One of them ruefully pointed out that while a spirit of discontent was not easily quelled among the best-regulated troops, it was even more difficult among men unused to the "Yoak of Military Discipline."[28]

This confusion and delay caused the Fincastle division to

---

[26] Draper Collection, 3QQ70.
[27] Thwaites and Kellogg (eds.), *Dunmore's War*, xviii, xix.
[28] Draper Collection, 2ZZ71.

which Jim Harrod and his men belonged to arrive at Camp Union, the regimental headquarters on the levels of the Greenbriar, much later than the rest. Because of their tardiness Harrod had to move his company to the rear guard, which was to follow several days later with baggage and supplies.[29] It was disappointing and embarrassing, particularly to Jim, since his men could have joined the earlier, front-rank companies had they not wanted to show their personal loyalty to him.

Regardless of this disappointment there was an important job for them to do. The difficulty of supplying an army of this size had forced the commissaries to scour the countryside in order to buy sufficient flour, beef, and bacon to afford a safe reserve; and no one could predict how long the campaign might last nor how soon the army could return to the base. The unexpectedly large enrollment had already strained their reserves to the limit.[30]

To his even greater unhappiness, Harrod did not receive marching orders until a week after the regimental commander had left Camp Union. Since his men were impatient to be in the thick of whatever occurred, the division moved as rapidly as possible along the winding mountainous trail, hampered as they were by the necessity of moving nearly 350 beeves and several thousand pounds of flour. The officers expected to find orders from Lewis in a tree hollow at the mouth of the Elk, but they were disappointed.[31] Fearing that delay might prove disastrous, they ordered the regiment to proceed to Point Pleasant.

The spirits of the men seemed to rise as they marched along, singing their well-worn English tunes for which they concocted new words to fit the occasion;[32] but on the afternoon of October 10 they were startled by a runner who dashed up with the surprising news that a large body of Indians had

[29] Thwaites and Kellogg (eds.), *Dunmore's War*, xviii, xix.
[30] Draper Collection, 3QQ146.
[31] *Ibid*. See also *ibid*., 3S44-49, 3QQ122.
[32] Thwaites and Kellogg (eds.), *Dunmore's War*, 433-39.

that morning at Point Pleasant attacked Lewis' regiment. This information brought exclamations of disappointment and fear.[33]

However, the end of the battle was not in sight, the runner explained. The attack had begun at dawn with two battle lines of Shawnee who had crossed the river during the night advancing on Lewis' men.

Since speed was now more important than before, Harrod and the other captains pushed on, allowing the supplies to bring up the rear. If, as the messenger had said, there were thousands of Indians in the attack their presence was absolutely essential. But it was almost midnight before they arrived. The battle was over. While their army had been victorious, many soldiers had been lost, and there were few medical supplies and doctors to care for the wounded. Harrod's men had no time now to bemoan their tardy arrival. They began at once to assist the wounded, to give what aid they could to the dying, and to bury the dead. What every soldier in the lot really wanted to do was to chase the "bloody red men" without delay. But when Jim and his friends reminded them that other red men might approach the camp at any moment, the frontier soldiers continued their unpleasant and sorrowful work.

Meanwhile, it was painfully evident to anyone who had his wits about him that the white man's victory had been far from decisive.[34]

When Will's men at the Hockhocking learned that all was over without their having so much as fired a gun they too were disappointed.[35] Eager to play some part in the campaign, however tardy, they and others of McDonald's regiment suggested that they repay this surprise attack with an immediate march on the Indian towns at Chillicothe. Dun-

[33] Draper Collection, 33S44-49.
[34] *Ibid.*, 3QQ128, 2ZZ71.
[35] Thwaites and Kellogg (eds.), *Dunmore's War*, xxii; Draper Collection, 27CC32-33.

more stoutly refused, on the ground that it would only stir up needless trouble. Cries of "Treason! Treason!"[36] rang through the camp as an undercurrent of resentment spread rapidly among the dissatisfied men, increasing as the other regiments straggled into camp. At a council which Dunmore and his officers, including Clark and both the Harrods, held as a preliminary peace meeting, a rifle ball whizzed through the tent, narrowly missing Dunmore and one of the Shawnee representatives.[37]

The leader of the Indian delegation was Chief Cornstalk, who arrived in full war regalia—a topknot of red feathers, a beaded forehead ornament, half-moons of red paint across his cheeks, and bone and silver rings in his ears. When it came his turn to speak, Cornstalk lashed out against the white men seated around him. Bitterly he described their crimes against his people, with particular emphasis upon the many unprovoked murders committed by the whites.[38] The spirit of the Indians had been lowered by the irreparable losses at the Battle of the Point, but this brave, haughty Shawnee "had his say" in a beautiful, sonorous voice that was heard throughout the camp. It was evident that the Indians had expected some retaliation for the attack. As the conference progressed and Dunmore did not mention punishment the Indians seemed to relax somewhat, losing their tense fear and gradually becoming more and more friendly in their apparent anxiety to settle the terms of the preliminary treaty as speedily as possible.

In glancing around at the assembled chieftains, Dunmore remarked that one of the more famous in the federation was not present. The Mingo tribal chief Logan had refused to attend the negotiations, but had sent a belt of wampum with a message to signify his acceptance of the terms to be agreed upon by his fellow chieftains.[39] There are several versions of

[36] Draper Collection, 27CC32-33.
[37] *Ibid.*
[38] *Ibid.*, 3Dxvii.
[39] Thwaites and Kellogg (eds.), *Dunmore's War*, xxii.

this message as repeated by white men who were present, but there is no radical difference which could not be accounted for by on-the-spot interpretation. According to a version published in contemporary newspapers, Chief Logan said:

> I appeal to any white man to say that he ever entered *Logan's* cabin but I gave him meat; that he ever came naked but I clothed him. In the course of the last war *Logan* remained in his cabin, an advocate for peace. I had such an affection for the white people that I was pointed at by the rest of my Nation. I should have even lived with them had it not been for Colonel *Cresap*, who the last year cut off, in cold blood, all the relations of *Logan*, not sparing women and children. There runs not a drop of my blood in the veins of any human creature. This called upon me for revenge; I have sought it—I have killed many, and I have fully glutted my revenge. I am glad that there is a prospect of peace, on account of the Nation, but I beg you will not entertain a thought that anything I have said proceeds from fear! *Logan* disdains the thought! He will not turn on his heel to save his life! Who is there to mourn for *Logan?* No One.[40]

Although Logan was mistaken as to the identity of his relatives' murderer, the message he sent has gone down in American history as an inspired example of Indian eloquence. For many years there were scholars who believed it the work of a white associate, but it is now established as the true expression of the sorrowing chief.[41] Jim, Will, and the other officers present were so impressed by the speech that they rehearsed it among themselves, attempting to recall word for word what Logan had said.[42] After the signing of preliminary peace terms,[43] calling for surrender of white prisoners and Indian hostages as well as the establishment of the Ohio River as the northern Indian boundary, Dunmore

---

[40] Peter Force (comp.), *American Archives*, Ser. 4 (Washington, 1837-1846), I, 1020. There is reason to doubt that Logan mentioned Cresap in his speech.

[41] *The Olden Time*, I (1846), 49-67. See Kenneth P. Bailey, *Thomas Cresap, Maryland Frontiersman* (Boston, 1944).

[42] Thwaites and Kellogg (eds.), *Dunmore's War*, 305-306.

[43] Draper Collection, 3QQ130; and Dunmore's account, Draper Collection, 15J4-48.

disbanded the regiment with instructions for the men to return home, living "on their guns."⁴⁴

The hardships which this summary although customary procedure caused the soldiers can scarcely be overdrawn. They were far out on the edge of the wilderness, with no provisions and no responsible officer to organize their safe return. As a result, many of the raw recruits suffered greatly from exposure, fatigue, and hunger. On the other hand, the runaway who had outfaced McDonald accepted his first chew of tobacco and was so refreshed by it that he was able to lead the march to the Ohio.⁴⁵

Before the regiment broke up, however, news of the Boston Tea Party and actions of the Continental Congress reached the Ohio, and the leaders felt that instead of returning home with their men immediately, they should draw up some kind of statement to demonstrate their patriotic sentiments. Jim and Will Harrod, Clark, and a number of other prominent frontiersmen took an active part in the discussions.

The council of officers meeting at Fort Gower pointed with great satisfaction to their record, declaring proudly that men who could live for weeks without bread or salt, and sleep in the open without covering "but that of the canopy of Heaven," who could march and shoot "with any in the known world," were entitled to respect. They would use these talents "to no purpose but for the honour and advantage of *America* in general, and of *Virginia* in particular."⁴⁶

Since it was still not clear that the colonies would renounce their allegiance to Great Britain, the frontiersmen declared their most faithful allegiance to His Majesty, King George III, as long as he should choose to reign over "a brave and free people," and that they would, at the expense of life and everything dear and valuable, exert themselves in support of the Crown and the dignity of the British Empire.⁴⁷

⁴⁴ Draper Collection, 27CC33-34.
⁴⁵ *Ibid.*
⁴⁶ Force (comp.), *American Archives*, Ser. 4, I, 962-63.
⁴⁷ *Ibid.*

Having safeguarded themselves on that side, they proceeded to the heart of their resolution: "But as the love of Liberty, and the attachment to the real interests and just rights of *America* outweigh every other consideration, we resolve that we will exert every power within us for the defence of *American* liberty, and for the support of her just rights and privileges." This they resolved to do, with a bow toward the contemptuous East, "not in any precipitate, riotous, or tumultous manner, but when regularly called forth by the unanimous voice of our countrymen."[48] They closed with an expression of confidence in Lord Dunmore's loyalty and with their testimony that he had had no motive other than the interest of America when he assumed leadership in the recent campaign. In this way the backwoods leaders served notice on everyone that their men had accused Dunmore of duplicity without their approval.

This, their first act as a politically conscious unit aware of more than local interests, was signed by the clerk in behalf of the corps.

When the general disappointment over the shortness of the campaign had subsided Jim began to realize that from his point of view the engagements known as Dunmore's War had been a success. At least for the time being, and regardless of any question as to the legality of the officers' council, his men were free to settle Kentucky unhampered by the most ferocious of the Ohio tribes. The borderers who had fled from their Allegheny homes could return to their plows; determined leaders like himself had discovered new recruits around the evening campfires. Many soldiers, eager to glimpse the marvelous new country, declared that they would return to their homes by way of Kentucky.[49]

Officials in Old Virginia were pleased with the outcome, too. The president and faculty of the College of William and Mary sent two messages to the governor—one congratulat-

[48] *Ibid.*
[49] Draper Collection, 27CC33-34; Thwaites (ed.), *Wither's Chronicles*, 190-91.

ing him on the victory, the other on the birth of a daughter.[50]

Colonel McDonald expressed the general sentiment in a letter to Will Harrod a few months later from Williamsburg. He declared that all the country was well pleased with the governor's expedition, but at the same time he referred to strained relations with the home government, observing that the colonies were preparing for war.[51]

The last American battle under the flag of England had come to a close; the beginning of the Revolution was already in the air. In pushing Virginia's frontier to its greatest limits, Dunmore, the loyal Britisher, had unwittingly performed a vital service to his future enemies.

Although the Battle of the Point cannot be called the first battle of the Revolution, as a few Western historians have termed it, it did serve as a training ground for some of the most skillful participants in that later conflict.[52] In Dunmore's regiments were seven men who rose to the rank of general in the Revolutionary army. Other writers have said with greater truth that had it not been for Dunmore's War, the victorious colonies might have found their western boundary fixed at the Allegheny Mountains.[53]

[50] Force (comp.), *American Archives*, Ser. 4, I, 1019-20.
[51] Draper Collection, 4NN22.
[52] Thwaites and Kellogg (eds.), *Dunmore's War*, xxv-vi.
[53] *Ibid.*, xxvi-viii; Roosevelt, *Winning of the West*, I, 244-46.

Chapter VI

A LAST FAREWELL

(1775)

"What a Buzzel is amongst People about Kentuck? to hear people speak of it one would think it was a new found Paradise. . . ."[1]

BY THE time James Harrod and his men returned from Dunmore's War, the whole country was "ringing from one end to the other of the beautiful Kentucky and the banks of the pleasant Ohio." As one enthusiastic soldier said, "Those who had been there gave the most enticing accounts of its beauty, fertility, and abundance of game. The Buffalo, Elk, and Bear were said to be rolling fat, and weary for the rifle shot."[2]

News spread rapidly of the agreement between Dunmore's forces and the Indian chieftains. Although this "treaty" could guarantee no more than a temporary lull in tribal hostility, it offered more favorable conditions for immediate Western settlement. Interest multiplied when Lord Dunmore announced that thereafter provincial soldiers would be eligible for bounty lands previously restricted to colonial veterans.

It was certain that the first warm days would bring a rush of surveying parties bound for Kentucky, and James Harrod wanted his company to be among the first settlers to reach the country. Immediately following his return from the officers' council at Fort Gower, therefore, he began preparations

[1] Statement of the Rev. John Brown, in Draper Collection, 4QQ15.
[2] Draper Collection, 27CC33.

for an early spring expedition. During this period Jim never relaxed his efforts to induce other members of his family to join the company.[3] Although Will, Levi, and Thomas were enthusiastic over the "new-found paradise," many years were to pass before any of them actually made his home in Kentucky—a fact which was due to their wives' natural reluctance to move deeper into the wilderness, and to their satisfaction with their own plantations.[4] Other less fortunately situated neighbors did not have the same incentive to stay in the Monongahela country.

Most of Captain Jim Harrod's company were young men without land or families.[5] They could not depend on sharing fortunes from fathers or fathers-in-law, whose farms were just large enough to support their own large families and never so extensive that they could be parceled out among all their children. But Harrod's men had youth, health, and industry, and these were considerable fortunes in those days. The highly advertised wealth of Kentucky was ready-made for the fulfillment of their ambitions. Danger from hostile Indians faded into insignificance beside the abundant opportunities for proving a man's ability to maintain a family.

If mothers were not as enthusiastic over these prospects as their sons, they usually gave no prolonged resistance to plans for moving westward, for they had left their own homes in the same fashion, with little more than a "bed well stocked with blankets and rugs, a cow and a calf and young mare."[6] Indeed, many had started married life with less. If a young suitor had more than daring and ambition to offer, along with a horse and a good rifle, he was the exception. Why should anyone ask for more?

The Widow Sarah certainly would not. She had been as enthusiastic about pioneering as had her sons. When her hus-

---

[3] Swainson records; Darling Papers.
[4] See Draper Collection, 12C25. Numerous references to this view are found in this collection.
[5] Draper Collection, 1CC21-102; collection of H. L. Leckey.
[6] McAfee, "Life and Times," *loc. cit.*, 12.

band died in 1754, leaving her with a houseful of children, she had not returned to Baltimore to live comfortably with her family. She was ever loath to sit by another's fireside. She had gone on with her children, moving to the newly opened country east of the Tuscarawas, and later to the Monongahela with Will and Jim.

No pioneer mother could have asked more for her children. Her girls were married well, into good families long associated with the Harrods and Moores; her boys, excepting James and Samuel, were married, too—their wives had been raised on the frontier, and their parents the widow knew.[7] The Harrods were good soldiers, good farmers, and leaders among their people. Although Sarah could not pioneer with James, she had lived to know that Ten Mile was not the end of the trail for her sons.[8]

There is a persistent legend, supported by meager evidence, that a few years after the family moved to Ten Mile, the Widow Harrod married a man named Brown and at the age of fifty bore a child, a girl who later moved to Harrodsburg, Kentucky, and married in the fort there. According to the gossip, Sarah's two eldest daughters acted as midwives at the baby's birth.[9] If this story is true, this was Sarah's thirteenth child. But Sarah did not live to rear her, because sometime during this fall and winter, when the girl would have been ten years old, the mother died at her home on Ten Mile. It is not known whether Indians killed her or she died from a malady. With but scanty knowledge of medicine, many pioneers fell victim to a "fever" or "flux" or to severe "stomach pains." Sarah was sixty then—a good age for a woman whose life had been strenuous with work and child-

---

[7] Collection of H. L. Leckey; Swainson records.

[8] Interview with John Harrod, of Pewee Valley, Ky.

[9] Both Mrs. Atkins and Mrs. Swainson have been told of this tradition by various persons claiming descent. Mrs. Swainson's studies indicate no actual record in support. It may refer to a second generation Sarah Harrod, of whom there were several.

bearing, so perhaps it was natural that her sons should accept her death quietly and without later comment.[10]

The boys must have realized that they owed much to her upbringing—their book knowledge, slight as it was; their strong sense of fair play; their zest for adventure—and undoubtedly James in particular felt a pang of regret that Sarah had not lived to see Harrodstown.

It was early March when James gathered his men on the banks of the Monongahela, ready to return to their new Kentucky settlement. The journey took much planning and work. The men and their sisters, mothers, and wives had spent the winter accumulating spare hunting shirts, new hats, and stocks of other necessities such as lead, gunpowder, salt, flour, kettles, and extra moccasins for the trip. The men had also built several keelboats and acquired fishing gigs and a few necessary tools. They had sharpened their versatile axes, cleaned and oiled their firearms, and, now that the first heavy spring rains were swelling the river tides, were ready to push off for Kentucky.

All day Sunday and Monday before their departure the men camped at the mouth of Ten Mile, dressing and packing sheep, and doing various last-minute jobs, while the womenfolk searched cupboard and rafter for additional supplies of bullet lead and linsey patches. One old settler recalled that "every gill of whiskey I had was stowed aboard 'Harrod's Terrior.'" Then at last, at about ten o'clock on that bright March day, the men pulled their boats into the current of a fresh rise in the river and departed, amid tears and promises, singing, "God Bless Old Virginia," and "God Save the King."[11]

Many of these men had been among Harrod's party of settlers the year before or with him when he surveyed with

---

[10] Even William Harrod, Jr., her grandson, omits any reference to her death in his sketch of the family. Draper Collection, 37J168-74.

[11] Interview with A. L. Moredock, Waynesburg, Pa., summer of 1947. Mr. Moredock was quoting a pioneer named George Teegarden.

Bullitt, but because some of them were new to Ohio River travel, Harrod had taken the precaution of calling a council the night before their departure in order to warn of the dangers ahead and to issue a few last-minute instructions.[12] Regardless of all the fine promises, there was no guarantee that the Indians would let them pass unmolested.[13] Chieftains were powerless to stop solitary braves from stealing out of camp to avenge a dead brother or father. Now that they were going down the river to stay, Harrod's men had many more trappings than when they had gone, in 1774, to survey or to build cabins. This meant that greater caution would be necessary. Navigation on the Ohio was no daydreamer's occupation. Harrod chose experienced hands to sit in the prows, men who would listen carefully for the sound of riffling water, who were quick-witted enough to steer away suddenly to avoid hidden rocks or fallen trees, and who would, when the course of the river permitted, keep their boats in the middle of the stream, heading straight and never relaxing their watch for a second.

Jim had seen to it that the boats were loaded carefully, not too heavily on one side or the other, with the weight evenly distributed between men and cargo. The men must stay in their assigned positions, for the risk of overturning the heavily packed boats was great. Since there was not a single white man's cabin between Grave Creek and Kentucky—a journey of over three hundred miles—every man and every article must arrive unharmed.[14]

There was a different spirit about this 1775 expedition. Jim's party were going to homes, to cabins already built, where they had staked claims and cleared small patches of ground. Although they might not foresee everything that

---

[12] According to depositions in Mercer County Records. See Draper Collection, 27CC32-33.

[13] In September, 1775, a great force of Indians assembled at Fort Pitt, pledging peace and friendship. Reuben G. Thwaites and Louise P. Kellogg (eds.), *The Revolution on the Upper Ohio, 1775-1777* (Madison, 1908), xiii-iv, 25-127.

[14] McAfee, "Life and Times," *loc. cit.*, 22; Draper Collection, 14J58-84.

was ahead of them, they had the power in their hands and heads to deal with whatever they might have to face. There were more men and more guns; and brothers and friends would join them later in the summer. In the fall, when the time was best for travel and settling, pilots would go back to bring their wives and sweethearts down the river. Families would be together again and new homes started.

The current was strong and the trip down the Ohio swift; the men reached the Kentucky River before they had time to realize the greatness of the distance they had covered. They must have thought Jim Harrod had been overcautious in his lecture about the dangers, for they had been able to go ashore at night to cook their suppers of mutton, or to kill a buffalo calf or a few turkeys they happened to see along the bank; they had rolled up in blankets under a shelving rock at night —if it looked like rain—or close to smoldering campfires when the night was clear. There had been no trace of hostile Indians.

Jim discovered that the path he had made in 1774 from Landing Run across country to the new settlement was now overgrown with head-high weeds and cane which seemed to shoot up as he walked along—the soil was that fertile. Indeed, the heavy growth slowed progress through the ten miles to Harrodstown, and the men dragged their heavy loads with difficulty.

As he walked along with his men single file, Captain Harrod was preoccupied with the task of reaching the old camp and depositing the supplies in the cabins. Therefore, he was greatly surprised as he neared the Big Spring to hear sounds of men's voices, the heavy clap of axes, and the crackling of burning weeds and brush within halloo distance of his settlement. Jim investigated and found to his astonishment that another party had arrived ahead of his.[15] The McAfee brothers, his partners in the survey work under Bullitt, had returned with a few others to survey, clear land, and prepare

[15] McAfee, "Life and Times," *loc. cit.*, 24.

for a settlement on Salt River near Harrodstown. They were working hard, planting apple and peach seeds, and putting in corn behind their hastily erected brush fence. Jim knew that the McAfees had been enthusiastic over Kentucky in 1773; but since they had not returned the next year while he was laying out Harrodstown, and since it was not unusual for surveying parties to give up claim to land which they had marked in a spurt of enthusiasm, he thought that they, like many others, had changed their minds about moving into the wilderness. Not all wives were anxious to risk their scalps.

The McAfees explained to Jim that they had not given up their plans for moving to Kentucky. Preparations for Dunmore's War had kept them at home in 1774; but this year they had plowed early, put in corn on their Botetourt County farms, and started to reclaim their new land. And it seemed odd to them, they said, that Harrod's men had overlooked their markings, because they had carved their initials as plain as could be on large oaks and piled brush high around good springs which now apparently lay within the boundaries of the Monongahelans' claims. They had been greatly shocked to find surveyors' poles only a few feet from their land.[16]

Certainly, an unexpected crisis had arisen, and it took all of Harrod's ability as a peacemaker to calm the men.

The McAfees were Scotch-Irish and proud of it. The traits that came to be associated with the frontier were characteristic of these immigrants who had landed in the American colonies with a long tradition of political and religious struggle behind them. Although they had been forced to move from Scotland to northern Ireland over a hundred years before, the Scotch had managed to keep their individuality. In the process of moving and living in strange lands, first in Ireland, then in America, they had developed a love of independence in thought and action, as well as an ideal of self-government, which had increased with the years.

There is no accurate count of the Scotch-Irish in the late

[16] *Ibid.*, 23-24.

eighteenth century, but it has been estimated that in 1790 they numbered only 7.1 per cent of Virginia's population and scarcely more than 25 per cent on her frontier.[17] Most of the backwoodsmen were English, sons and daughters of earlier pioneers from the Eastern seaboard. Many Scotch-Irish in search of good land and freedom from religious intolerance came into Pennsylvania and across to the western ridge, along with small numbers of other nationalities. Among these were Poles, Germans, Irish, English, and Welsh—all represented in Harrod's company.[18] Although these groups intermarried with the Scotch-Irish, it was not unusual for those of purely Welsh or Irish background to migrate with them and join Presbyterian congregations, where they soon lost their identity.

The Presbyterians' strong faith in the Bible as a guidepost to salvation carried over to new frontiers, where these followers of Calvin became leaders in a region unblessed with facilities for education. Those aggressive traits known as "typically Scotch-Irish" were developed through long years of hardship, which saw these rugged people conquer a hard environment. The Calvinist concept of a planned universe, where God's will is worked out in orderly fashion, developed in them a strong belief in predestination, while the convenient handle of foreordained action only enhanced their courage.[19]

The son of one of the McAfee brothers remarked that his pioneer forebears were fully aware of the dangers and difficulties they would have to encounter in Kentucky, but that the prospects of making future fortunes and "the honor of being among the first adventurers in the western wilderness

---

[17] Bureau of the Census, *A Century of Population Growth from the First Census of the United States to the Twelfth, 1790-1900* (Washington, 1909), 116-20.

[18] Collins, *Kentucky*, II, 517.

[19] "Calvinism," *New Schaff-Herzog Encyclopedia of Religious Knowledge*, 13 vols. (New York, 1908-1912), II, 359-63; William W. Sweet, *The Story of Religion in America* (New York, 1939), 172-83.

consoled and supported them, together with a firm reliance upon an over-ruling Providence."[20]

The McAfees found need for their religious faith the day James Harrod and his inspired but less devout followers met them face to face on the banks of Salt River. Jim and his men soon let them know that they had a feeling of ownership, too, because after all, their cabins were already built; they had raised corn in 1774; and had it not been for Dunmore's War, their families would be there that very minute.

Fortunately, Jim's men had done most of their surveying south of the McAfees' claims, but there was sufficient overlapping to necessitate a general discussion and some individual bargaining. Within a few days Harrod and the McAfees managed to come to a preliminary agreement, and the two parties settled down to work in general harmony. Although they straightened out most of the conflicts, it was many years before the courts settled the last claim.[21] In a country where man power was wealth and land was rich and plentiful, reasonable people were often able to reach sensible decisions without resorting to violence or extensive argument. But this was not always the case in Kentucky, particularly in later years when the pioneers were confronted by ambitious newcomers, skilled in the ways of court and eager to take advantage of those whose efforts and bloodshed had built Kentucky. Even in the first years, not all disputes were as easily quieted as those between Jim Harrod and the McAfees—as both parties soon learned.

Only a short time after Harrod's arrival, Daniel Boone and a party of settlers from North Carolina came to Kentucky. They had gone ahead to build a road across the mountains for their employer, Colonel Richard Henderson of the Transylvania Company, who at the same time was concluding a "treaty purchase" with the Cherokee at Sycamore Shoals for the very land that Harrod and the McAfees were clearing.

[20] McAfee, "Life and Times," loc. cit., 13.
[21] Ibid., 23.

Boone's road builders arrived on April 1, when Harrod's party were settled in the town cabins, working on preparations for bringing out their families. If Jim asked Boone for any particulars about Henderson's plans and claims, Daniel no doubt parried, since he was never one to indulge in open argument.

Henderson was a man of importance back in Carolina—a colonel in the militia, a noted orator, a judge—a self-made man who cherished dreams of a great fortune to be made in Western lands. His Treaty of Sycamore Shoals providing for the purchase from the Cherokee of the land south of the Kentucky River was not a treaty at all, but a deed, a purchase clearly in violation of the Royal Proclamation of 1763, which forbade private persons from engaging in land deals with the Indians. To make matters worse, he was negotiating for land not ceded by the Indians through the usual treaty formality. The other land companies such as the Vandalia, the Ohio, and the Loyal had at least confined their purchases to land ceded through authorized agents of the Crown.[22]

The "treaty-purchase" conference lasted four days, with speeches by Henderson and the assembled chieftains. After ten wagonloads of goods including coarse woolens, metal brooches, rum, flour, guns, and ammunition were handed over to the Cherokee along with £2,000 in British money, the Transylvania proprietors were handed the deed to land lying along the Ohio River from the mouth of the Kentucky southeast to the top ridge of Powell's Mountain and west along the ridge to the headwaters of the southwest branch of the Cumberland to the Ohio River.

Scarcely had word of the purchase reached Williamsburg when the governor issued a proclamation strictly charging all justices of the peace, sheriffs, and other officers, civil and military, to prevent the "illegal designs"[23] of Henderson, and pointing out that the King would not sanction any arrange-

[22] Lester, *Transylvania*, 35-47. See Abernethy, *Western Lands*, Index.
[23] Lester, *Transylvania*, 39-40.

ment whereby Indians gave land titles to private purchasers. Down in North Carolina, Governor Josiah Martin, who had also issued a proclamation against Henderson, informed Lord Dartmouth that his purchase was contrary to the express words and meaning of the Royal Proclamation of 1763.[24] So far as is known, Henderson had made no actual attempt to obtain approval of the royal government for his proposed colony, although he later expressed the hope that the project would "be acceptable to his most gracious majesty."[25]

Following their "treaty-purchase," Henderson and his co-proprietors wasted no time but started out immediately to claim their newly acquired empire. They had not proceeded far when they discovered that the company's trace would not permit wagon travel. In fact, it was all a man or horse could do to get through the spring mires, along the swollen streams, up the steep hills, and through the tortuous crags that formed the Wilderness Road.[26] So they stored their wagons and most of the goods which they had counted on to supply their settlement, packed what they could on their horses, and started for Cumberland Gap.

It was near this point that the proprietors met about forty persons returning from Kentucky and heard from them the first news of Indian attacks. The numerous surveying parties and land speculators who had rushed to the West in the spring, eager to claim land under military warrants, had aroused the northern Indians as no hunting parties had ever done. But instead of raiding the infant settlements, they had so far contented themselves with attacking isolated surveyors who happened to wander too close to war roads or main streams.

Henderson had to move fast in establishing his "colony," or the Indians would drive him out. As he recorded in his journal, he approached Kentucky with considerable anxiety

[24] *Ibid.*, 25, 26, 29-47.
[25] *Ibid.*, 25.
[26] *Ibid.*, 66.

A LAST FAREWELL

lest his experiment be wrecked at the outset. But he had more to fear than Indians. He worried most about James Harrod. He could not risk an open argument with him; he must and would win his support.[27]

[27] Henderson's Journal, in Draper Collection, 1CC21-102.

Chapter VII

TRANSYLVANIA

(1775)

"... we have a right to make ... laws without giving offense to Great Britain, or any of the American colonies, without disturbing the repose of any society or community under heaven...." [1]

JIM HARROD had to face another challenger that spring. This was Colonel Thomas Slaughter, who brought a party of land seekers from North Carolina to Harrodstown. When they arrived, Jim greeted them enthusiastically, as usual, and sent the newcomers out in high spirits to begin their search for unclaimed land. However, as soon as they discovered that Harrod's men had already marked vast acreages, they began to grumble and accuse Jim of unfair tactics.

One Sunday while Harrod was scouting at the head of Salt River, he came across Slaughter wandering around in the woods in a very bad humor. The North Carolinian declared that the captain's men had no right to "ride through the country, mark every piece of land they thought proper," [2] and secure all the good springs in the area.

Harrod replied that Slaughter was exaggerating. After all, his men had arrived first and had started a town; and those who were riding around the country marking land were not working for themselves alone but also for those who had re-

---

[1] Judge Henderson's speech to the Transylvania Assembly, quoted in Collins, *Kentucky*, II, 502.
[2] Draper Collection, 1CC21-102.

turned to the settlements in order to bring out more supplies or their families.[3] Of course, everybody wanted good land. Soil wore out with constant use here as well as in Old Virginia. Kentucky was a new country, with plenty of land for them all.

In the midst of this argument, Jim was surprised by the arrival of Colonel Richard Henderson, who was riding by; so, feeling the need for a mediator, he outlined the difficulty and asked advice. When the Judge suggested that both of them go with him to Boonesborough, where they could talk at more leisure, the men agreed.

Monday was a dismal, rainy day, but the Judge never relaxed his efforts to cheer his guests and encourage them to come to an understanding. Although, as Jim learned later, Henderson secretly favored Slaughter,[4] he appeared to be absolutely impartial, pointing out that in a rapidly growing country arguments such as this one were bound to arise, and suggesting that everyone join in forming some kind of government to make laws and rules for preventing trouble. There were four distinct settlements—Boonesborough, Harrodstown, the Boiling Spring, where Harrod intended to live, and St. Asaph's, which John Floyd and several other Virginia surveyors had started. The Judge proposed that in about two weeks representatives from these groups should meet at Boonesborough to form an assembly with power to draw up a constitution and make laws for governing the settlements.

Harrod and Slaughter, declaring Henderson's idea good, agreed to invite their leaders to co-operate. The next morning Harrod was to notify in person those around the fort and at Boiling Spring.[5]

When he left Boonesborough at dawn with Slaughter, Jim was joking and laughing in high spirits, for what might have developed into a serious rift was now resolved into construc-

---
[3] *Ibid.;* Collins, *Kentucky*, II, 499-500; Lester, *Transylvania*, 86-88.
[4] Draper Collection, 1CC21-102.
[5] *Ibid.*

tive action. Although his ready acceptance of Henderson's plan had surprised the Judge, as Jim learned later,[6] it was characteristic of Harrod, who was always willing to step aside in favor of what he considered superior talent and education. While this trait usually worked for the general good, in this case Jim was to learn a hard lesson—that experience, sound judgment, and an understanding of men are as desirable as book learning and enterprise.

Harrod would have been shocked had he read the Judge's own thoughts on this subject. Earlier, Henderson had written that he was unable to learn on what "terms or pretense" the Monongahelans meant to hold land. Since he knew that "so large a body of Lawless people" would cause "trouble and require the utmost exertion" of his abilities to manage them, it had been with "considerable anxiety"[7] that he wished to meet Captain Harrod, but following the discussions at Boonesborough the Judge recorded that "Captain Harrod is a very good man for our purposes."[8]

The proponents of the Transylvania government issued their invitations and set an early date for the first meeting of the new Transylvania Assembly. While they regretted that there was no imposing chapel to house the delegates, they found the shade of a "giant divine elm" not far from the unfinished Boonesborough fort to be a suitable meeting place—plenty good enough, as Henderson expressed it privately, for "a set of scoundrels, who scarcely believe in God or fear a devil."[9]

However, Henderson must have had a change of heart about the delegates, for on the opening day of the Assembly he publicly expressed satisfaction with the type of men at the meeting.

Jim Harrod and the other delegates from the various settle-

[6] *Ibid.*
[7] *Ibid.*
[8] Henderson to the Proprietors, quoted in James Hall, *Sketches of History, Life and Manners in the West*, 2 vols. (Philadelphia, 1834), II, 267.
[9] Collins, *Kentucky*, II, 500.

ments arrived at six o'clock in the morning, ready and eager to start their deliberations. Among them was the Reverend John Lythe, a Harrodstown settler and Anglican minister, who opened the meeting with a solemn prayer.

As soon as this was over, Judge Henderson arose and addressed the group in his most impressive courtroom manner, calling attention to the fact that they were assembled for a noble and honorable purpose, which, however ridiculous or idle it might appear "to superficial minds," was indeed "of most solid consequence."[10] From there he proceeded to a discussion of the problems facing the new Assembly. By referring to English law and not speaking of the governments of either Virginia or of North Carolina, Henderson neatly skirted the touchy subject of prior land claims, which he well knew had already aroused much comment in the Southern colonies.

The governor of North Carolina, amplifying his earlier remarks, had termed Henderson's venture a "daring, unjust and unwarranted Proceeding,"[11] that was also illicit and fraudulent, while one of the Judge's colleagues had asked, "Pray, is Dick Henderson out of his head?"[12]

Following the Judge's address, a three-man committee, including James Harrod, drew up a statement in which they acknowledged the wisdom of the Judge's reasoning and expressed an earnest desire to meet their legislative tasks with vigor. The first order of business was to draft a constitution for the Transylvania "Colony." Henderson's prearranged plan for this constitution called for an elected assembly, with perpetual quitrents and a power of veto reserved for the proprietors. Regardless of any misgivings James Harrod or the other representatives may have had about the feudal overtones of the constitution, or compact, as the proprietors

[10] W. L. Saunders (ed.), *The Colonial Records of North Carolina* (Raleigh, 1886-1890), IX, 1267-69.

[11] Lester, *Transylvania*, 29-47.

[12] Archibald Henderson, "Richard Henderson and the Occupation of Kentucky, 1775," in *Mississippi Valley Historical Review* (Cedar Rapids), I (1914-1915), 341-63.

chose to call it, he and the other delegates approved the instrument and began to carry out its provisions.

Jim served on a number of committees, including the one on lands, of which he was chairman. He drew up regulations for a militia, helped amend a bill prohibiting "profane swearing and Sabbath breaking," and also served on a committee for conserving game.[13]

Daniel Boone introduced a measure for improving the breeding of horses—a laudable, farsighted idea, but one which proved difficult to administer because of the constant inroads by Indians who either killed or stole most of the domestic animals.

One of the few major triumphs for the backwoods philosophy was a law providing for freedom of worship. This passed in spite of the fact that at this time the Church of England was a state institution in Virginia; and further, the only minister present was a member of that congregation. Therefore, this religious provision must be accredited to the temper of the frontier delegates themselves, many of whom, like the Harrods, were dissenters, Scotch-Irish Presbyterians, or indifferent churchgoers.

After agreeing to meet again in September, the delegates adjourned and returned to their surveying, clearing, and planting. In Harrodstown they erected more cabins south of the Town Fork and chinked the old buildings. Harrod cleared land at the Boiling Spring, but spent most of the summer at the other stations, talking with new settlers, advising them on locations, and helping novice hunters supply their parties with food.[14]

The settlers ran short of flour and suffered for lack of greens until the vegetable patches began to mature.[15] The Transylvania proprietors provided much ammunition for the men but could help little with other needed articles because of

[13] "Journal of the Delegates," as printed in Collins, *Kentucky*, II, 501-508.
[14] Draper Collection, 48J10; Collins, *Kentucky*, II, 518-20.
[15] Draper Collection, 1CC21-102.

their inability to bring out the bulk of the provisions they had packed in the wagons, still on the other side of the pass. Henderson reported great suffering in Boonesborough, particularly for want of flour; but he managed to get salt from Harrodstown.[16]

Early in the summer a party of men from Piedmont Virginia asked James Harrod to survey for them.[17] One member of the group kept a journal in which he recorded the high ambitions of his fellow travelers as they crossed the mountains to Fort Pitt and went down the Ohio by canoe to Harrod's Landing. He told of many hardships along the way, largely due to their lack of skill as hunters and to fog and much "violent dew." But when they arrived at Harrodstown, he said, their enthusiasm for Kentucky brushed aside unpleasant memories, and immediately the men asked Harrod to help them locate unsurveyed land.

Captain Jim made a good impression. The Virginians were especially happy over his detailed knowledge of the country, his affable ways, his undoubted efficiency; but above all they were delighted with Harrod as a cook. His "excellent stew of buffalo and as much lettuce and young endive as they could eat" pleased them more than any food they had consumed in months, recorded one man in his journal. Also, the work of surveying under his guidance progressed rapidly. The men located several good tracts, and Jim marked claims for one of his Moore cousins, as well as ten thousand acres "for some gentlemen in Virginia," by order of Council.[18]

Before Harrod started out with the party, he talked over with Henderson the points for survey.[19] Interestingly, the Judge's diary made no reference to any argument or difference of opinion between the two leaders. But whether the newcomers observed it or not, all was not peaceful in Transylvania.

Almost as soon as the Assembly had adjourned, the Harrods-

[16] *Ibid.*
[17] Nourse, "Journey to Kentucky in 1775," *loc. cit.*, 121 ff.
[18] *Ibid.* [19] *Ibid.*

town settlers voiced dissatisfaction with the new regulations. Jim tried to calm them as best he could. Backed by Fincastle County officials with whom he kept in touch during the summer, and influenced by George Rogers Clark's wait-and-see attitude, Harrod was trying to mark time while waiting for official opinion on Henderson's purchase to crystallize.[20] Even if Great Britain should decide in Transylvania's favor his men would not lose out. And had it not been for the proprietors' own highhanded and arbitrary measures late in the summer, Harrod might have allowed matters to drift until the next meeting of the Transylvania Assembly.

Since Jim left no record of his thoughts on this subject, his reasoning can be explained only by his actions. From these it is apparent that in all his dealings during these first years in Kentucky, Harrod's first loyalty was to the men who had chosen him as their leader; for while John Floyd of St. Asaph's grew more sympathetic with Henderson's cause, accepting the commission of company surveyor, Harrod's attitude grew increasingly cool.[21] His men, who were never inclined to follow orders merely because of the authority behind them, were unwilling to obey what they considered unnecessary and arbitrary restrictions on their movements.[22] Newcomers, seeing the muddled state of affairs in Transylvania, either ignored the rulings or returned to their old homes rather than risk their efforts on uncertain claims.[23] But as fast as they went back East others came out, and as the summer progressed, more and more of them turned to Jim Harrod for authority, leaving Judge Henderson in an increasingly depressed state of mind which he attempted to bolster through a combination of pretense and minor compromise. Finally, disheartened and ignored, the Judge returned to North Caro-

[20] Abernethy, *Western Lands*, 125, 129.
[21] *Ibid.*, 164; Lester, *Transylvania*, 133-34.
[22] Max Savelle, *The Foundations of American Civilization* (New York, 1942), 217, 416; Thomas P. Abernethy, *Three Virginia Frontiers* (University, La., 1940), 66-68; J. F. D. Smyth, *A Tour in the United States of America* (Dublin, 1784), I, 217-18.
[23] Hall, *Sketches of the West*, II, 266-67; Draper Collection, 1CC195-97.

lina for consultation with his coproprietors who, to worsen matters, were quarreling among themselves.[24]

In addition to voting Daniel Boone two thousand acres of land for his "signal services" to the company, the proprietors announced an increase in land prices from twenty shillings to two pounds ten shillings per hundred acres. Previously, they had done a good land business—mostly with people who had no money and were consequently in debt to the company. But when they announced the new ruling, and John Floyd started charging two dollars Continental money for an entry, business began to slump.[25]

The crowning insult as far as James Harrod was concerned was the surveying by the company then going on at the Falls of the Ohio.[26] Harrod, like Connolly, Bullitt, and numerous others who had surveyed near the site of Louisville, realized fully that a town of importance was bound to develop there sooner or later. But when Harrod learned that Boone had orders to survey large acreages for the proprietors only, he was indignant. This selfish move overshadowed even the advance in land prices.

Harrod's growing antagonism so worried Judge Henderson's brother that he wrote a letter to one of the proprietors, praying for assistance: "I acknowledge the task is hard," he said, "but hard as it is, if you or my brother dont personally attend at this place this fall there will be reason to fear that matters will not go on so smoothly as you may imagine . . . upon the whole, Sir, you . . . ought to be here."[27]

In spite of this urgent letter, Colonel Henderson did not appear at Boonesborough until after Christmas.

Meanwhile there had been important additions to the population. During the summer Daniel Boone had returned

[24] Lester, *Transylvania*, 81-82, 107; Draper Collection, 1CC21-102.
[25] Lester, *Transylvania*, 127-29.
[26] W. L. Saunders (ed.), *North Carolina Colonial Records*, X, 384; Abernethy, *Western Lands*, 162.
[27] Letter in the Duke University Archives, quoted in Lester, *Transylvania*, 112.

to the Holston, bringing his family. With them came friends and neighbors bound for Harrodstown. Among these was Hugh McGary, a hot-tempered, loud-talking but able Scotch-Irishman from the undermountain country, who brought his wife and three stepsons, as well as several other families, to join Boone's party in Powell's Valley.[28]

Since Jim Harrod had spent considerable time in North Carolina, his plan for starting a town in Kentucky was well known to people there. Now that it had actually been started, McGary's company had "sold out" their individual holdings to join their old friend, Captain Jim. Men could plow the ground, fence in new clearings, and erect cabins, but only the arrival of women and children could give permanency to settlement efforts.[29] Jim learned that McGary had gotten lost at Dick's River after leaving Boone's party. This river, like the Kentucky, flowed through a limestone canyon which was steep and difficult to climb. Realizing that it would be foolish to wander aimlessly looking for a way out, McGary had left the stock with his fourteen-year-old stepson, James Ray, and two other boys, and taken the rest of the party ahead. Finally he made camp for them too, and hurried alone through the woods, hoping to find Harrodstown. Fortunately, as he was following a path to the Boiling Spring station, he met a settler who offered to guide the women and children.[30]

In all this excitement over the arrival of families, the September date set for the second Transylvania Assembly passed almost unnoticed. Although the Proprietors had transferred the land office to Harrodstown in an effort to pacify Jim's settlers, the move had done no material good. When the company announced that the postponed Assembly would meet in December, Captain Jim would not enter his name on the list of candidates who were to represent his settlers.[31]

[28] Draper Collection, 12C34, 36J3, 17CC195, 7J45, 1C51.
[29] *Ibid.*, 12C34; Mann Butler, *A History of the Commonwealth of Kentucky* (Cincinnati, 1834), 28-29.
[30] Butler, *Commonwealth of Kentucky*, 28-29; Draper Collection, 12C15.
[31] Lester, *Transylvania*, 114, 132-33.

GENERAL JAMES RAY OF HARRODSBURG, AS A CHILD, A MEMBER OF A PARTY OF SETTLERS LED BY DANIEL BOONE. FROM A CONTEMPORARY SKETCH. *Wisconsin Historical Society.*

The dispute reached a climax shortly after Will Harrod rushed down from Fort Pitt with news that relations between the colonies and Great Britain were getting worse. At this point two new elements entered the Transylvania dispute. Apparent to the Westerners was the certainty that no decision Great Britain might make favoring Henderson could have any lasting effect if war came between England and the American colonies.[32] Also, regardless of Indian conferences and treaties aimed at pacifying the uneasy tribesmen, warfare between them and the Kentuckians was certain, because the Britishers had already begun to hand out arms and ammunition.

Jim Harrod and his followers had but one course open to them: they must appeal to Virginia for help against the Indians; and to ensure the necessary wholehearted effort in defense, they must at once clear up the land-title quarrel and see that Kentucky was recognized as a real part of the Virginia colony.

Late in December Jim's settlers drew up a remonstrance to the Proprietors, protesting against the injustices of the company and condemning the large Louisville grants reserved by the owner.[33] With this formality out of the way, they drafted a petition which was signed by eighty-four landholders, including William and Levi Harrod and numerous Moore and other relatives by blood or marriage.[34] The petition opened with a survey of the proprietors' activities, including the promises they had made to lure people to the country and the increase in land rates on tracts to which the company had no just claim. Harrod's party called attention to the fact that Henderson's purchase conflicted with Virginia's charter rights. They pointed out that the Cherokee could have had no legal basis for making the sale in the first place, since the land had already been turned over to Vir-

[32] Abernethy, *Western Lands*, 162-63.
[33] Lester, *Transylvania*, 127-28.
[34] Abernethy, *Western Lands*, 162-63; Collins, *Kentucky*, II, 510-11.

ginia by the Six Nations at Fort Stanwix. Fortunately, they did not attempt to explain the legal basis of the Six Nations' title to Kentucky—a territory which they had claimed by conquest but never by occupation. The Kentuckians warned that should the Transylvanians be granted title to the country, all prior claims would be invalid and the purchasers subject to almost any demand by the Company.

It is doubtful that Henderson could have understood the true basis of this petition. To James Harrod and his fellow frontiersmen, it contained the very core of their existence.

For two and three generations these pioneer families had faced westward, confident in the belief that their own hands could obtain for them all that was necessary for their existence. Across the Blue Mountains they had found new land that needed only to be cleared and planted and perhaps, when the time came, recorded to become their own. They could plow the soil, plant their seeds, raise their crude cabins, fence in their pastures, ride into the woods on their autumn hunts, and return to harvest their crops. Their lives were marked by constant danger and new excitement. They made friends with Indians who smiled on them; they fought those who opposed their coming. They looked on the red men's land ownership much as they did on their own, belonging to them while they stayed, passing on to the next occupant when they had gone. Kentucky was open to settling; for, by the Indians' own admission, almost a hundred years had passed since any of them had lived in this favorite hunting ground. The settlers were willing to work with Richard Henderson in opening this wilderness; they would join in its defense and meet with him under the giant elm to devise measures for the common safety and the common good. They would treat with the proprietors as equals; but pay them homage, as owners of the soil entitled to annual quitrent—they would not![35]

[35] Collins, *Kentucky*, II, 509-10.

Chapter VIII

VIRGINIA CREATES A COUNTY
(1776)

"All that part thereof which lies to the south and westward of a line beginning on the Ohio at the south of the Great Sandy Creek . . . to the Great Laurel Ridge or Cumberland Mountain . . . to the line of North Carolina shall be one distinct county and called and known by the name of Kentucky."[1]

JIM HARROD'S truce with Henderson ended abruptly. After the December meeting at Harrodsburg, as the first settlement was now generally known, he became an outspoken, unflinching opponent of the Transylvanian scheme, winning followers in other stations as well as in his own. Consequently, by spring many people in Boonesborough were either moving to the older settlement or expressing sympathy with its cause.[2]

This rising opposition evidently disturbed the Transylvania surveyor greatly: ". . . the Harrodsburg men have made a second revolt and Harrod and Jack Jones at the head of the Banditti," he reported to one of the proprietors. "God knows how it may end," he added hysterically, "but things at this time bear but a dull aspect—they utterly refuse to have any Land Surveyed or comply with one of the office rules. . . ."[3]

John Gabriel Jones, who joined Harrod in leading this

[1] *Journal of the Virginia House of Delegates* (Williamsburg, 1776), December 20, 1776.
[2] Lester, *Transylvania*, 133-34.
[3] Draper Collection, 1XX10, as quoted in Lester, *Transylvania*, 133.

second revolt, was a young lawyer, the son of a prominent Valley family, and a pepper-spitting little man.[4] His arrival in Harrodsburg during these crucial months provided Captain Jim with skills to supplement his own natural leadership and persuasive abilities; for Jones could phrase arguments gracefully and logically, easily matching those of the most polished Transylvania attorney, while his knowledge of legislative methods was of great assistance to Jim.

More far-reaching aid for Harrodsburg came with the arrival of George Rogers Clark, who had shown a deep interest in Kentucky during the previous summer. He appeared suddenly in the forest outside the town one fine spring day, much to the surprise of fifteen-year-old James Ray who had just finished turning his stepfather's horses into a new pasture and was about to set his teeth in a fine, juicy duck he had killed and roasted near a small spring.

"My name is Clark," the Virginian explained in a soft, kindly drawl. "I have come out to see what you brave fellows are doing in Kentucky, and to lend you a helping hand, if necessary!"[5]

Having noticed that the tall, red-haired man was eyeing his duck hungrily, Ray handed it over and invited the newcomer to take a few bites. To James's amazement, Clark devoured the meat completely, leaving scarcely a bone for him to pick. When the last bit had disappeared, Ray led the way to Harrodsburg.

Both Jim and Will had served with Clark in Dunmore's campaign, Will having been in the same company with him on McDonald's expedition. Moreover, both the Harrods had participated with him in the Fort Gower meeting. In the course of these adventures, Jim had grown to respect the

[4] John Redd, "Reminiscences of Western Virginia, 1770-1790," in *Virginia Magazine of History and Biography* (Richmond), VI (1898-99), 337-44; VII (1899-1900), 1-16.

[5] This quotation is from Butler, *Commonwealth of Kentucky*, 37 n., and is, according to Butler, based on General Ray's own narrative. See also Draper Collection, 12C16-17.

VIRGINIA CREATES A COUNTY 93

energetic young soldier, recognizing in him abilities far above the average for his age and experience;[6] it was natural, therefore, that he should turn to Clark for advice on the Transylvania land problem.[7]

After listening to Jim's chronicle of the year's events, Clark suggested a meeting of the settlers to consider the Transylvania dispute.[8] Harrod told him that he had already planned such a gathering. The people were to elect delegates to represent them in the Virginia Assembly; further, they expected to ask for separation from Fincastle County, which was entirely too large to have but two delegates. Since Virginia had taken no action on the Harrodsburg petition, it was plain that the Kentuckians needed to have delegates of their own to assure their side a fair hearing. Gossip had it that Henderson's men were going to Williamsburg to push for recognition of their Cherokee land purchase, and if their plan were successful it would cheat the firstcomers out of their legal rights. Harrod was going to make sure this did not happen.[9]

Clark had a different proposal for dealing with the threat. He too wanted an election, he said, but he believed it would be wiser to send representatives who would have no official status as delegates, and who would therefore be in a better position to bargain.[10]

While it was true that many influential Virginians, includ-

[6] Draper Collection, 12C23.
[7] George Rogers Clark Memoir, written about 1791 or later, Draper Collection 47J1, *et seq.* This "Memoir" has been printed in a biography of Clark—based largely on Virginia State Papers (Richmond, State Archives)—by Consul W. Butterfield, *A History of Lieutenant Colonel George Rogers Clark's Conquest of the Illinois* . . . (Washington, 1904), 208-302. The account of Clark's thoughts and actions on the Transylvania problem which follows in the text has been based upon the "Memoir" and supplemented by Butterfield's interpretation in his biography. The Clark "Memoir" has also been published in James Alton James (ed.), *George Rogers Clark Papers, 1771-1781*, Vol. VIII of Illinois Historical Collections (Springfield, 1912), 208-302, and in William Hayden English, *Conquest of the Country Northwest of the River Ohio; and Life of Gen. George Rogers Clark* . . . (Indianapolis, 1896).
[8] Butterfield, *Clark's Conquest*, 26.
[9] *Ibid.*, 29.
[10] Clark "Memoir," in Butterfield, *Clark's Conquest*, 208-302.

ing Patrick Henry, had shown sympathy with Henderson's cause, most of them had now turned against the Transylvanians.[11] However, Clark believed that the Council was still reluctant to assume responsibility for the welfare of these distant settlements.

But Jim was depending on Virginia, and, besides, he had announced his plan for sending delegates to Williamsburg.[12] It was too late to do anything about it.

The election was a long-drawn-out affair, lasting five days, and when the last settler had voted, Captain Jim announced that George Rogers Clark and John Gabriel Jones would represent them.

In preparation for their delegates' departure, Harrod planned two petitions for presentation to the Virginia Assembly. With Jones as chairman, he and the other men formulated the first document as a defense of their land claims, basing it on bounty warrants granted by Governor Dunmore and on regular prior-occupancy laws of the colony. Characterizing Henderson's purchase as illegal, on the ground that Virginia had a right to it under her charter, they pointed out that her citizens had "fought and bled for it," and that had it not been for the defeat of the bloody Shawnee at the Battle of Point Pleasant, the region would still be largely uninhabitable. In conclusion they asked that their delegates be recognized, stating that they had already elected a committee of twenty-one to maintain order in the district.[13]

Harrod's second petition was on behalf of the new committee and pointed out how impossible it was for two delegates to represent adequately all of Fincastle County.[14] It said pointedly that it would be "impolitic" for the Convention to permit "such a respectable body of prime Rifle men to re-

[11] Lester, *Transylvania*, 44-47, 123-26; Abernethy, *Western Lands*, 165.
[12] Clark "Memoir," in Butterfield, *Clark's Conquest*, 28-29.
[13] Draper Collection, 14S2.
[14] James R. Robertson (ed.), *Petitions of the Early Inhabitants of Kentucky to the General Assembly of Virginia, 1769-1792*, Filson Club Publication, No. 27 (Louisville, 1914); Draper Collection, 4B63.

main even in a state of neutrality,"[15] particularly since at that very moment a group of men from North Carolina were preparing to challenge Virginia's charter rights. Everyone in the West knew that the Indians were planning an attack on Virginia's borders.

At the head of the list of signers to this petition was the name of James Harrod—the only one among the eight men who had represented the Boiling Spring and Harrodsburg settlements at the Transylvania Assembly. Others were as dissatisfied as Jim, but they were less willing to express themselves openly at this time.

No longer were the Kentuckians to be looked on as "poor relations" fit for charity; the West had begun to feel its own strength for contributing to the general colonial welfare. Harrod's days of temporizing were over; he was now rejecting Henderson's claim openly and completely.[16] A short time later he learned that Colonel Preston had sent word that Virginia was now ready to maintain her claim against Transylvania. When this became generally known, others who had been shy about signing the petition denounced the proprietors.[17]

In the midst of these explosive events, runners from the Delaware tribes on the Wabash brought a disturbing message. Word had come to their chieftains that the Kickapoos were about to sign a treaty with the English, a move which the Delawares were powerless to stop.[18]

This was ominous news for Captain Jim, who had counted on the friendly Delawares to maintain a buffer against hostile tribes. Obviously, once the Kickapoos had gone over to the British, other tribes, including the Delawares, might follow. Many of the younger chieftains were already restive. For

---

[15] Robertson (ed.), *Petitions*, 40.
[16] Lester, *Transylvania*, 130-34; Abernethy, *Western Lands*, 163.
[17] Abernethy, *Western Lands*, 163.
[18] Draper Collection, 14S2; "Deposition of John Gibson in regard to Delaware Indians," in *Virginia Magazine of History and Biography*, XIII (1905-1906), 423-24; Thwaites and Kellogg (eds.), *Revolution on the Upper Ohio*, 43-44.

several months it had been apparent that the Shawnee were listening to British flattery and accepting bribes in return for sympathy with their cause.

The Delawares now declared the situation critical and suggested to the "lone Long Knife," as they affectionately referred to Harrod, that he send a reliable man to confer with their chieftains.[19]

The possibilities for Kentucky were so serious that Jim decided to go in person to see what could be done and invited Garret Pendergrass, a friend from Monongahela days, to accompany him.[20] What Harrod learned at the Delaware village caused him great anxiety. The Kickapoos were determined to make war on the white men who had stolen their favorite hunting ground. Remembering their promises after Dunmore's War, some of the Shawnee were willing to remain quiet, but others were restless. Even some of the Delawares had been accepting guns and rum from the British. With this uncertain state of affairs, it was plain to Jim that anything might happen.[21] There was little he and Pendergrass could do but thank the Delawares for their pains and return to the settlements. One point was clear, however: there could be little doubt that Kentucky must have help, and quickly, if the settlers were to hold out. More than ever it was necessary to settle the question of Virginia's jurisdiction, for on this point depended any future assistance the Assembly might grant.

Prior to Harrod's return, Clark and Jones left for Williamsburg, hoping to reach the capital a short time before the summer session of the legislature had adjourned. The Wilderness Road appeared the safest and quickest route, so the two men set out on horseback. On the second day they discovered Indian signs which caused them to speed their trip as much as possible. Then Jones's horse gave out, and the two took turns

---

[19] Thwaites and Kellogg (eds.), *Revolution on the Upper Ohio*, 43-44.
[20] *Ibid.*
[21] *Ibid.*

riding. The weather was very rainy, as Clark reported later to Harrod; their feet were wet for three or four days, with no chance of drying them because of the danger from making a fire. Both the men developed "scald feet," a most shocking complaint which caused the soles of their feet to feel hot and tender.[22] But Clark cheered his companion with the prospect of finding relief at an advanced station across Cumberland Gap.

"Grievously disappointed" over their failure to find anything but a few hogs there to greet them, the men sat down on a log to consider what they should do next. They decided to fortify themselves in a cabin and wait for their sore feet to heal, meanwhile applying to them a mixture of pork fat and oak-bark ooze. Within a few days they had recovered sufficiently to continue their journey as far as Fincastle, where they learned to their dismay that the Virginia Assembly had already adjourned. Once more they had to review their situation.[23] There was no point in returning to Harrodsburg with nothing accomplished; nor could they expect to receive any definite assurances of help from Virginia as long as the Assembly was not in session. They must wait until fall.

Clark and Jones did not know it, but at about the time they left Harrodsburg, the Virginia Convention had taken into consideration the December petition and had passed a resolution restating priority of settlement as the basis for land claims and denying the validity of titles conveyed by Indians in violation of Virginia's charter. The Convention had also denied an appeal by James Harrod, Evan Shelby, and others for additional pay allowances for their men who had served in Dunmore's War.

While the announcement restating the basis for land claims apparently closed the matter,[24] Richard Henderson and his coproprietors issued a statement at Williamsburg, forbidding

[22] Clark "Memoir," in Butterfield, *Clark's Conquest*, 208-302.
[23] *Ibid.*
[24] *Journal of the Virginia Convention* (Williamsburg, 1776), May 28, June 24, 1776.

any person to take up Transylvania land during the controversy.[25]

The Virginia legislature then appointed a commission to study and report on the controversial problem.

Although Clark had learned that the new governor of Virginia, Patrick Henry, was ill at his home in Hanover, he nevertheless made a trip there in order to secure his backing for the Harrodsburg cause.[26] This he was able to do. Delighted with the approval, Clark appeared before the Council at Williamsburg with a letter from the governor. But he soon discovered that these gentlemen were not all of like mind. Among them were one or two aristocrats who had little sympathy with the idea of frontier expansion, believing that it drained the Eastern seaboard of manpower and material at a time when there was little to spare. But finally, after much argument, they agreed to lend Clark five hundred pounds of powder.[27]

This was a great disappointment to the Harrodsburg delegate. He wrote immediately to the Council, informing them that it was out of his power to convey the stores at his own expense over such a distance and he must therefore reject their offer. He pointed out that a country that was not worth protecting was not worth claiming.[28]

This statement jolted the Council out of its lethargy, and the members ordered that the five hundred pounds of gunpowder be sent forthwith to Pittsburgh—with no strings attached.[29]

Overjoyed, Clark wrote at once to Harrod, telling him the good news and asking that he send a party of men to convey the powder.[30]

Harrod never received the letter.

---

[25] Palmer and others (arrs.), *Virginia State Papers*, I, 271-72.
[26] Clark "Memoir," in Butterfield, *Clark's Conquest*, 208-302.
[27] *Ibid.*
[28] *Ibid.*
[29] *Journals of the Council of Virginia* (Williamsburg, 1776), August 23, 1776.
[30] Clark "Memoir," in Butterfield, *Clark's Conquest*, 208-302.

THE COMMITTEE OF SAFETY FOR THE COLONY OF VIRGINIA.

To *Lev Harrod [?]*
William Harrod Gentleman

BY Virtue of the Power and Authority invested in us, by the Delegates and Representatives of the several Counties and Corporations in General Convention assembled, we, reposing especial Trust and Confidence in your Patriotism, Fidelity, Courage, and good Conduct, do, by these Presents, constitute and appoint you to be *Captain* of the Militia of the *District of West Augusta* ; and you are therefore carefully and diligently to discharge the Trust reposed in you, by disciplining all Officers and Soldiers under your Command. And we do hereby require them to obey you, as their *Captain*. And you are to observe and follow all such Orders and Directions as you shall from Time to Time receive from the Convention, the Committee of Safety for the Time being, or any superior Officers, according to the Rules and Regulations established by the Convention.

GIVEN under our Hands, at *Williamsburgh* this *27* Day of *March* ANNO DOMINI 1776.

John Page
Dudley Digges
[Harrington?]
Tho: Lud: Lee
Jr: Jones
Thomas Walker

WILLIAM HARROD'S COMMISSION FROM THE VIRGINIA COMMITTEE OF SAFETY, DRAPER COLLECTION, 4NN27. THE NAME WHICH HAS BEEN STRUCK THROUGH IS THAT OF LEVI HARROD, WILLIAM'S BROTHER. *Wisconsin Historical Society.*

Here matters stood when on the opening day Clark and Jones presented their two petitions to the Assembly, requesting at the same time that they be seated as delegates from the "Western Part of Fincastle County." No county by that name being in existence and the legal representation for Fincastle having been provided, the authorities refused to grant the Harrodsburg request.[31]

Henderson, whose purchase had been disallowed, tried a new point of attack by attempting to have his claims validated under Virginia law at the expense of other companies—Harrod's in particular.[32]

Thomas Slaughter, who had opposed Harrod's activities when he first came to Kentucky, also had a petition on behalf of himself and other "inhabitants situate near Kentuckke."[33] It was a lucky turn, because Slaughter not only reinforced the Harrodsburg pleas, but called attention to the need for organized and well-functioning militia. By dramatizing the danger of Indians, the Kentuckians showed that they actually were forming a line of defense for the older settlements. This argument succeeded. That same day the House of Delegates began consideration of a bill for creation of a new county.[34]

The strongest friends the Harrodsburg people had in that official body were Thomas Jefferson and George Mason, who saw eye to eye with Governor Patrick Henry on the Transylvania-Harrodsburg controversy and speeded the bill to its third reading.[35]

At this point the opponents got busy, for Henderson, rival land companies, and certain western delegates did not want a new county created out of "their" territory.

In spite of this activity Jefferson managed to bring out the bill. After almost a month of jockeying, arguing, and closed-door maneuvering, the bill passed the House and Senate. On

[31] *Ibid.*
[32] Lester, *Transylvania*, 148-49.
[33] *Ibid.*, 145-46.
[34] *Ibid.*
[35] *Ibid.;* Abernethy, *Western Lands*, 166.

the last day of December, 1776, the legislature created the new county of Kentucky, embracing that part of Virginia south and west of a line from the Ohio below the Big Sandy to the Laurel Ridge, thence to the line of North Carolina.[86]

It was too bad that James Harrod and his men, who had been the first leaders of the Henderson revolt, could not have been there that day. Clark and Jones had represented them well, but the triumph was theirs. The creation of the county of Kentucky prophesied doom for their adversaries. It was a victory for the little man against the domination of a feudalistic land company, and as such it gained in importance beyond the immediate result.

On Virginia's old settlement law Jim's company of forty men had staked their future. Now that the House of Delegates had agreed that they themselves had an obligation to help defend Kentucky and had demonstrated that willingness by sending powder and lead and creating a new county, little else mattered. It could be only a short time before Henderson's priority claim would be exploded.

Harrod and his men knew how to deal with Indians. All they needed was powder and lead; their guns would do the rest. Virginia had recognized their right to band together as a political unit in defense. Kentucky at last was more than a river.

[86] For boundaries, see quotation at beginning of this chapter.

Chapter IX

TWO RESCUES

(1776-1777)

"I am no politition yet I can see that we are in no posture for deffence."[1]

GEORGE ROGERS CLARK and John Gabriel Jones, having finished their business in Old Virginia, prepared to return immediately to Kentucky by way of the Wilderness Road, but when a messenger from Fort Pitt reported that Harrod had not sent the expected party to convey the five hundred pounds of powder, they changed their plans and started for Fort Pitt instead.

This was the first hint Clark had that his letter to Captain Jim had gone astray. The quantity of ammunition might have appeared trifling to people in the East, but it was of vital importance to the Kentuckians. Clark knew it must be conveyed to them as soon as possible.[2] At Fort Pitt, however, the Harrodsburg delegates learned that the Indians expected to waylay the powder escort boat on its trip down the Ohio. This news posed another difficulty which delay would only aggravate, so Clark and Jones, hastily enlisting several hands to load the twenty-five kegs of powder into their flat-bottomed boats, set out as quietly as possible in order to slip by the hostile Indians. They managed to pass their enemies in the night without being detected, but as they approached Limestone Creek they discovered that they were still being followed.

---

[1] The Rev. John Brown to Col. William Preston, May 5, 1775, Draper Collection, 4QQ15.
[2] Clark "Memoir," in Butterfield, *Clark's Conquest*, 208-302.

During the night, therefore, they hid the stores in four or five places at considerable distances apart along the banks, ran their vessels a few miles lower and set them adrift,[3] and started for Harrod's fort where they expected to make up a rescue party. They went by way of the Blue Licks to a point on the west fork of Licking Creek where there was an old cabin. Here they posted guards and sat down to rest.

Within a short time Simon Kenton and three other scouts happened to come along.[4] They suggested a plan for saving the powder. There was a larger hunting party in the vicinity, and if the two groups could join forces, they might be able to rescue the stores. Help from Harrodsburg would not be needed. But whereas the probability of running into the other hunters was uncertain, the danger of the Indians finding the hidden powder was imminent. Clark therefore proposed that he take half the men and proceed, with Kenton as their pilot, to Harrod's settlement, while Jones and the others waited at the cabin on the chance that they might recruit sufficient strength to rescue the stores.[5]

Clark and Kenton had scarcely disappeared in the forest when the other hunters arrived at the shelter. After a short consultation, Jones decided that although he had but ten men in all, the need for speedy action made an attempt at rescue worth the risk. Following the buffalo trace to the lower Blue Lick, they had gone only a few miles when Chief Pluggy and a band of Mingos confronted them. The short skirmish that followed was tragic for the white men. Pluggy's band killed three of them, including the brave but impulsive John Gabriel Jones, and took several prisoners. The rest escaped to tell Harrod and Clark what had happened.[6]

Leaving Clark to organize the fort defenses, Captain Jim rounded up a rescue party of about thirty men, including Simon Kenton, and marched by way of McClelland's Fort,

[3] *Ibid.*
[4] Collins, *Kentucky*, II, 445.
[5] *Ibid.*
[6] *Ibid.*; Clark "Memoir," in Butterfield, *Clark's Conquest*, 208-302.

where Kenton had been living in recent months. From there they went north to the Ohio, striking the shore not far from the point where the cargo lay hidden.[7] Harrod's men dug up the powder and packed it on horses while Kenton reconnoitered the country for Indians. Kenton returned with the news that although he had not actually seen any tribesmen there were signs of them in the neighborhood. Believing that it would be too risky to go home by the war road, Jim led his party downstream several miles and took a short cut through the woods to an old buffalo road which joined the route they had used coming up.[8] The plan worked perfectly, but Harrod's joy over the safe arrival of the ammunition was overshadowed by his fear of more raids from Pluggy's band.

His fears were well founded, because a few days later Indians attacked McClelland's Fort, killing the leader and a number of others. Simon Kenton piloted the remaining settlers to Harrodsburg, where added strength made up in part for the loss of one more wilderness station.

It was abundantly evident to Will Harrod that although the Shawnee under Chief Cornstalk appeared to be intent on keeping their pledge of friendship, small bands of their people showed increasing signs of hostility. Beyond doubt there was little hope for more than a temporary neutrality. Only recently the Delawares had reported that hostile tribes were already threatening to make war on them because of their friendliness to the Virginians. But, as any intelligent frontier captain well knew, the fault was not all with the Indians.

A few months earlier the militia commander in the Monongahela region had notified Will Harrod that a number of white people had crossed the Ohio and killed some of the Indians as they were returning to their homes from the treaty

---

[7] Draper Collection, 15C25; Collins, *Kentucky*, II, 445; Butler, *Commonwealth of Kentucky*, 40-42.
[8] Butler, *Commonwealth of Kentucky*, 40-42.

meeting at Fort Pitt. An action of this kind would destroy forever the faith of the Indians. The commander suggested to Will that should he find another such uncalled-for action "in the wind," he should exert every effort to "frustrate it."[9]

The previous September, on his return from Kentucky with a party of fourteen men, including his brother Levi, Will had been surprised to find no hostility visible along the Ohio. True, he had met several Indian hunting parties, but, as he reported to Colonel Dorsey Pentecost at the time, the red men "were very sivle."[10]

While this report had quieted the minds of the settlers to a degree, the militia officers had continued to work feverishly, building new forts along the Allegheny ridge. Under Pentecost's orders Will supervised a part of this work but spent a larger amount of time buying cattle and laying in provisions against attack.[11]

Colonel Pentecost, an able executive and a Connolly appointee, was doing his best to build adequate defenses. At one time he ordered Will to take fifty men for scout duty along the Ohio. Harrod was to draft ten men from his company, as well as ten each from four other captains, and to watch for any hostile Indians who happened to cross to the south side of the Ohio. These he was to treat as open and avowed enemies and, if necessary, he was to "Chastize them."[12] The colonel also cautioned Will to protect the settlers as best he could, to take sufficient provisions along, and to march the men to his new Grave Creek command, where he was to erect a fort. Pentecost added a warning that Harrod was to be frugal in the expediture of money but assured him that he knew he would give "a good account of those Rasculs that may attempt to Attack our Lives Libertys or property."[13]

As always, Will set out with appropriate energy to comply with orders, but this time he met a snag. Some of the men

[9] Draper Collection, 4NN34.
[11] Ibid., 4NN34.
[13] Ibid.
[10] Ibid., 3ZZ6.
[12] Ibid., 4NN28-29.

who had enrolled under other captains and were now to transfer to Will's outfit looked on the county lieutenant's orders as a personal affront to their chosen leader. Twenty-five men under the daring Captain David Owens made up a petition which they promptly forwarded to Harrod.

In it they expressed their unwillingness to join his company unless they could have David Owens, the captain of their choice, to lead them. Since they had entire confidence in his ability, they would "never forsake him" until they found sufficient cause.[14] They punctuated this demand with a request that Captain Harrod disclose the reason for official dissatisfaction with their leader.

The need for concerted action had certainly been made clear to Owens and his men, and there was no time for further explanations. Will was eager to carry out his orders promptly, but he knew from firsthand experience how insistent frontiersmen were about serving under their own captains. In this case, because of the general knowledge of the situation, he had expected the men to be more reasonable; the need was urgent, and they knew it.

Colonel Pentecost refused to be alarmed by the petition and wrote Will that he did not doubt that the proper number of men would soon arrive at Grave Creek. Once more he reminded Harrod to be careful and to "use good Oeconomy" and not be too adventuresome. He warned him to be on guard because there was no doubt that Harrod and his men were in great danger. Then, in an apparent attempt to soothe Will's injured pride, he added, "I place the greatest confidence in your abilities, all the fear I have for you is that you will be too rash."[15]

Additional orders which arrived at Grave Creek a few weeks later directed Harrod to keep the post well guarded at all times and to allow no furloughs except in cases of real necessity. The men were to assist the inhabitants by guarding them during harvest; scouts were to reconnoiter the river,

[14] *Ibid.*, 4NN31.   [15] *Ibid.*, 4NN36.

being careful to remain at work and not engage in hunting, as they were always tempted to do; while Harrod was to enclose the fort with a picket fence as soon as possible. In a final warning note, the colonel admonished Will not to neglect "the Dutey we ow to our Creator," and to be sure that the men did not "Practice of prefain Swearing or Brackng the Sabat Day by hunting or other wise."[16]

With these general and specific orders at hand, Harrod speeded work on his fort and the preparations for defense. He must have been amused by the final admonition, however, and it is unlikely that he tried to enforce any distinct Sabbath behavior, for to the frontiersmen one day was like the next, and activities were seldom governed by religious dicta during times of peril.

Late in January of 1777, Will received an important letter from Pentecost, referring to orders from Governor Henry.[17] Two men had gone to New Orleans to buy powder for the Allegheny forts and had not been heard from since they left Fort Pitt six months earlier. Apparently they had been expected to return before winter; the governor was concerned over their whereabouts.[18]

It developed that the men had reached New Orleans safely and succeeded in buying ten thousand pounds of gunpowder, but one of them had been captured and thrown in jail. He escaped by water to Virginia, carrying a large portion of the powder. The other man, William Linn, had started up the Mississippi in September with the remainder of the cargo.

After a hastily summoned council at Fort Pitt, Pentecost ordered Will to raise a company of fifty privates and to proceed immediately down the Ohio, "taking all possible Care to examine Stricktly the mouth of all Creeks and Rivers" as he passed, and upon arriving at the mouth of the Kentucky or at the Falls of the Ohio to send a messenger to Harrodsburg to inquire about Captain Linn and the cargo. If it should

[16] *Ibid.*, 4NN38. [17] *Ibid.*, 4NN46.
[18] *Ibid.*, 1SS43.

happen that he was there, Will was to conduct him "with the utmost Safety" to Fort Pitt. Before Will could get his expedition under way, however, word came from Harrodsburg that Linn had arrived there after wintering at a Spanish post on the Arkansas. A few weeks later Linn and his cargo arrived safely at Fort Pitt—no doubt to the great relief of Pentecost, Will Harrod, and the other militia officers, since all of them had regarded the rescue trip with considerable anxiety.

During this period, Will remained at his Grave Creek post, where he organized spy work and obtained supplies and ammunition for equipping the blockhouse. Late in the spring he received orders to send his scouts down around Fish Creek to watch for war-painted Indians. The Colonel told him that should he discover "any of the Dam theeves cuming in"[19] he was to notify him immediately. This was a more or less routine order. Spies and hunters continually brought word that hostile tribes were on the warpath here or there. In the midst of everything, moreover, when his mind was completely taken up with these day-to-day emergencies, a message arrived which troubled Will Harrod more than any he had ever received. Two captains had charged him with embezzlement of the Commonwealth stores of ammunition and beef, and Will was to appear one month from that date to answer to these charges.[20]

The accusation might appear insignificant to modern readers, accustomed to scandals involving millions of dollars and many thousands of soldiers' lives, but to Will it was a matter of the deepest concern. His career, military and civil, was based on his reputation for honesty and ability, and this charge against him could not pass unchallenged. Since that wrestling match he had won as a boy of twelve Will had been able to look after himself. But he was always more sensitive than his brother Jim, so that these charges against his character were unbearable. He was now face to face with accusations no fisticuff battle could settle.

[19] *Ibid.*, 4NN54.   [20] *Ibid.*, 4NN18-21.

Greatly disturbed, he wrote at once, expressing concern and resigning his commission.

In return, the colonel sent word that in his opinion the charges were "but trifling and without foundation," and that he would see to it that the case was dismissed.[21]

But Harrod replied that he was unwilling to let the matter drop, for after all, true or not, the charges constituted a slight on his character, and his reputation as a soldier and keeper of accounts could not be cleared in this manner.

At this point, Pentecost came to the rescue. Having appeared before the commission appointed to audit the accounts for Dunmore's expedition, he recalled that Will's purchase books were examined carefully at that time. Pentecost now took a particular interest in these charges of dishonesty against one of his officers. He issued a certificate of service, as he said, to do justice to Harrod and to counteract any damage to his reputation resulting from the reports.[22]

This certificate, which Will carefully preserved among his papers, stated that Pentecost had been present when all the books were audited and that none bore a better character than Harrod's, a fact which the Colonel thought was greatly to Will's credit, since his accounts were "Very Long and Intricate." Then he added for good measure that he had also "frequently heard Lord Dunmore say, that the said Harrod was Exceedingly Abel and active in his duty." Pentecost further spoke of Will's work during McDonald's campaign and in the scouting activities which followed. "Upon the whole," he declared, Harrod's various accounts "gave general Satisfaction at the Time . . . the Commissioners much applauded him for the fair, Honest and Accurate manner in which they were ajusted."[23]

Will had been particularly upset over a specific accusation involving a horse which had arrived in such bad condition that he could neither use it nor return it to the owner. After

[21] Ibid., 4NN55. [22] Ibid., 4NN18-21.
[23] Ibid.

clearing the fog over this little transaction, Pentecost further certified that while Harrod was under his command at different times and at different places he had "deported himself as a good officer . . . and from the Long Experience I have had of him I Verily believe him to be a good Soldier and Honest man."[24]

At last Will was satisfied. This was the final paper on an embarrassing subject. Now he could resume his military career without bowing to any man.

Taken all in all, the winter had been a good one for the Harrods. Jim had his precious cargo of powder, and at least for the immediate future Kentucky was safe; while his brother Will, with the help and understanding of superior officers and good friends, had managed to save his valued reputation.

[24] *Ibid.;* Zach Morgan, the officer who was to have presided at the court-martial, also issued a signed certificate acquitting Will of misconduct, Draper Collection, 4NN58.

Chapter X

THE SIEGE OF FORT HARROD
(1777)

"Accounts from Kentucki tell me of the most distressing & deplorable condition of the surviving Inhabitants in that Quarter. Your Movements I trust will prove the best Defence to them."[1]

ALTHOUGH the appointment of General Edward Hand[2] to take over Continental operations in the West brought joy to the hard-pressed Monongahela inhabitants, to Jim Harrod in Kentucky it meant little more than occasional consignments of lead and ammunition or the arrival of an express from Fort Pitt with word of far-off battles in the East. Captain Jim and the other Kentucky leaders—Boone, Logan, and the farseeing George Rogers Clark—still had to carry the burden of their own defense.

The most important defense measure James Harrod undertook that year was the completion of a fort where settlers and livestock could enjoy a measure of safety against increasing Indian attacks. Several fortifications were under construction and many others were being planned, but at this time there was no finished stockade in all Kentucky.[3] A few men had put up small enclosures around their cabins, but these frail structures housed too few guns to guarantee against mass attack. Fully aware of the need for strong defense, Jim had

---

[1] Gov. Patrick Henry to Gen. Edward Hand, Williamsburg, July 27, 1777, Draper Collection, 18J26.
[2] Thwaites and Kellogg (eds.), *Revolution on the Upper Ohio*, x.
[3] Draper Collection, 4CC85, 12C26-29, 4B102-103.

begun early to plan his fort, but after the arrival of women and children he gave it more serious thought.

In Old Virginia he had seen stone blockhouses, also brick ones—long lasting and secure, but he knew that in Kentucky, where trees were close at hand, a log fort would be more practical.

Having started as a simple two-storied house-fort back in New England,[4] this type of fortification had gradually expanded with westward migration until it included at least one row of houses with in-slanting roofs and with back walls connected to form a continuous line, flanked by corner blockhouses commanding a view of the outside along a fence of high log pickets. There was nothing fancy about these rectangular forts, but they were practical. The settlers made them from the best hardwood available—black locust if they could get it, oak if there was any handy—and rarely did they use a piece of metal in the entire structure.[5]

Harrod had expected to put up his buildings on the slope above the big town spring, where he and his men had camped in 1774, but when he had come back in early March of 1775 to find water gushing and bubbling over, soaking the land all around, he was forced to find a high place in order to avoid the possibility of being washed out.[6] Jim chose the hill on the south side of the town fork, where there were several springs, as well as a good view of the country round about. As soon as the men had cleared the ground and marked off a rectangular space, Harrod directed them to raise three corner blockhouses with overhanging second stories and carefully measured loopholes. Since one corner of the rectangle sloped downhill, and a small spring ran off at that point, they had to omit a fourth blockhouse; but this mattered little because

---

[4] See William E. Barry, *The Blockhouse and Stockade Fort* (Kennebunk, Maine, 1915).

[5] Benjamin Van Cleve Memorandum from 1773, in the private possession of Lloyd Waddell Smith, Madison, New Jersey; Draper Collection, 17CC206, 27CC35; depositions in the court records of Mercer County examined by Major Chinn.

[6] Draper Collection, 12CC22, 12CC45. See Chaps. VI and VII.

the other buildings would be on higher ground to give a clear view.

Harrod's site proved to have great advantages over others in Kentucky. The corner spring, together with the one inside the enclosure, but near the crest of the slope, assured the people a fair supply of drinking and cooking water during times of siege, except in very dry seasons, while a third spring outside the fort, at the foot of the hill, served as a wash tub when it was safe for the women to go outside to work.[7]

Jim and the others had many good ideas to work out when they could get around to it. They wanted a fire walk in all the blockhouses, as well as along the picketing, to give even the shortest man a chance to level his rifle in the loopholes or in the V of the pickets. Double safety doors that could be let down in a hurry with a snip of rawhide pulleys would be a good addition, too, when the men had the time—and ambition. Actually they added all these refinements later; for the present it was all Harrod could do to get the men to put more logs on the fort cabins.[8]

Everyone was too conscious of the need for land clearing, cabin building, or hunting to take time off for work on common fortifications. To be sure, every time Indians attacked an outlying station during the winter and spring of 1777, the men showed a little spurt of interest, working feverishly on the fort until matters closer to their hearts again captured attention. But gradually they managed to complete the buildings, even to putting up a schoolhouse in the fort, where good Mrs. William Coomes, an educated woman for those days, taught the younger children their ABC's and numbers one to ten, charcoaled on the hornbook, a paddlelike affair made of clapboard and a piece of horn, which was steamed and flattened to provide a smooth writing surface.[9] The hornbook also came in handy when contrary youngsters took to

[7] Van Cleve Memorandum.
[8] Information furnished by Major Chinn. See Bakeless, *Daniel Boone*, 163.
[9] Lester, *Transylvania*, 253-54.

BLOCKHOUSE IN FORT HARROD (RESTORED). *Kentucky State Department of Conservation, Division of Publicity.*

dreaming of the woods or fishing, and would not learn their sums.

Mrs. Coomes called the children with a brass bell that had once hung around the neck of a cow she had brought across the Wilderness Road. Indians had long since shot or stolen the animal, but her bell continued its cheerful tinkle—serving also to notify folk that evening supper of cornmeal mush and milk was ready in the big iron pot at the center of the fort.

Between the schoolhouse and the row of buildings on the southwest the men placed a sycamore hominy block, where they ground the corn for mush. It was of good size and well balanced, and gradually, with frequent use and careful scraping, it became a perfect bowl. In fact one visitor pronounced it "one of the best I have seen anywhere."[10] The women were proud of it and kept it covered from the weather by a deerskin held down by flat roof boards.[11]

Jim had added reason for thinking of defense when, in the spring, commissions arrived for the new Kentucky county militia. Somehow this gave reality to the new civil status. Harrod, Boone, John Todd, and Benjamin Logan received captains' commissions. In order to make the most of the spell cast by this event, Harrod and McGary rounded up the men and older boys around the fort to organize them for spy and guard duty, as well as for fort building.[12]

There was plenty of other work to be done, too, for they must plant vegetables, clear more ground, and bring in additional meat to dry for winter. To furnish needed clothing, the women resorted to an old frontier practice of weaving a

[10] Van Cleve Memorandum.
[11] W. W. Stephenson, "The Old Fort at Harrodsburg," in *Register of the Kentucky State Historical Society*, VIII (1910), 47-50. Apparently an L was added after Van Cleve's visit, since his sketch made about 1792 shows rectangular construction. He also omits some of the cabins at the sides and lower end, described by early inhabitants and included in Draper's sketch of the fort based on interviews. Draper Collection, 12C29.
[12] Draper Collection, 1A313; James Ray Pension Record, Revolutionary Pension Office, S 31314, National Archives, Washington.

cloth from buffalo wool and shreds of rotted nettle, which they broke out in a wooden trough, in much the same way that they prepared linen for spinning. All winter Jim's people worked, hardly conscious of danger from Indian attack. But one day in early March they had a tragic surprise. Hugh McGary sent his stepsons James and William Ray with one other boy and a man named William Coomes to clear a piece of ground near the Shawnee springs.[13] There was a sugar camp not far away, and at noontime the tired and hungry boys called out to Coomes that they were going over to the camp to rest and drink a little sugar-water. While they were lying down, talking aimlessly, they heard the sound of voices coming from behind them.

Since there were a great many surveying and hunting parties around, the boys did not at first suspect any danger, but when in a few moments the voices came closer, they turned around and to their great surprise saw a party of forty-seven Shawnee warriors running in single file with trailed arms, only a few yards away from them.

William Ray had his gun with him, but his older brother James and the friend had left theirs at the clearing. All three boys sprang up at once. James seemed to possess much presence of mind and immediately pointed out a course for them to run, as he started in a different direction to rescue his gun.[14]

James had gone only a short distance when he noticed that the Indians had managed to get between him and his rifle, so he then turned his course the way he had directed William and the other boy to run. He easily overtook William, but their friend was not in sight.

The two boys ran together for some distance. William, being a trifle on the plump side and having a heavy rifle to carry, could not make the necessary speed. Realizing this,

---

[13] The following account is based on a number of sources, particularly on Draper Collection, 12CC136, 12C15, 12C16, 4B118, 26CC55, 48J10, 4CC92.
[14] *Ibid.*, 12C17.

James told him to throw down his gun and surrender to the Indians before they killed him.

William was puffing too hard to answer, but he shook his head and kept on running, holding tightly to his prized rifle, while the Shawnees came closer and closer. Suddenly the boy turned round, stopped, and raised his gun to his shoulder.

At that instant an Indian fired and the younger brother fell.

Knowing that he could no longer help William and would indeed be lucky to save his own scalp, James Ray set out at full speed. After running nearly a mile, he found that his leather leggings were cramping his knees. As he ran he drew his butcher knife; then, darting behind a large tree, he cut loose his leggings and tore them off. While he was hiding, the Indians passed on ahead of him. As James sprang forward to continue his escape, the tribesmen commenced firing and throwing war clubs in a desperate effort to slay the boy. Ray soon outdistanced them, however, and the tribesmen gave up the chase and turned back.

When James discovered that he was well ahead of them, he circled back toward the camp to see, if possible, what had happened to his brother and their friend. Although he hid in the bushes for a long time, he could see nothing. Finally, racing on, James reached Harrodsburg, four miles distant, a little before nightfall.

Meanwhile the Indians, having lost track of him, had returned to camp amid jeers from those who had stayed behind. Blackfish, their chief, told Daniel Boone a little later that some boy at Harrodstown outran his fastest warriors.

Captain Jim sent out an alarm to all the cabins and clearings, warning the men that a large party of Indians was in the neighborhood, and telling them to bring their families and livestock to the fort.

Hugh McGary rushed up to Harrod, shouting excitedly that if Harrod had organized their defense properly this thing would never have happened. What if the men had refused to do guard duty? As leader it was Jim's duty to *make* them do it! Then he demanded that thirty guns be dispatched to find "those red rascals."

Seconded by Clark, who had been working at the fort headquarters, Jim tried to calm McGary by pointing out that it would be foolish to send so many men away from the settlement. James Ray had said that there were a great many Shawnee in the party. They might attack the fort at any moment. Did McGary want to leave the women and children unguarded on the chance that he might save Bill? After all, the other wood choppers were probably dead. Ray had seen his brother fall.

McGary would not listen to reason. All he could think of was revenge. His charges of inefficiency finally aggravated Captain Jim beyond endurance. The Harrodsburg leader shouted angrily that he would stand no more of this. No man could call him a laggard. McGary lifted his rifle. Harrod grabbed his.

Frail, weeping Mrs. McGary ran between the quarreling men and begged her husband to listen to reason.

Harrod, dropping his gun, announced wearily that he and McGary would take a party of thirty men to rescue any of the wood choppers who had survived.

Calmed at last, McGary rounded up the rescue party and they set out. At the sugar camp the men saw a body lying on the ground.

"See there!" blurted out one settler, "they have killed poor Coomes."

"No, they haven't killed me," came a voice from beneath a log by the side of the camp. "By Job, I'm safe!"[15]

Harrod and McGary then discovered that the body was that of William Ray, scalped and robbed of hunting shirt and hat. They could find no sign of the other boy.

While McGary and James Ray buried William, Harrod

[15] Collins, *Kentucky*, II, 611-12.

INTERIOR OF FORT HARROD (RESTORED). *Kentucky State Department of Conservation, Division of Publicity.*

SIEGE OF FORT HARROD

and the others set to work, filling the gaps in the palisades and hanging the fort gates. The job took all night, but the settlers worked fast, each doing his assigned task quietly and efficiently. Harrod had never seen them work like that before. By dawn they were ready for the expected attack.[16]

But the Indians did not appear that day. As usual, they hoped to surprise the whites—to catch them off guard.

Some of the settlers actually thought that the Shawnee had left the neighborhood and that everyone might as well go back to his job, but Harrod and Clark kept them in the fort. The next day, while everyone was lolling about talking, the guard shouted that one of the old cabins was on fire.

The settlers rushed to their posts.

Captain Jim, McGary, James Ray, and several others ran outside to investigate. As they neared the burning cabin over on the east side of the town, the men in the fort shouted to them that they were cut off.

Harrod and his men then retreated to "a piece of woods" south of the fort, each one taking a tree, as the Indians crept towards them in the brush.

One by one the fort party managed to dodge from tree to tree until they were near enough to race in the fort gate, which the guards were holding ajar.

McGary, who saw his stepson's hunting shirt and hat on one of the attackers, vowed to "get that devil," which he did—but not until he had received a wound in his arm.

This skirmish was not the end of Harrodsburg's troubles that summer. Many raiding parties lurked in the neighborhood, and almost every day a man was killed or wounded by Indians. Captain Jim kept in close touch with Boone's and Logan's forts, which the Indians also attacked frequently.[17]

After a number of these unsuccessful forays, the hostile Indians apparently realized that harassing the forts would not

---

[16] *Ibid.;* Martin Spalding, *Sketches of the Early Catholic Missions of Kentucky* (Louisville, 1844), 37; Draper Collection, 4B118, 26CC55, 12C26-29, 12C16.

[17] Draper Collection, 4CC30.

drive the settlers out, and that they must starve them from the Indian hunting ground. Accordingly, a tribe from north of the Ohio moved into Kentucky and made camp only a half mile from Fort Harrod, where they kept constant watch for venturesome settlers. They managed to kill or steal nearly all the livestock the settlers had brought across the mountains, and to prevent them from harvesting their corn and other grain crops.

About the only crop which escaped destruction was a turnip patch. The Indians knew nothing about this food and allowed it to reach maturity. One day, when the men were working there under heavy guard, tribesmen fired on them, forcing a hasty retreat. The next day, George Rogers Clark, Harrod, James Ray, and a few others stole out of the gate on the far side of the fort and crept around behind the high weeds beyond the clearing. Just as they had suspected, the Indians were hiding there.

At Clark's signal, the men fired, dropping four tribesmen and sending the others away in headlong confusion. Without waiting to scalp the fallen Indians, the men followed the other tribesmen to a creek bed, where they found the remains of a camp.

There was no sign of any Indians, but Clark, Harrod, and Ray were convinced that this camp had served as headquarters for the summer-long siege of their fort.[18]

Harrod also knew that there were still large numbers of hostile warriors in the near-by woods, ready to take pot shots at any whites who might walk more than a few hundred yards from the stockade. During this period hunting had to be done at night, and Harrod and Ray did a large share of it, taking turns at going out after dark on the one old nag that had escaped destruction. They would ride far enough that their shots could not be heard and return the next evening with their kill.[19]

[18] *Ibid.*, 12C16.
[19] *Ibid.* See also 12C17, 4B118, 26CC55, 23J166-67, 48J10, and 12C26-29.

According to a story told by an early English writer who collected legends from pioneer Kentuckians, Harrod visited Boonesborough at about this time to see how that fort was making out.[20] Daniel was away on one of his long excursions, hunting or attending to business down in Carolina. Finding that the Boonesborough settlers were as "hard put to it" for meat as were his own people, Captain Jim suggested that some of the men go with him on a hunting expedition. They did not want to leave the women unprotected, however, so Harrod went alone, telling the settlers to keep up their spirits and he would bring them meat.

Jim rode a considerable distance without finding game, and from the many Indian signs about he knew that he would be lucky to bring in anything—turkey, bear, or deer. Having circled the woods a few times, he came on a small herd of deer running about restlessly as if they had been frightened—a sign to Jim that Indians must be in the neighborhood.

Dismounting and tying his horse, Harrod walked along cautiously for some distance, taking care to expose his body as little as possible, and using trees and shrubs to hide his movements. Ahead of him a deer came into view. Jim waited.

Suddenly there was a whistle; the ring of two rifles close by and to his left warned Jim that he had a little competition in the deer hunt. As he peeped around a tree, a rifle ball whizzed through the heavy mass of black hair which fell down his shoulders. Crouching low, he waited for his assailants to come out of hiding.

After a long time Harrod cautiously raised his hat on the muzzle of his rifle.

Three guns fired simultaneously as the heads of the Indian hunters came into view.

Jim took quick aim, killing one Indian before he could drop out of sight. He was able to repeat this trick once more, but the third red man darted away through the brush. Har-

[20] Charles W. Webber, *The Romance of Forest and Prairie Life* (London, 1853), 167-69.

rod ran back for his horse and then rode with the deer back to Boonesborough.

On another occasion during this siege, Harrod was out hunting near the Kentucky when he saw several fine deer feeding in a small glade in the forest.[21] Creeping cautiously within gunshot, he had started to raise his rifle to take aim when suddenly the buck leader of the herd scented some human being and produced that shrill note which means danger.

Jim was too good a woodsman not to notice that the deer turned his head in the direction opposite to his, showing that another person was near.

Then a rifle cracked on the other side of the glade; the buck sprang into the air and fell lifeless. At that instant a tall Shawnee chieftain sprang into view and ran toward the deer. A second later Harrod fired, killing the Indian.

Captain Jim must have had many adventures similar to these, all of which would have lent themselves to florid Victorian narratives. But he related his exploits to few people. In his life of almost continuous action, each day brought its own immediate problems that required concentration and forethought, rather than contemplation. Only on long hunts in the forest, when all was quiet, did Jim have time for reflection on his adventures—and on these excursions his only companions were his English mare and a hunting dog. It was later, when hunting was no longer good in Kentucky, and problems of Indian defense had given way to intricacies of state politics and other matters of more casual interest to the early pioneer leaders, that most of them found time and occasion for reminiscences.

But Jim Harrod's story had to be told by others.

[21] *Ibid.*

Chapter XI

A CLOUDED SKY

(1777)

"By virtue of the power and authority to me given ... I do assure all such as are inclined to withdraw themselves from the Tyranny and oppression of the rebel Committees, & take refuge in this Settlement, or any of the Posts commanded by his Majesty's Officers, shall be humanely treated. ... God save the King."[1]

CAPTAIN JIM was never wounded in an Indian skirmish, although he suffered two broken bones during hunting excursions.[2] Curiously, the accidents were almost identical and were the result of Harrod's preference for hunting on horseback, which gave him the advantage of speed, so important in chasing buffalo, deer, and other swift-footed game. But managing his long rifle while mounted on a moving animal was risky business. Twice, as he fired, the horse jumped and threw him, breaking thigh bones. These minor tragedies never seemed to deter Jim, however, because all his life he rode to the hunt.

Diaries of this period show that there were more serious results of many such pioneer adventures.[3] Scarcely a week

---

[1] Governor Hamilton's proclamation to the frontiersmen, Detroit, June 24, 1777, quoted in Reuben G. Thwaites and Louise P. Kellogg (eds.), *Frontier Defense on the Upper Ohio, 1777-1778* (Madison, 1912), 14.

[2] Draper Collection, 37J168-74.

[3] Diary of John Cowan (1777), Draper Collection, 4CC30; "Clark's Diary" (December 25, 1776 to March 30, 1778), James (ed.), *Clark Papers, 1771-1781*, 20-28. (All subsequent references to "Clark's Diary" are to the same dates.)

passed without the loss of one or two lives, often in the course of ordinary activities near the fort or at home stations. The settlers, expecting attacks as part of their everyday lives, became so accustomed to the ever-present dangers that some of them took unnecessary chances, and there were many deaths due to outright carelessness.

This was certainly true in the case of Barney Stagner. Captain Jim had named this little Dutchman as keeper of the fort springs, and while this was not a lofty appointment, it was an important one which Barney took very seriously and, in Teutonic fashion, performed thoroughly. The boys, particularly the younger ones, liked to tease the old fellow by throwing gourds and rocks into the water, mainly to hear Barney scold.

Stagner had an idea that he led a charmed life. "The Indians can't kill me," he often boasted; "I'm too old."

James Ray, who was standing near Stagner one day, happened to hear Barney make this remark. Indians were firing away at the fort and bullets were popping like hail on the clapboard roofs, so Ray suggested, "Now Barney, you say the Indians can't kill you, suppose we hoist you on top of the Fort now and see what will be the consequence."[4]

Barney begged to be excused and quickly changed the subject. But he had not changed his opinion of his own powers, because a short time later he carelessly wandered outside the gate, against Harrod's instructions, and was killed and scalped. For years after that, the boys living near the fort used to say that at night when the moon was full they could see Barney's ghost around the old fort spring.[5]

In spite of these gruesome happenings, Harrod managed to keep most of his settlers happy. For instance, when he discovered that a newcomer had lost his horse, Jim would quietly disappear in the forest for a day, and frequently return in the evening with the animal—much to the joy of the frightened

---

[4] Draper Collection, 12C16.
[5] *Ibid.*, and 12C26-29, 26CC55, 4CC30.

settler who would rather do without his horse than look for it in the strange, Indian-infested woods.

Jim's well-meaning attempts to keep things running cheerfully and smoothly could not do away with the fact that it was no fun to be cooped up in the fort all summer. Nerves got on edge. One traveler who visited the Kentucky forts during this year of almost constant siege said that he was shocked by the way the people lived: the women were quarrelsome and gossipy; they pestered him with their "impertinent interrogations" of happenings back in Virginia; they were dirty and their children unkempt, their cabins and clothes greasy.[6]

This squeamish foreigner did not stay long enough to learn the reasons for this disorder and uncivilized way of living. Captain Jim could have told him how starved for news of their old homes his people really were, how little they had to occupy their thoughts during the summer-long Indian sieges. Harrod could have tried to make him understand the emotional effect of daily killings, the meaning of life in a place where danger and sorrow entered every cabin door. Probably the stranger would never have understood what it was like to go down to the wash-tub spring outside the fort walls, to rub dirt out of greasy clothing with his bare hands scuffing against the stones while he wondered at what moment a bullet would whizz across the clearing. The women were never safe outside the fort in those days, but in spite of danger they could stand the dirt just so long, then they would pull the smelly shirts off their scrubby youngsters and head for the spring.

As James Ray was sauntering by the spring on one such occasion, he spied an Indian near the stockade, clutching his gun as he crawled on his side and evidently trying to get within range of an unsuspecting housewife.

Ray's unerring aim cut short the Indian's plan.[7]

These were almost daily occurrences—too much for timid

[6] Smyth, *Tour in America*, I, 136.
[7] Draper Collection, 12C16.

people unused to constant danger, and many of them hurried across Cumberland Trace to the shelter of older, less-remote settlements. Fearing that this exodus might prove fatal to their long efforts, Harrod and Clark speeded the organization of the new Kentucky militia, meanwhile waiting impatiently for the arrival of their new county lieutenant, Colonel John Bowman, and his reinforcements.

Early in June Captain Jim and another settler set off to meet Bowman and bring him on to Harrodsburg. After waiting a month at the pass they had to return alone, but a few days later an express arrived with the cheering news that the new county lieutenant was on his way out.[8]

Once more Harrod went in to meet Bowman, and this time his trip was a happy one;[9] although he returned to Harrodsburg alone, he could tell the eager settlers that their new commander would arrive as soon as he had finished inspecting Boone's and Logan's forts. Furthermore, Bowman was bringing a large company of volunteers.

This was good news; however, the settlers were soon depressed again, for Bowman told them that his men had enlisted for only a short time—a large part of which had already elapsed.[10]

Only with considerable difficulty had Harrod been able to coax many of his younger men to stay on militia duty throughout the summer, and now that reinforcements had arrived they could not see any reason for remaining longer. They needed to get back to the settlements, where their mothers and wives would make them new moccasins, hats, and hunting shirts. One man needed a new rifle—an Indian had made away with his. Another said he was sure his folks were worried about his safety, that he must tell them he was all right. And so it went. But finally, after considerable persuasion, the

[8] *Ibid.*, 4CC30; "Clark's Diary," James (ed.), *Clark Papers, 1771-1781*, 20-28.
[9] Draper Collection, 26CC55, 4CC30.
[10] Humphrey Marshall, *History of Kentucky* (Frankfort, 1824), I, 53; Draper Collection, 4B131.

new arrivals under Bowman agreed to stay on a while longer to relieve the homesick and tattered regular militia.[11]

Massive, brave, trumpet-voiced Colonel Bowman, assisted by Harrod, Logan, and Boone, plunged into his job of coordinating the defenses for the three forts.

George Rogers Clark had other matters on his mind.[12] For many months he had been roaming the country, talking to this person and that, trying to figure out the best solution to Western defense problems. He finally decided that the only way to stop these Indian attacks was to hit at their source—out in the Illinois, and at Detroit, where the red men were supplied by the British, who never stopped in their efforts to win over Indians, French, and even the frontiersmen themselves. As a preliminary to his plans, Clark sent out two spies—Lieutenant William Linn and Samuel Moore, a cousin of the Harrods—to find out the condition of the Illinois forts of the British and, if possible, the nature of activities there.

The men did their work well. There is a tradition that Jim's brother Sam served as go-between for Moore and Linn, prying secrets out of the Indians and French, listening to talk around the campfires, and getting plans of the various forts.[13] The spies learned that the British had told the French that frontier people were shocking barbarians who intended to force them out of the Illinois.[14] Some of the French appeared to believe these tales.

Moore and Linn discovered the strength of the British garrisons. They also found that the enemy had several cannon. British Governor Hamilton was planning to transport one of these on a boat along the Ohio and up the Kentucky River

[11] Draper Collection, 4B131; "Clark's Diary," James (ed.), *Clark Papers, 1771-1781*, 20-28.
[12] *Ibid.;* Clark "Memoir," in Butterfield, *Clark's Conquest*, 208-302.
[13] Photostatic copy of Lord Henry Hamilton's Journal, Filson Club Collection, Louisville.
[14] *Ibid.*

in order to fire on near-by forts. If this happened, the Lord help the settlers, because no picketing in the country could stand up against cannon balls.

One piece of news was good: the British did not expect any attack from the Virginians.[15]

When his spies returned to Harrod's fort with this information, Clark made his final decision. Sitting in the blockhouse at the top of the hill, he charted plans for an expedition against the unsuspecting Illinois towns and formulated the best arguments for appealing to Governor Henry and the Council—who must be convinced that an Illinois expedition was the only way to protect the Virginia frontiers.

While Clark was planning all this, he consulted occasionally with Will Harrod as well as with Jim, for Will had made a quick trip from Fort Pitt, along with Joseph Bowman, a brother of the county lieutenant.[16]

The returned spy, Lieutenant Linn, celebrated by taking a wife. This occasioned great merriment, according to Clark, who always had time for a little fun.[17] However, Clark did not mention the name of the man who read the ceremony. It could have been the Reverend John Lythe, who had prayed so ardently for the success of the Transylvania "Colony," or perhaps a Baptist minister who had recently come out to make his fortune in land.

Between Indian skirmishes Hugh McGary, a newly appointed justice in Kentucky's first court, also married couples.[18] The pioneers may have had short romances and unorthodox ceremonies, but they were enthusiastic about marriage. Even widows, who were more plentiful in the first years than unmarried girls, found that a month was quite long enough to mourn in a country where lone women only added new burdens to the men left to provide for them. They were

[15] Clark "Memoir," in Butterfield, *Clark's Conquest*, 208-302.
[16] English, *Life of Gen. Clark*, I, 83.
[17] "Clark's Diary," James (ed.), *Clark Papers, 1771-1781*, 20-28.
[18] Draper Collection, 12CC26-29.

only too glad to find their protectors in the form of second husbands.

Babies were born in the wilderness that summer, too, and one of them, who tradition says was the first white child born in Kentucky, was named Harrod Wilson. While a later generation pronounced him a worthless man, certainly Captain Jim regarded him with satisfaction.[19]

Harrodsburg had its share of romantic gossip. One of the most noted cases, which furnished chatter for many a month, involved a not too reluctant widow whom the "respectable women" accused of "carrying on" with one of the more prominent pioneers. Once, while her lover was away on military duty, the people amused themselves by concocting a mock marriage between her and a more than usually eligible bachelor who laughingly agreed to stand in as groom. Everything proceeded in fine fettle, but soon after the ceremony the joke took on a serious mien, for the "bride" claimed that the ceremony had taken place in all seriousness. The gun was now turned on the "groom" who had to part with good cash to unscramble the knot he had tied in foolishness.[20]

Although the arrival of Bowman's trained company had impressed the Indians so deeply that they attempted no large-scale attack on Harrodsburg for many months, there was never any real peace for the settlers that summer. Ammunition ran low at all three forts, and after Boone's settlers had suffered a heavy attack, and Logan's garrison of fifteen guns showed definite signs of weakening, Captain Jim made plans for another trip into the settlements—this time in search of supplies. Ben Logan said he was anxious to keep his small group of families together and agreed to join Harrod on his expedition.[21] While it seemed a foolhardy thing to do—leaving their forts for a dash through the wilderness alone when

[19] Lester, *Transylvania*, 251; Draper Collection, 4CC85.
[20] Draper Collection, 4CC85.
[21] *Ibid.*, 4B105-106; Lester, *Transylvania*, 192-96.

they knew that hostile Indians were as thick as cane along the Cumberland—their need was desperate.

Because red men were sure to watch the Wilderness Trail, Harrod, Logan, and their men cut across country, far from any path, in the hope of reaching the settlements unnoticed. It was a rough trip. The rocks were sharp and steep and the wilderness undergrowth so dense that they had to hack their way through, but they made it, arriving at the Holston less than ten days after they had left Harrodsburg. Harrod and Logan bought 100 pounds of powder and 176 pounds of lead. The generous settlers offered to furnish them an escort so that they could return in safety along the Wilderness Trail.[22]

Early during that year the over-the-mountain folk had come to Kentucky's aid. They had sent a detachment of men to Boonesborough to help fight Indians. Now they were ready to share their own limited supply of powder and lend men besides.

The Kentuckians accepted the proposal eagerly but feared that there might be some delay in recruiting the men. Since Logan was particularly worried over the safety of his garrison, he started for home at once, leaving Harrod to bring the cargo across a mountain short cut with the help of the Holston men.

Two weeks after Jim and Logan had left their homes, Jim returned with powder and lead for all the forts.[23]

Early in September the first court in Kentucky opened in Harrodsburg. Although the cases were not spectacular, the sessions were taken seriously by the settlers, who went to great lengths to follow accepted legal procedure as far as their knowledge or abilities permitted. Harrod in particular called on the best-educated men in his settlements, asking their advice on legal problems.

John Todd, the chief justice of the first court, ordered a

[22] Lester, *Transylvania*, 196; Marshall, *History of Kentucky*, I, 52.
[23] Marshall, *History of Kentucky*, I, 52; Lucien Beckner, "History of the County Court of Lincoln County, Kentucky," in *Register of the Kentucky State Historical Society*, XX (1922), 170-90.

census, the results of which Captain Jim no doubt heard with pride. His was the largest of the three settlements (St. Asaph's and Boone's being the other two) and had 81 men in service, 24 women and 70 children, in addition to slaves and domestic servants—198 in all.[24] These numbers rose and fell with the changing winds of Indian hostilities and white migrations.

Even the departure of the twenty-seven men led by Clark, who was on his way to see Patrick Henry, had failed to dim Harrod's optimism, for nearly everyone had promised to rejoin his company as soon as possible.[25]

The problem of food and clothing was ever present for Jim in those first years. By the end of this first year of siege, the Indians had left the settlers with little grain and very little flax for spinning. They had burned most of the corn during the summer; what was left was in cribs at different plantations some distance from the garrisons, and there were no horses to haul it in. At this time, Jim's people had no more than two months' supply of bread.[26]

In spite of all these causes for gloominess, when December came and the year of "the bloody sevens" was at an end, Jim could look back with a just sense of pride. Many new settlers had come to his town, and even more had promised to join him; a system of defense under trained Virginia officers was now in operation; there was a court in Kentucky—even if it still had no house to call its own; and while the old dispute with Henderson was not closed, there was no doubt in Jim's mind about its final outcome. True, the Indians had been more bothersome than ever, but with more powder and lead, and salt to dry their meat, the pioneers would "make out."

Come Indians, come Redcoats, the county of Kentucky was here to stay.

[24] Draper Collection, 48J10-11, 4CC30; Collins, *Kentucky*, II, 606.
[25] "Clark's Diary," James (ed.), *Clark Papers, 1771-1781*, 20-28.
[26] Draper Collection, 3NN192-96.

Chapter XII

A SECRET WELL KEPT
(1778)

"The Indians have Done More Damige in the Interior Settlements this summer than ever was Done in one season before...."[1]

THE CLOUDS which hung heavy over Harrodsburg, causing Jim so much concern, were not local phenomena; the settlers around the Forks of the Ohio lived under them too. Although the "near Indians"—as the frontiersmen called the friendly tribesmen living along the Ohio—continued to serve as a convenient buffer against the more aggressive "far Indians"—the Shawnee, Wyandots, and others—the Continental commander as well as Jim in Kentucky and the officers along the Monongahela felt hostility in the sharp breezes blowing across their settlements from the Indian country.

This hostility could not be blamed entirely on war-hungry tribesmen. Jim learned from his brother Will that the powerful Shawnee Chief Cornstalk, who was being held as hostage at Fort Randolph at the mouth of the Great Kanawha, had been attacked and killed by a party of irresponsible backwoodsmen.[2] Jim and his brother knew that this outrage would stir up trouble even among the near Indians, and that there was no longer any hope for peace in the Ohio Valley.

To Jim's dismay the effects of the attack were almost im-

---

[1] Col. John Bowman to George Rogers Clark, October 14, 1778, Draper Collection, 48J42.

[2] Thwaites and Kellogg (eds.), *Frontier Defense*, ix-xvii; Draper Collection, 6NN105-12.

mediately apparent in Kentucky, along the Monongahela and near the Kanawha. He was not surprised to hear that his brother Will, who with an almost herculean effort had built and maintained the Grave Creek fort (Moundsville), had because of supply difficulties been forced to abandon it and take his company to the fort at Wheeling.[3]

While Will and his men were packing the supplies preparatory to leaving, the settlers, no longer afforded the protection of a garrison, made plans for moving closer to Fort Pitt or the Monongahela.[4]

At about this time Will received a wound in the leg from a stray Indian bullet and returned to Ten Mile to wait for the wound to heal and, incidentally, to receive new military orders.[5] His next assignment was as commander at Wheeling, or Fort Henry, where most of his old company was now enrolled. Trouble loomed almost immediately.

Chief White Eyes, a Wyandot whose spies kept him informed about the white garrisons, announced his determination to reduce Wheeling.[6] The Indians attacked fiercely for two days and nearly succeeded in carrying out their threat. Although friendly Delawares had warned the Virginians that a raid was imminent, when the Indians did not appear within a few days as predicted many of Will's companies left in the belief that it had been a false alarm. But when news of the attack reached the Monongahela and Virginia authorities, reinforcements poured into Fort Pitt for assignment to duty at Wheeling, Redstone, Fish Creek and other stations. Every able-bodied man in the area, it seemed, was now ready to volunteer for outpost duty.[7]

One company went out from an interior county which had not seen an Indian raid in twenty years.[8] But the tedious job

[3] Thwaites and Kellogg (eds.), *Frontier Defense*, ix-xvii.
[4] *Ibid.;* Draper Collection, 7NN19.
[5] Andrew House Pension Record, Revolutionary Pension Office, R 5261, National Archives, Washington.
[6] Draper Collection, 12CC236-67.
[7] Thwaites and Kellogg (eds.), *Frontier Defense*, xiii.
[8] *Ibid.*

of waiting for something to happen at Wheeling was not the exciting life they had expected, and the men became restive. To break the monotony, they planned a scouting expedition down the Ohio under Captain William Foreman, a brave leader who, like most of his men, was inexperienced in Indian warfare. Will agreed to go part way as their pilot and to lead them to his old post at Grave Creek. He hoped to locate supplies here, those he had been forced to leave behind for want of enough boats to transport them, but found to his bitter disappointment that the blockhouses and crops had been destroyed. Since there was no quick way to cross the river, and remaining at this point for more than a few hours was hazardous, Will talked the reluctant company into returning to Wheeling. They made camp for the night on the site of old Grave Creek fort and set out the next morning. They had not gone far when a party of Wyandots, who had been waiting in the tall grass beneath a ledge bordering the river bottoms, leaped out of the brush and began to fire. Several white men fell; the others fled in confusion up the river or climbed over the ledge to escape from the Indians.

Will, who with a few of the men had managed to reach the ledge unhurt, ran past the point of ambush and down the steep incline to attack from the rear.

The Indians, in expectation of this maneuver, had erected a wide screen of shrubs and branches as protection. As Will and his men began pushing through this defense, whooping and yelling, about ten of the Indians slipped out and ran for their canoes, which were tied on the opposite bank.

The white men dashed after them, reaching the river as the Indians were swimming in midstream.

Meanwhile, with Foreman leading, the other surviving members of the expedition, who had escaped upstream, returned in close file to the ledge to engage the main body of Indians. A blaze of fire greeted their arrival, and Foreman was killed. His men, confused by his death, halted.

The Indians poured in a second fire and the whites fled.

Will and his handful of men retreated in safety to Wheeling, where they arrived at noon. One of his party reported that as he ran he could hear "the tomahawks as if the Indians were cutting up beef." Another, who also escaped unhurt, arrived at Wheeling still carrying his gun, but minus his hat, which had been shot off his head. He was surprised to learn that any of his comrades had escaped; however, between sundown and night, others straggled in with the same mournful account of defeat.

The next day Will turned out with a party to bury the dead. Then he went on furlough to Ten Mile.[9]

Soon after this encounter George Rogers Clark arrived at Will's house on his way back from Virginia, to explain new plans he had for a Northwest expedition which he believed would help put a stop to the Indian raids.

Clark admitted that he had left Harrodsburg for the capital of Virginia with much more confidence than he had possessed on his first important journey. He had prepared his way by writing Governor Henry to suggest an attack on Kaskaskia in the Illinois. Such an expedition, he had pointed out, would cost the Commonwealth but little and, if successful, would save the frontiers from large-scale, heavy attack. Further, he had received assurance that there were land-company interests who favored westward expansion for their own profit and would consequently push his idea.

Clark's first job in the capital had been the settling of Kentucky's militia accounts, but after that he had gone immediately to the Governor.[10]

Henry thought that the proposed expedition would be too hazardous, but he and the Council finally agreed that it was worth the risk—provided it could be carried out with the secrecy necessary to its success. They gave Clark the rank of lieutenant colonel and provided him with two sets of instruc-

[9] Draper Collection, 7NN19.
[10] Draper Collection, 48J13; Clark "Memoir," in Butterfield, *Clark's Conquest*, 208-302; "Clark's Diary," James (ed.), *Clark Papers, 1771-1781*, 20-28.

tions—one written in vague terms, suggesting that the destination for the troops would be Kentucky; the other, which was secret, defining the Illinois as the real objective.[11]

Clark wanted to enroll Will Harrod as one of his four captains, to recruit men along the Monongahela and to purchase supplies.[12]

Although Clark said later that he had been careful to keep the real destination of his troops a secret from everyone, it is certain that Will knew they were going to the Illinois. Since otherwise his work of outfitting and providing food for the expedition could not have been carried out successfully, Will had to know where they were going, and how long they expected to stay—nothing could be left to chance.

Although the Continental commander at Fort Pitt knew about the proposed expedition and gave it his support, recruiting in the area went slowly and for obvious reasons. The old boundary dispute between Pennsylvania and Virginia, while officially quiet, was still embarrassing to Will in his efforts to obtain volunteers. Disappointed in Virginia's admission of doubt over her Monongahela claims, the settlers could see no reason for helping her now, particularly since the Continental Congress was increasing demands for men in the regular army. The Monongahelans were already short of men, and they were not willing to spare more guns to save a wilderness country, when their own settlements farther east were being abandoned because of inadequate defense.[13]

Handicapped by his inability to disclose the true objective, Will resorted to baiting the men with promises of good land as a reward for their services, but in the end the only ones who enlisted were teen-age boys and men who had relatives and friends in Kentucky or were anxious to see the country. In spite of this man shortage, Will rejected many volunteers who clearly were unable to stand great hardships.

[11] James (ed.), *Clark Papers, 1771-1781*, 33-36.
[12] "Clark's Diary," *ibid.*, 20-28.
[13] George Rogers Clark to George Mason, November 19, 1779, James (ed.), *Clark Papers, 1771-1781*, 114-54 (see also lix).

Clark planned to take supply boats from Wheeling to Redstone, which would be the point of embarkation. Soon Will received a letter from Clark, directing him to send the boats from Wheeling to the Monongahela for loading flour. "I have instructed the different Recruiting officers to send some of their men to whelin [sic] for that purpose," he wrote, "and hope that you wil get as many of your Company to go as you can." He closed with a suggestion that those who co-operated in this work should be subject to no other duty before they reached Kentucky. "I intended to have come by your house from Court but our common interest called me another way," he added.[14]

A month later, when Clark received word that Will had taken the boats to Redstone as directed, he wrote again, expressing his hope that at last the expedition would be ready to leave for Kentucky. He added that since this was the day Will's company was to assemble, ". . . I thought it necessary to get this intelligence to you as quick as possible as the men might not be uneasy."[15] Governor Henry, explained Clark, had sent word that he was fearful that the Indians might soon "make a brake on the Frontiers" and might attack the concentration of men at Redstone before the expedition could march into the Indian country.

This final note would indicate rather clearly that Will knew of the real purpose of the expedition. The letter also shows that Clark knew how important his commanding officers were to the success of the plan.

All four captains were men of strong leadership, equal to the undertaking. Will had had wide acquaintance and experience in the Monongahela country; he was masterful in persuading reluctant, home-loving frontiersmen to risk their lives in Indian fighting, and while his tactics were not the easygoing, kindly, persuasive ones which his brother Jim used so effectively, they worked as well. The other three cap-

[14] Draper Collection, 18J69.
[15] *Ibid.*, 18J72.

tains were Leonard Helm, John Montgomery, and Joseph Bowman, all of them prominent Virginia soldiers who had served with Clark and the Harrods before. Bowman was a relative of Clark's by marriage and a brother to Colonel John Bowman of Kentucky; Montgomery was a recognized leader in Botetourt County. All three of these names added prestige to the expedition, and, since they were known to the Kentuckians, the chances of obtaining enrollees in the country below the Ohio were thus enhanced. But the vagueness which surrounded the plans worked against all of the officers, and when the three companies "set sail for the Falls" of the Ohio, their first stopping place, Clark had only 150 men under his command.[16]

They left in the middle of May along with twenty families moving to Kentucky, who were happy to make the trip under heavy guard. The Monongahela country, as all knew, was "in great confusion, much distressed by Indians," [17] and the settlers expected Kentucky to be in the same condition. The regiment boats proceeded cautiously to Fort Randolph at the mouth of the Great Kanawha. Clark learned from officers there that a party of 250 Indians had attacked the fort the day before and were now on their way to the Greenbriar country to the southeast. The officers begged Clark and his captains to send at least a part of their men in pursuit. While the latter listened sympathetically, they turned down the idea, for although it was certainly true that an easy victory might result, the regiment would be certain to lose men badly needed for the more important Illinois campaign.

From the Kanawha the expedition followed the Ohio to the mouth of the Kentucky, where they landed a number of badly needed salt kettles which the Kentuckians had ordered. Some of the men thought this would be a good place for a supply station, but Clark, Will, and the others rejected the idea.

They were determined to keep their sights on a more dis-

[16] James (ed.), *Clark Papers, 1771-1781*, 114-54.   [17] *Ibid.*

tant goal, the Falls of the Ohio, which they argued would offer a better location. All river travel had to stop there in order to prepare for passing the rapids.

In those days, there was a small island in the middle of the Ohio River opposite the Falls. The constantly changing currents and extensive cultivation, which decreased the island's resistance to erosion, have since obliterated it, but in Clark's and Harrod's time this was an ideal spot for a station. There was plenty of rich, virgin soil, and the place could be defended easily. Fortunately it appealed to the accompanying families too, and they agreed to live on the island and raise a crop of corn and garden greens.

Will was to command the garrison, which was to have the job of protecting the inhabitants and the military stores. Acting under Clark's direction, Will divided the island into garden plots and set up a small guard to protect the people while final plans for the continuance of the expedition were under advisement. According to earlier arrangements, Colonel John Bowman arrived with part of his regular Kentucky militia, which was to join the regiment. But Captain Jim was not among them; he had stayed home to direct settlement defenses.[18]

He must have had serious misgivings about sending any of the Harrodsburg men, but he had promised and kept his word. The ultimate outcome would benefit all posts.

When Clark discovered that a large party had arrived from the Bluegrass country, clearly to the jeopardy of that area, he sent part of the regiment back to their posts, keeping only one company and part of another. He even declared his intention of replacing these later with expected reinforcements from lower southwest Virginia.

The secret of their destination could no longer be kept from the men, so Clark and his captains revealed their plans. To their surprise the soldiers almost unanimously praised the

[18] Clark "Memoir," in Butterfield, *Clark's Conquest*, 208-302; Draper Collection, 37J168-74.

projected undertaking. A number from Jim Harrod's fort under their leader's persuasion declared that this would be Kentucky's salvation. But as the hazardous possibilities of a march into unknown, hostile country, far from bases of supply, began to penetrate their consciousness, rumblings of discontent could be heard among the volunteers, who feared that the expedition was not strong enough to ensure success.[19]

Will suspected that this belated opposition was the work of enemy sympathizers, for in Kentucky, as he and Jim well knew, there were many loyalists, some of them refugees from the East, trying to find asylum in the less closely settled West.[20] Often they represented the best families in the colonies, people to whom the mere thought of independence was treason. In their associations with militia authorities around Fort Pitt, Jim and Will Harrod had seen many old friends, Connolly, for instance, fall into disgrace because of their sympathy with the British to whom they had all pledged their loyalty a few years earlier.

So many of the volunteers showed signs of deserting that the officers ordered the boats well secured and sentinels placed wherever there was even a possibility of the men swimming from the island to the southern bank.

But the frightened militiamen eluded these precautions. A group had gone bathing the day before and discovered that the channel opposite their camp might be waded; so, a little before dawn, a Harrodsburg lieutenant led his company down the bank and across the stream before the sentinels knew what they were about.

John Bowman had brought a number of horses from Harrodsburg, and the officers used these to chase the deserters. But the men scattered in the woods and only seven or eight were picked up. The lieutenant who led them nearly died from hunger and fatigue in the forest. By the time he arrived

---

[19] Clark "Memoir," in Butterfield, *Clark's Conquest*, 208-302.
[20] Draper Collection, 27CC33; Wilbur H. Siebert, "The Tory Proprietors of Kentucky Lands," in *Ohio State Archeological and Historical Quarterly* (Columbus), XXVIII (1919), 48-71.

at Harrodsburg, Jim had learned of the desertion and consequently refused for several days to admit the lieutenant to the fort. Nor would the settlers let him in their houses. Later the mounted volunteers returned to Corn Island, tied an effigy of the disgraced officer to a stake, and set fire to it—with Will's and Clark's good-natured approval.[21]

Cowardice was the worst possible offense on the frontier—and not only with the men. Just as enthusiastic were the women, who refused to make a shirt, sew on a button, or mend a bullet pouch for anyone suspected of this terrible vice.[22]

Clark's men set out on their march under an eclipse of the sun. Some looked on this as a bad omen, while others thought it meant success. The regiment was bound for the mouth of the Tennessee, where there was a small post, but on the way an express from Fort Pitt informed them that the American government had made an alliance with France—welcome news for Clark, who was planning to use the French in the Illinois to help him win his campaign. The march to Kaskaskia was strenuous and difficult. Water and rough ground had to be surmounted and new trails blazed. Because Clark planned to surprise the British, he could not take the familiar Warriors' Road. The guide engaged to take them through had assured the officers that he knew the country well, but he became confused and lost his way.

When the men showed that they suspected him of treason, and began to clamor for his scalp, the harried fellow asked leave to go out alone in order to get his bearings. In an hour he was back, happy and relieved that he had located a familiar landmark.

It was late afternoon, ten days after they had left the Falls, when they arrived within a few miles of Kaskaskia. Fearing that they would be discovered, they hid in the woods and waited for darkness.

[21] Clark "Memoir," in Butterfield, *Clark's Conquest*, 208-302.
[22] Draper Collection, 17CC207.

After capturing an outpost, Clark separated his regiment into three divisions under Harrod, Bowman, and Helm, and deployed them to surround the town. The commander entered by a rear gate, and, as easily as fishing with a net, he and his men took possession of the town without anyone having to fire a shot.[23]

A number of militiamen who understood French dashed through the streets warning the inhabitants that anyone who poked his nose outside his house would be shot down without question.

There is a legend that Will Harrod, painted like an Indian, and brandishing his long butcher knife, appeared in the doorway of the troop headquarters and shouted in thunderous tones, "A thousand Bostonians are now upon you!"[24] The term "Bostonians" was used by the French settlers to mean colonial soldiers.

Under Clark's orders, Harrod and his men went through the streets shouting and whooping like Indians. Awe-stricken, the French inhabitants peeped out of doorways or from between window shutters, cowed to utter submission by this savage display.

The French governor surrendered in his chamber. Owing to an unexpected sense of gallantry on the part of the invaders, his wife was allowed time to dress in private—an opportunity which she used either to destroy or to conceal the official papers.

Clark started an immediate campaign to win the confidence of French inhabitants, who had been told by the British commander that the Kentuckians were unmerciful in victory. While the lieutenant colonel was sitting with Harrod, Bowman, and the minor officers—all of them dirty, with torn clothes, bedraggled from their journey through the marshes—the village priest asked permission to wait on the Virginians.

[23] Clark "Memoir," in Butterfield, *Clark's Conquest*, 208-302.
[24] Draper Collection, 12C24.

He entered along with a half dozen other elderly gentlemen, who were all so shocked by the spectacle of their savage-appearing captors that it was some time before they would venture to take seats and longer before they would speak. Finally the priest asked as a special favor that he be permitted to hold service in the chapel.

When this had passed without incident the priest again "screwed up his courage" to approach Clark and his staff with a request—that fathers not be separated from their families.

Thereupon Clark rose to his full dignity and made a speech. He asked the Frenchmen just what they had expected of the Virginians. Were they the kind of men who shed innocent blood? Did the French believe them to be savages? Of course the families could stay together. Furthermore, all religious faiths would be tolerated in America.

The reaction was joyous among the French, but many of the Indians, upon hearing that the "long knives" had taken over, silently departed for more congenial settlements farther west or north.

Clark at once announced his intention of marching against Vincennes and Cahokia, although he and his captains knew that they lacked sufficient men for such a large operation. But the inhabitants, eager to spare the other villagers, offered to intercede in behalf of the Virginians. Before several weeks had passed, they notified Clark that they had talked the other towns into surrendering. At last the Illinois country was his —at least for the time being.[25]

Meanwhile Clark's army had become restive and eager to go back to "civilized country" and away from this Indian-infested land. To offset the bad effect of a major withdrawal, Clark began to talk loudly of reinforcements waiting at the Falls,[26] and soon he announced that he was sending Captain

---

[25] Clark "Memoir," in Butterfield, *Clark's Conquest*, 208-302.
[26] Draper Collection, 20S229, 49J33.

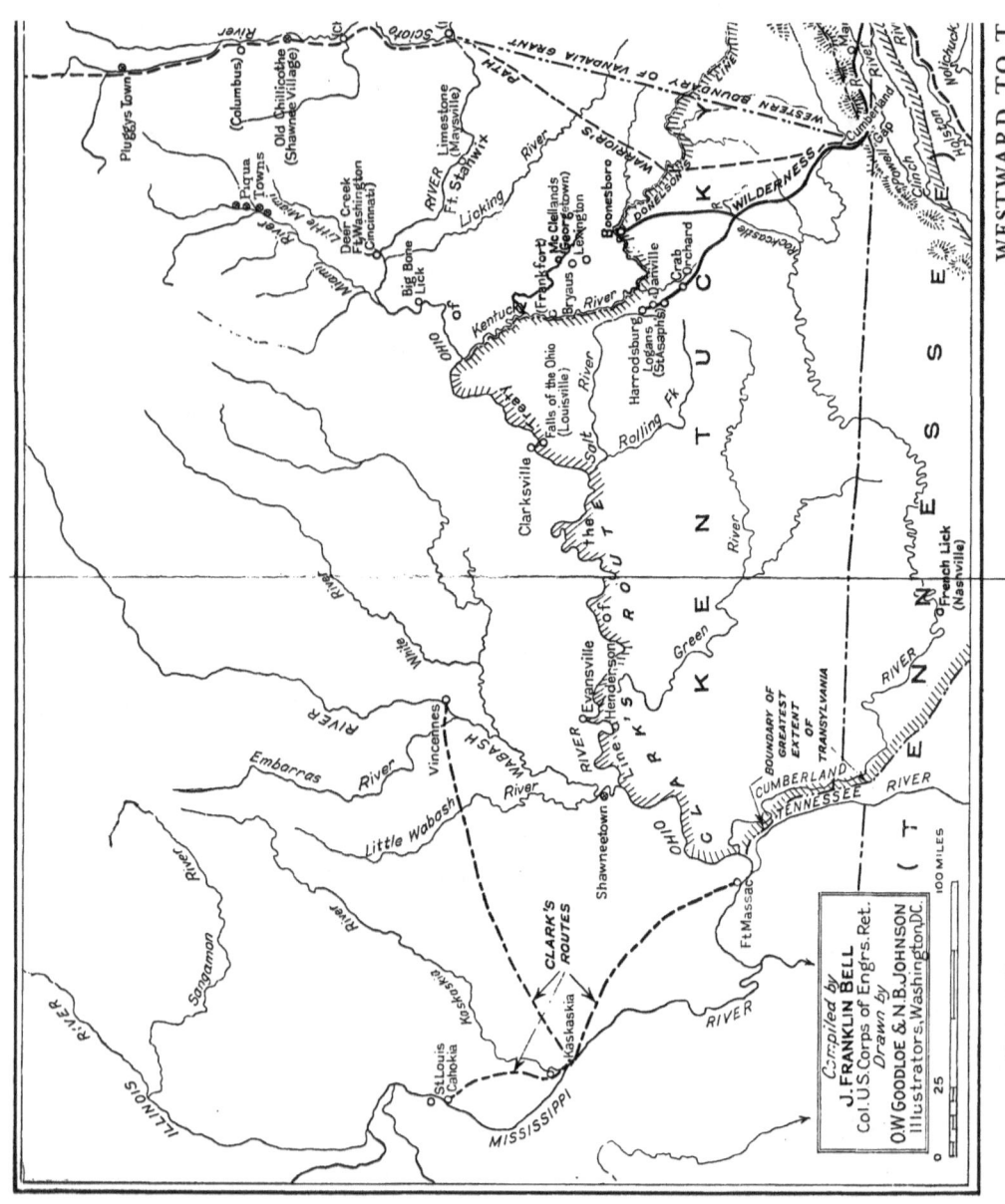

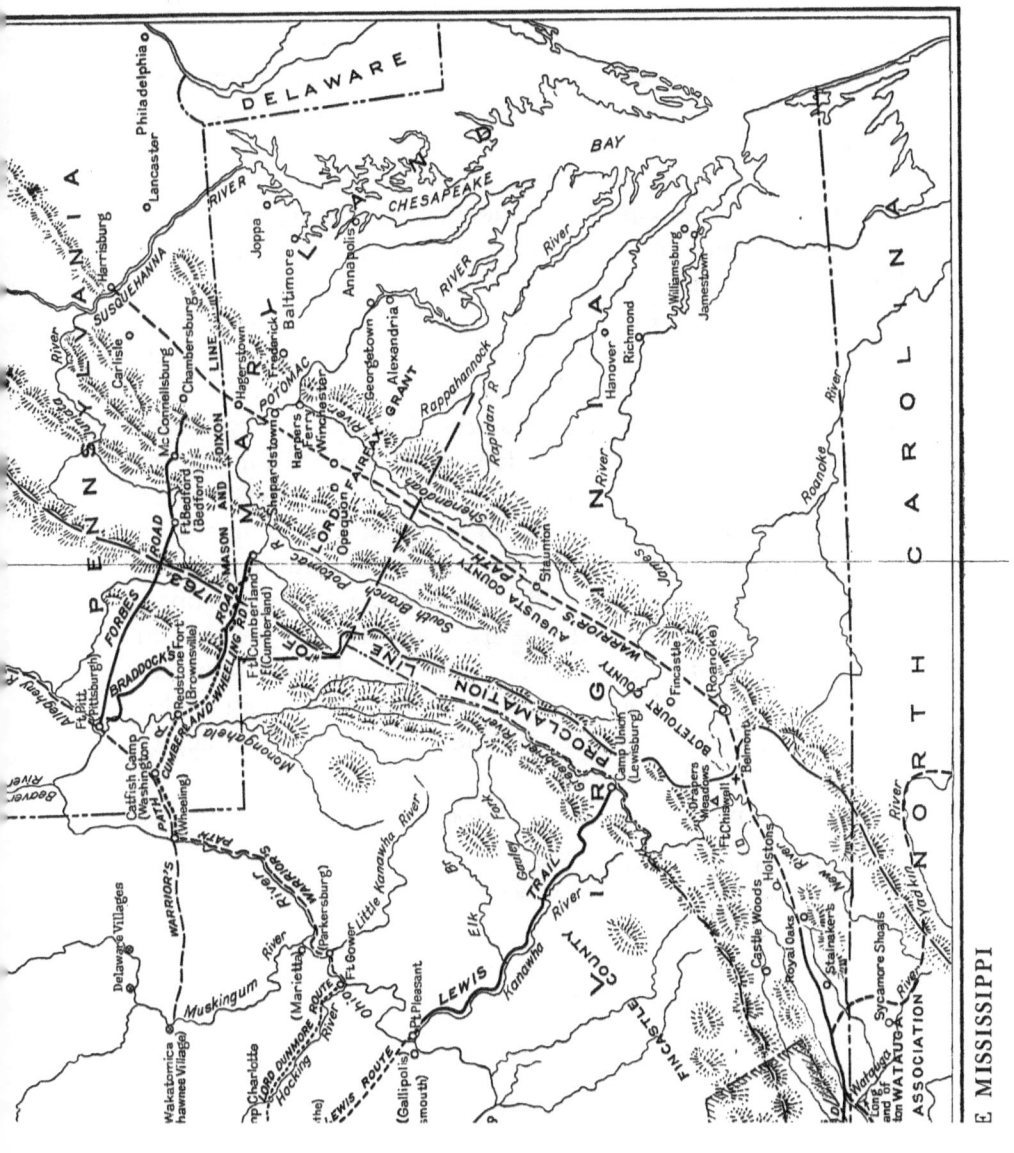

Will Harrod to that place to erect a permanent fort—which from now on was to serve as his supply base.²⁷ The other captains were to remain with their companies in Illinois.

It had all been so simple and easy. Only Detroit remained, and Clark had too few men to undertake this ambitious, ever to be desired expedition.

The Illinois commander and his officers and men received Virginia's official thanks "for their extraordinary resolution and perseverence in so hazardous an enterprise, and for the important services thereby rendered their country." ²⁸

The salutary results of the expedition were even more warmly received by Jim Harrod, who had lived in dread of invasion by the British troops from the Illinois garrisons. If Virginia could maintain her foothold there his own tasks would be lighter. The chief dangers now were the far Indians in the Ohio country and, to a lesser degree, the Cherokee from the South. If Detroit could be captured, so much the better. The steady filter of guns and ammunition into the northern Indian towns would be stopped, and Harrodsburg, with her neighboring settlements, could live in peace. Jim was overoptimistic—as even he must have known—but optimism was in his bones; it was the chief ingredient in his recipe for success. It was to be the frontiersman's legacy to the growing West.

²⁷ Reuben T. Durrett, *Centenary of Louisville*, Filson Club Publication, No. 8 (Louisville, 1893), 33.
²⁸ Butterfield, *Clark's Conquest*, 782, note 124. In addition to the other works cited in this chapter, the author has drawn on James Alton James, *George Rogers Clark* (Chicago, 1928).

Chapter XIII

CAPTAIN JIM TAKES A WIFE
(1778)

*Soldier, Brave, won't you marry me?
Now, now, soldier, won't you marry me?
Oh, by the fife and big fat drum,
How can I marry such a pretty girl as you
When I've got no coat to put on?*[1]

JIM HARROD was not a lady's man, but he knew a pretty girl when he saw one. The twenty-two-year-old widow, Ann McDaniel, was very good-looking, indeed, and even the most gossipy old Harrodsburg pioneer never denied it.

Ann was a fun-loving girl, a native of the Yadkin country in North Carolina and the only daughter of a hard-working frontiersman named Sam Coburn, whose family had migrated from the South Branch area of the Valley of Virginia. Ann had first married a young farmer, James McDaniel. The Coburns and McDaniels were well off for undermountain folk, but when their Scotch-Irish relatives started moving to the west where land was rich and easy to obtain, they could not resist the temptation to go along. This was in the fall of 1775, soon after the first white women and children had gone to live in Kentucky.[2]

Ann's family had more than the usual share of bad luck in the wilderness country, and there were times when she won-

---

[1] A stanza from "Soldier Brave," among the early American songs filed in the Music Division, Library of Congress, Washington. This particular version is still sung in mountain areas of Virginia.
[2] Draper Collection, 12C16, 4CC114, 4CC85.

dered why on earth they had left their comfortable Carolina home for this rough country hundreds of miles from civilization.³

The first bad luck that the girl had was to lose her husband, who was killed by Indians while making salt near Drennon's Lick. After that, Ann took her year-old baby James and moved to Logan's Fort, where she would have more protection than in her father's isolated station on Gilbert's Creek.

Anyone as pretty as the Widow McDaniel could not stay unmarried long,⁴ for women were as scarce as nails then; so poor McDaniel was hardly in his grave before bachelors began visiting Ann, offering to fend for her and bring in meat, maple sugar, and other necessities.

Jim Harrod often visited Logan's Fort, and he took a fancy to the young widow. In the past, this thirty-four-year-old bachelor⁵ had been too busy and often too far from the settlements to find a girl to marry, but now that he was established in this growing country, he thought it would be nice to have a household and a wife to make it cozy. Harrod proposed and Ann accepted.

The widow had made a good match. Besides being one of the handsomest men in Kentucky, Captain Harrod was desirable for other reasons. He was refined and gentle mannered, strong, energetic, and smart;⁶ furthermore, he had arrived early enough to take his choice of the best land in the country.

The wedding took place in February at Ben Logan's, with Robert Todd reading the ceremony.⁷

February was the quiet time on the frontier. Indian tribesmen were in their camps and towns, waiting for spring when they could raid Kentucky stations; the settlers had new supplies of meat jerked and stowed away; ground was not ready

---

³ *Ibid.*, 12C23-25, 12C22, 12CC53, 17CC192, 4CC80, 29S142.
⁴ *Ibid.*, 12C23, 9J35-37.
⁵ *Ibid.*, 12C22, 37J168-74.
⁶ *Ibid.*, 17CC192, 12CC45, 12CC112. See notes for Chap. XX.
⁷ *Ibid.*, 12C22, 12C25.

CAPTAIN JIM TAKES A WIFE 145

for planting. It was an ideal time for a big celebration. Other gatherings such as log rollings, sugar makings, corn huskings, and cabin raisings were all good fun, but these were connected with labor. At weddings the settlers could forget their troubles, hard work, and danger. In those days folks had to make their own celebrations and provide amusement as best they could. This should have been easy, since all they needed to have fun was to gather with friends they seldom saw except by chance. But cabins were often isolated, and, excepting during times of siege or in the summer when there was always plenty of other work to do, the settlers had little opportunity for exchanging news and dancing or singing.

If Harrod's was anything like the usual frontier wedding, it was a long-drawn-out affair, beginning with the groom's arrival just before noon and lasting until the next day.[8]

To the casual visitor, accustomed to the refinements of older settlements, Jim's and Ann's wedding must have been a drab affair, for there was no silver, no fine Delft china, no pure Irish linen to decorate the dinner table. Nor were there any beautiful flowers or soft music—only the seesaw of a screechy violin, accompanied by tapping feet and clapping hands to the tune of "The Mouse Trap":

> Of all the simple things we do,
> To rub o-ver a whim-si-cal life,
> There's no one fol-ly is so true
> As that ve-ry bar-gain a wife.
> We're just like a mouse in a trap,
> Or rat that is caught in a gin;
> We start and fret, and try to escape,
> And rue the sad hour we came in.[9]

Ann had at least one pretty, ruffled dress she had packed

[8] The following account is based on numerous descriptions of typical weddings among pioneers of English ancestry. See Joseph Doddridge, *Notes on the Settlement . . . of Virginia* (Wellsburg, Va., 1824), 102.

[9] Early American Dance Music Collection, Music Division, Library of Congress.

across the mountains, and she probably had a brooch, too. This was far more than many frontier brides possessed.

Jim wore a new hunting shirt and jeans. It would have been nice had he owned a fine broadcloth coat and shiny silver-buckled shoes, but it was several years before this kind of elegance was available on the Kentucky frontier. There is reason to believe that his eldest brother Tom was the only son of the widow present on this occasion, although Sam could have been there. Will was busy in the Monongahela country, helping to outfit Clark's Illinois regiment; otherwise he would have attended and had a rousing good time.

Since there was no way of getting a marriage license without a long trip to Williamsburg, Jim did not have one. This fact so disturbed Ann in later years, when she was involved in lawsuits over her inheritance, that she took pains to prove the legality of her wedding. But it could not have worried her much on her marriage day. Few frontier brides could boast of licenses to wed.

The ceremony preceded a dinner which consisted of the very best the settlers could get together. The "false spring" of early February had brought a new flow of maple sap, so the bride and groom had hasty pudding, a favorite dessert made of corn-meal mush, baked with treacle, or molasses. Bear meat and venison with kraut were always favorite dishes. Gourds and wooden plates held the food, but if there were any pewter spoons or cups to hold milk and toddy, these were few and undoubtedly a little the worse for travel and hard use. No one minded that, least of all Jim Harrod. When anyone called, "Where's Black Betty? I want to kiss her sweet lips!," a large bottle made the rounds, without anyone being afraid of germs.

"Here's health to the groom, not forgetting myself," a shouting guest would add, "and here's to the bride, thumping luck and big children!"[10]

After dinner the fun really started. Dancing—three- and four-handed reels—with the bride and groom jigging off the

---

[10] Doddridge, *Notes*, 102.

first set to the tune of "Roger de Coverley," danced longways for as many as cared to, or "Simple Simon" or "Huddle-duddle," danced longways for eight. "An Old Man a Bed Full of Bones" or "A Soldier's Life" started off a nightlong celebration which shook the rafters.[11] It took a stout pair of lungs to call out the places above the din of joking, stamping, and singing, which accompanied the dancers, and pitied be the fellow who tired easily amid all this hilarity; he had to parade up and down the floor until he dropped from exhaustion.

Jokes and games were on the rough side, but Captain Jim could take his share and give it back in full measure. However, a becoming blindness overtook the men when the girls pulled the bride to one side and led her up the ladder to the cabin loft.

When she was tucked securely under the warm bearskin rugs covering the high bed, the men carried the groom up the ladder and dropped him on the cornhusk mattress beside his bride.

Dancing went on in the room below.

Now and then a hearty settler would take "Black Betty" aloft. And toward morning the women placed before the couple a bowl of kraut and pork, or hominy; this held enough to feed six or seven hungry men, but the newlyweds had to eat it all before the intruders would leave them alone.

Along toward midmorning the last guest returned to his clearing, and the bride and groom went to their own station, where another crowd waited to give them a rousing welcome.

Jim's new station at Boiling Spring was too isolated for safety, so he took Ann to the fort at Harrodsburg, where they lived until the next fall.

Although relieved to find herself in the security of this larger fort, Ann had a sense of uneasiness—almost a foreboding that her stream of tragedy had not run out. Like most frontier people, Ann was superstitious, although she later

[11] Early American Dance Music Collection, Music Division, Library of Congress.

denied this. Frontiersmen regarded dreams as having special significance, and one particular dream she had that spring, Ann never forgot.

"I dreamed one night," she told an early Kentucky historian, "that the Indians attacked some of our men outside the fort; and that my husband ran out to help them. I saw an Indian shoot him, and, when he fell, stoop over and stab him. The very next day three men were chopping upon a log on the creek alongside the old Harrod's fort, close by, when we heard guns fire and saw the three men killed and the Indians scalping them."

While Captain Jim was calling the men to join him as he rushed to the gate, Ann's dream came into her mind. "I clung to him," she related later. "He forcibly tore himself from me and hurried out. I ran up to the highest point and looked out."

Terror-stricken, Ann watched the encounter. Jim was firing on the Indian nearest him. The tribesman, wounded, ran along the creek for a short distance, then fell.

"I plainly saw," Ann continued, "my husband stoop over (just the contrary of my dream) and stab him. When he came back, he did not exult but seemed distressed, and said he wished never to kill another of the poor natives, who were defending their fatherland; and that this feeling was forced upon him by the rebound of his knife, when he plunged it into the heart of the fallen Indian, who looked up so piteously into his face. He shed a tear when telling me."[12]

Ann's father was killed by Indians at about this time, while "packing corn" between Logan's and Harrod's forts. There was little time for grieving, however, for the new Mrs. Harrod was too busy helping her husband greet the many new settlers arriving during the summer. She had to teach the women how to make linsey, where to find the best herbs for the itch, and what to do for snakebites and fever. But she never could do much with a gun. "I *have* tried it often, but never could

[12] Collins, *Kentucky*, II, 615.

succeed," she used to say. "I did manage to kill a *cow* buffalo and a *bear,* or the girls would never have done laughing at me."[13] The hunting she was willing to leave in her husband's capable hands.

That task had been easy in the first years, but now the big game was pushing farther and farther west. Jim found, too, that getting enough salt to cure meat and season porridge was an increasingly hard problem.

Saltmaking was one of the most dangerous and tedious jobs a man could undertake[14]—dangerous because the Indians, particularly when in a scalp-collecting mood, made a business of watching the licks. This meant that a company must post guards day and night. The saline content of the springs was generally too low to make salt quickly. At large licks there were three or four furnaces going all the time, but it took eight hundred to a thousand gallons of this brackish water to produce even a bushel of salt. The pioneers had a saying that a lazy man was not worth his salt; in fact it took a cow and a calf to balance the scales against a bushel of this vital commodity.

Jim talked the problem over with men around the fort, and sixteen of them agreed to go with him to buy or make salt. Harrod had visited the lick at the mouth of the Ohio as a boy while trapping in the Illinois and lower country with Sam.[15] It was a large spring, about three miles west of Kaskaskia, across the Mississippi, but Jim knew the French and Indians there and believed that in spite of the long distance it would be a safer place to work than in Kentucky, where hostile tribesmen from Ohio lay in wait.

Harrod's party started out the middle of October, going directly to the Falls, where they bought a keelboat—a light craft, sharp at both ends and sixty or eighty feet long and eight or ten feet wide in the beam. It was fitted with a long

[13] Draper Collection, 12C25.
[14] Thomas D. Clark, "Salt, a Factor in the Settlement of Kentucky," in *Filson Club History Quarterly* (Louisville), XII (1938), 42, *passim.*
[15] Draper Collection, 12CC65-98, is the basis for the anecdotes which follow in the text.

cabin, removable mast and sails, and running boards along the sides where the men could stand as they poled the boat upstream.

The captain stood in the prow, directing the course. As they went, Jim told the men about his early life in the Illinois —how he had first come out in 1766 with his older brother Sam and had lived with the French and among the Delawares, learning to speak their tongues.[16] This was not so unusual; many trappers could speak with the Indians to a limited extent. Nor was it strange to find a red man who had at least a smattering of English. During attacks at the Fort, Harrod had heard the tribesmen use English swearwords, or short sentences such as, "Go on—fire your big gun!," or "Where's McGary? Send *him* out!"[17]

Once during this salt excursion, Harrod tied up at the bank and went ashore to get his bearings from a couple of Delawares and their squaws who had a camp along the river. Jim took with him a bottle of taffa, or rum, but kept it behind him so the Indians would not see what he had as he sauntered up to the group and in a casual manner began talking with them.

The Indians pretended they could not understand and held their heads down, but when Harrod produced the rum it was no time until they found their tongues and began talking freely. When the atmosphere was entirely friendly, Jim grew more impressive in his speech, asking them their names, then solemnly announcing that their father was his father.

The Delawares nodded and replied solemnly, "Capitan Harrod my brother," and appeared very proud of their newfound relative.[18]

Jim passed the bottle until the Indians were thoroughly and happily drunk, then he approached the real objective of the occasion.

[16] *Ibid.,* 12CC65-98, 18J59, 18J84-88.
[17] Spalding, *Sketches,* 39 n.
[18] Draper Collection, 12CC65-98.

CAPTAIN JIM TAKES A WIFE

Yes, the tipsy Delawares agreed, one of them would be glad to go with their white brother as guide and protector. The peace emissary staggered along behind Harrod to the boat—where he promptly fell asleep. He lay there a long time, and before he awakened, the keel had gone fifty or sixty miles downstream.

Because of the great distance they had covered, it was plain to Jim and his party that the Indian would be little help, so, telling him that they had gone only five or six miles, they let him out of the boat and sent him on his way. Evidently he was a steady drinker—a habit he had learned from white men who used alcohol freely as a means of bribing Indians. This one had probably learned to drink from close association with the French and Spanish living close to these western Delaware tribesmen.

As the salt hunters went farther and farther into the wilderness they became more conscious of their danger. In order to keep their minds off the subject Jim kept up a fire of amusing anecdotes or devised games for the occasion. One of these latter was "cobbing," a ribald sport in which every man who did not manage to pull off his coat or roundabout within a split second had to bend over the side of the boat "with his fundament protruded," and receive a wallop. This procedure continued until every man in the boat was naked. Far from objecting to the roughness of the sport, the men thought it great fun. "Harrod was a lively-pleasant-hearted friendly sort of man," commented one of the party.[19]

Jim also liked to play practical jokes; for instance he "put fire" to Billy Bush's red beard and burned another man's "britches." "He was always," the saltmaker recalled, "playing some prank on the men which passed off in perfect good humour."

When the party reached St. Louis, Jim bought a stallion, which he stabled, carefully fed, and nearly every day ran in a race against French horses. For his rider Jim chose one of

[19] *Ibid.*

his company, a very small man. Since the French usually caught their entries fresh from the range and made no effort to put a lightweight in the saddle, naturally Harrod's horse always won.[20]

If, as one writer reported, the first Kentuckians were half alligator and half horse, they soon lost the first half of the appellation.[21] The first track in Kentucky was at Harrodsburg, and about 1783 Hugh McGary and others were fined and denounced by pious magistrates who were trying to outlaw the sport. Nevertheless, horse racing continued to grow in popularity in spite of official displeasure.

At the saltworks the men found furnaces blazing and water boiling in leaden and iron kettles. Jim bought all the salt they had, paying for it in Continental money, since the Indians were not inclined to take goods in exchange for so valuable a commodity. They did not know in this far outpost that the papers were worth only one fourth their usual value.

On their return up the Ohio, Harrod's party met two Frenchmen paddling canoes from O'Post, or Vincennes. These men reported that there were four hundred Cherokee waiting at the mouth of the Cumberland to kill the Kentuckians. A little farther on Harrod met another Frenchman who confirmed this story. This being too large a number for a party of his size to deal with, Jim planned to avoid meeting them by having the men wrap the oars with cloth. They traveled in this manner all night, until they were far above the danger point. The next day Harrod met a squaw standing on the bank and went over to talk with her, to discover what information, if any, she might have concerning the Cherokee war party.

The squaw was surprised to hear about the Cherokee and grateful to the white man for telling her about them, since, as she explained, they were enemies of her tribe. She would tell her husband of the danger as soon as he returned from the hunt.

[20] *Ibid.* [21] *Cincinnati Miscellany*, II (1846), 33.

CAPTAIN JIM TAKES A WIFE 153

Men like Jim, having lived and hunted with Indians, knew that enmity between tribes was at least as deadly as that between red men and white, so by doing them small favors they won friends who were often of great help, while irresponsible, hotheaded backwoodsmen frequently nullified their efforts through rash attacks on any Indian who came in sight. The tribesmen knew their friends and did their best to protect them. Even the Shawnee, who hated Kentuckians, were known to repay acts of kindness. When Daniel Boone was captured while making salt at Blue Licks, he was unusually well treated —a fact he later attributed to Jim Harrod's gentle handling of a Shawnee warrior a few months earlier.[22]

According to the story, Captain Harrod went out on one of his long, solitary trips to the Indian country above the Ohio and ran into an ambush of Shawnee. He had to race for his life. By dodging in and out of brush Jim managed to keep ahead as far as the river, where he discovered there were but three warriors continuing the chase. Harrod swam to the opposite bank, got behind a tree, removed the waterproof cover of deer's bladder from the lock of his rifle and prepared to make a stand.

Hesitating at first, the Indians finally began to cross. When they had reached the halfway mark, Jim fired. One Indian sank; another floundered, wounded. The third, through skillful diving and rapid maneuvering, managed to get out of range.

Harrod "made off" through the woods, then reconnoitered two hours later to see if the other Indians had crossed the Ohio. On a small pile of driftwood, gathered at the mouth of a tributary, he saw the figure of a tall Indian, unarmed and bleeding heavily from the shoulder. After making a circle and creeping toward the wounded man from behind, the Kentuckian reached a large tree, propped his rifle against the trunk, rose to his feet, and with spreading arms showed he was unarmed. Then he spoke a few words in Shawnee.

[22] Webber, *Romance of Forest Life*, 173-76.

At first the Indian acted as if he would try to swim, but being too weak gave up the attempt.

Jim helped him to the bank, tore his own shirt into strips and bound the wound with herbs. Since the warrior was unable to walk, Harrod threw him across his broad shoulder and took him to a limestone cave, where he often deposited meat. It was a deep, well-like cave, with a very small entrance covered with briars which made it invisible. Harrod had discovered it when a wounded bear tried to hide from him there. He had fashioned a pole ladder from a sapling by cutting off the limbs within six inches of the trunk to leave footholds. Having carried the Indian down this ladder, Harrod dressed his wounds, fed and cared for him until he was well enough to return to his tribe. Harrod bade him farewell, telling him to remember "Lone Long Knife."[23]

According to Boone it was this grateful warrior who saved him from torture.

After leaving the squaw, Harrod's party continued their homeward journey unmolested. The success of his salt trip was not the last of Jim Harrod's "lucky streak." About Christmastime he heard good news from the capital of Virginia. Once more the determined and now desperate Judge Henderson had presented a memorial to the house, asking for validation of his title. But the house refused his request, resolving instead: "That all purchases of lands, made or to be made, within the chartered bounds of this commonwealth, as described by the constitution or form of government, by any private persons not authorized by public authority, are void."[24] However, in consideration of the company's very great expense in making the purchase and settling the lands, they further resolved that it was "just and reasonable"[25] to allow Richard Henderson and Company a compensation for their

---

[23] *Ibid.*
[24] See Lester. *Transylvania,* 229-36, for details. *Journal of the Virginia House of Delegates* (Williamsburg, 1778), October 30–November 4, 1778.
[25] Lester, *Transylvania,* 229-36; *Journal of the Virginia House of Delegates,* October 30–November 4, 1778.

trouble and expense. The senate, concurring in the resolution, voted to allot them land on the Green River—land far inferior in quality and location to Henderson's original claim.[26]

With this final enactment Jim Harrod achieved complete victory. While the creation of Kentucky County two years earlier had voided the Transylvania claim in effect, now it had been voided by law.

At last the promises Captain Jim had made his party of forty men back in 1774 would hold good; they could claim their land under old Virginia law, and no proprietary government would take it from them.

No longer was James Harrod a mere adventurer, a lone hunter. He was now a man of property and—what he had dreamed of being—a planter and a gentleman, surrounded by friends and "kinsfolk." He had a wife and a little boy as dear as if he were his own; and soon, at the Boiling Spring, he would move into a fine new home, the first frame house in Kentucky.[27]

But, like most dreamers, Jim had to face a harsh reality. With twenty years of carefree wilderness-living behind him, thirty-four-year-old James Harrod was too old in experience and too set in habit to enjoy the role of a gentleman.

[26] *Journal of the Senate of Virginia* (Williamsburg, 1778), November 14-17, 1778.
[27] Draper Collection, 12C25.

Chapter XIV

THE MONONGAHELANS
(1778-1779)

*"I now send two Belts to all the Nations,
One for Peace and the other for War."*[1]

WHILE James Harrod was making his dreams come true in central Kentucky and Clark was continuing military operations in the Illinois, the corn grew rapidly on the small island opposite the Falls. The twenty families who had come down the Ohio with the Monongahelans huddled snug and secure in their new stockade at the lower point where land was high and the island narrow. They had put up cabins, marking them off with a neat row of pickets which, with the perpendicular banks on the other sides, made a natural fortification.

Will Harrod's already difficult task of provisioning Corn Island was further complicated by the arrival of many new families during the summer. Realizing that if people kept coming at that rate, there would not be enough tillable soil to grow greens and corn for the population, Will began to make plans for the construction of another fort as soon as he returned from Kaskaskia.[2]

News of Will's undertaking was received with enthusiasm by Jim Harrod and other leaders in the older settlements, since the fort would afford a convenient, safe stopping place for newcomers bound for central Kentucky. Up to now, Jim

---

[1] George Rogers Clark to the Lake Tribes after his capture of Governor Hamilton, quoted by Clark in a letter to George Mason, November 19, 1779, in James (ed.) *Clark Papers, 1771-1781*, 114-54.

[2] Draper Collection, 37J168-74, 11C7; Durrett, *Louisville*, 30-32.

Harrod had been forced to send out pilots to wait at the Falls for boats floating down to Kentucky; now, with the fort on Corn Island, he would be less apprehensive about his new arrivals. There was always at least one scout at the Ohio River garrison who would lead the way to Harrodsburg.

The new fort was to be on the southern shore, opposite the Falls, where close watch on river travel would be easiest. Similar in outline to others in Kentucky, it had no pickets; instead, there were rows of cabins on all sides of the parallelogram, held together by protruding blockhouses at all corners.

When the fort was finished Will turned to problems of a civil nature such as the calling of an election of trustees.[3] At the public meeting where the inhabitants chose Will and six others to govern them, strict attention was paid to the new rules that had been laid down by the Kentucky county court in an effort to regulate the establishment of towns in conformity with old Virginia practice and new frontier experience.[4]

The "town" which Will, as first trustee and commander of the garrison, ordered built, consisted of 116 half-acre lots to follow the course of the river. The lots were all numbered, of course, but if the design was to produce a numerical puzzle, as one historian has commented, the success was perfect.[5] However, drawing proceeded with enthusiasm, and Will pulled a number for himself and one for his brother Sam. It developed later that one section of the town was on John Campbell's old military grant, while the other was on John Connolly's. This fact, which was certainly well known to Will Harrod and Clark at the time, must have appeared unimportant to them;[6] but several years later, hardfisted John Campbell insisted on his rights and had the properties confiscated, forcing all those who had drawn lots in the bend of the river to lose their titles. Undoubtedly, Connolly would have taken similar action had he not, as a Loyalist sym-

[3] Durrett, *Louisville*, 33.
[4] *Ibid.*, and Appendixes E, F.
[5] *Ibid.*, 35.
[6] *Ibid.*, 54-56, 134-36.

pathizer, lost his land through forfeiture.⁷ Sam's lot was on Campbell's grant; Will's in the other section.

It is doubtful that either of them ever seriously planned to live at the Falls, for Sam liked the Illinois wilderness too well, and Will's Amelia agreed with Tom Harrod's wife that moving to Kentucky was "a gloomy prospective." Like many others, the Harrods drew their lots as pure speculation.

When Clark returned, the men at once made plans for a housewarming, sending invitations to Jim Harrod and Ben Logan and urging everyone to join in a celebration.⁸

Everything seemed so promising to the settlers that Jim and Ben had no trouble gathering a group to attend the housewarming. Logan took his party to Harrodsburg where they spent the first night of their journey; then, early in the morning, he, Jim and Ann Harrod, Hugh McGary, and a number of others—twenty-six men and women in all—started for the Falls. They had gone only a mile when Dan Trabue, a young Virginia boy who had come along to do business with the Falls commissary, discovered Indian traces. As soon as Dan had reported the news Jim halted the company and sent McGary to examine the signs.

On his return McGary reported to Harrod that he had seen the Indians, and that while the settlers could probably defeat them, it would be foolish to fight with the women along. Jim agreed, ordering the company to retreat, while he sent a party out to scout for the tribesmen, who by now had disappeared in the forest.

The next morning the celebration party again started out, but with only fifteen men and three women. All were in high spirits. For fun as much as for need, Jim killed a buffalo, which he packed along.

They all arrived safely at the Falls where Clark, Will Harrod, and the resident families had prepared the ingredients

---

⁷ *Ibid.;* Collins, *Kentucky*, II, 183.

⁸ Durrett, *Louisville*, 30-33; the "Journal of Colonel Daniel Trabue," in Lillie DuPuy Harper (ed.), *Colonial Men and Times* (Philadelphia, 1916), 19 ff. The manuscript of this journal is in the Draper Collection.

for a real celebration, including rum and sugar, which the Colonel had brought in a keelboat from Kaskaskia, and a large room for dancing.

"When these Fort Ladys came to be dressed up they did not look like the same," commented Dan Trabue. "Everything looked new; we enjoyed ourselves very much. Col. Harrod & his Lady opened the ball by dancing the first jig. We had plenty of rum Toddy to drink...."[9]

A French violinist who had stopped at the Falls to repair his boat before continuing to Kaskaskia offered to play for the dance. He began with a fashionable European tune for a step called a "Branle," which required considerable skill in execution—wide, leaping circles—too much for the inexperienced frontier women. Next he tried a minuet, but the sight of the women holding their dresses out from their sides like sails, skipping across the floor, and bowing their heads like geese dodging stones, brought the poor Frenchman to despair. Declaring that he would sooner be in hell than playing for this ungraceful lot, he gladly turned over his task to an old Negro named Cata, whose fiddling of a familiar tune, a Virginia reel, then an Irish jig, was more in keeping with the celebration.

The Frenchman had a change of heart, or at least an eye for business, because he returned to open the first dancing school in Louisville. As for the Negro fiddler, he was later hanged for killing his master—much to the sorrow of the young folk, who missed his playing at their dances.[10]

Clark went back to the Illinois soon after this celebration, but Will Harrod stayed on, providing food for the steady flow of new arrivals, some of whom remained at Louisville, while others merely rested or stocked up for journeys to more-distant Kentucky settlements.[11] However, Harrod's commissary duties ended abruptly when he learned that Clark had captured the British governor, Lord Henry Hamilton, who

---

[9] "Trabue Journal," in Harper (ed.), *Colonial Men and Times*, 19 ff.
[10] Durrett, *Louisville*, 32-33.   [11] Draper Collection, 20S229.

would be sent to the capital by way of the Falls. Dropping all his other tasks, Will made ready for the arrival of this important personage.

When all was in readiness, he went down the river with thirteen oarsmen to take over the custody of Hamilton and the twenty-two other prisoners who were established in a camp a little above the mouth of Salt River. Here he made out a receipt for the valuable captives and proceeded with them to the Falls.[12]

Lord Hamilton and his fellow prisoners were prepared for almost anything. Will put them in a log house, where they shuddered in fear of their lives, while the joyful inhabitants celebrated by firing their cannon at intervals throughout the day. This glee over their capture made Hamilton recall Clark's admonition, that they would be running the risk of their lives in passing the frontier settlements.

Clark was right. The settlers had nicknamed Hamilton the "hair buyer," and every man, woman, and youngster in the country believed that he bought scalps from the red men. Captain Will managed to restrain any violent tendencies, but the settlers took their spite out on the captives in other ways. For instance, they made the British pay for their food; a supply of bread cost the governor his good feather quilt. When Will set off with the prisoners for Harrodsburg, there was not a single day's provision in their packs, the plan being to send out hunters on the march between stations.

The trip between the Falls and Harrod's fort was uneventful, excepting a brief and peaceful encounter with a band of Shawnee warriors on their way to attack the Cherokee. Will and his party arrived at Harrodsburg after dark on the sixth day. Hamilton observed that the people there "were in hourly apprehension of attacks from savages, and no doubt these poor inhabitants are worthy of pity. Their cattle were brought into the fort every night, horses as well as cows. They dared not go for firewood or to plow, without their arms; yet in

[12] *Ibid.*, 49J12.

spite of this state of constant alarm, a considerable quantity of land had been cleared, and as their numbers were increasing fast, they will soon set the savages at defiance, being good marksmen and well practiced in the woods...."[13]

Although Hamilton and his fellow prisoners fared better at Jim's fort than they had at Will's, their accommodations were not fancy, since they had the same "victuals" as did the settlers—Indian corn and milk for breakfast and supper, Indian bread and bear's flesh for dinner.

When the Britishers first arrived, the Harrodsburg people considered them little better than savages, which Hamilton admitted was excusable, considering their reputation for inspiring Indian raids.

At Logan's fort, where Will conducted them on the next leg of their journey to Williamsburg, the people, particularly the women, vociferously accosted the prisoners "in pretty course term," said Hamilton, although he excepted Ben Logan and his wife from this accusation.

From this fort, Will led the march through rich cane country, up steep heights and down ragged stony crags, across swamps and clayey grounds to the Rock Castle branch of the Cumberland. "The scene is very beautiful," Hamilton observed, "the trees being in high beauty, the water bright, the weather clear ... I could not but enjoy this romantic prospect ... while our poor fatigued pack horses were towed through the rapid stream by their wearied journey leaders. We encamped about 7:00 P.M., when we were joined by Colonel Calloway, who took upon him, the charge of the prisoners, and their escort, hitherto commanded by Captain Harrod."[14]

Succeeding entries in Hamilton's journal contain indictments of Colonel Richard Calloway's actions, of his great military display, and of his rigid discipline and harsh treatment, which were apparently in strong contrast to those the prisoners had experienced under Harrod.[15]

[13] Lord Hamilton's Journal, photostatic copy in the Filson Club Collection.
[14] Ibid.   [15] Ibid.

Meanwhile Will returned to Louisville, where plans were under way for a proposed expedition to Detroit the next spring. Prospects looked good to John Bowman, who reported his belief that more than three hundred Kentucky militiamen would be at Clark's disposal. Will's men from the Monongahela country liked the idea of obtaining a little Indian booty before returning to their homes. Enthusiasm ran so high that Colonel Bowman planned an advance campaign against the Ohio Shawnee towns—an undertaking which he expected to smooth the path for Clark's more ambitious plans. He told the settlers to plant their corn early in preparation for a rendezvous at the mouth of the Licking. Will Harrod was to recruit men at the Falls and have boats ready to carry the entire body of troops across the river.[16]

The absent Clark could not be consulted on Bowman's plan, but it appeared reasonable to Will, who tried to win support for it by pointing out the importance of an offensive expedition. Shrewdly he told of the opportunity it would present to acquire large amounts of booty. As usual, Will's persistent arguments and harangues brought large enlistments. Four companies turned out from various other stations, including Logan's, Harrodsburg, McAfee's, and Bryan's—a new fort located near the present town of Lexington. Although Bowman had expected to draft regular militiamen, this proved unnecessary. Three hundred volunteers agreed to go.

Corn was knee-high when Will and the Monongahelans went ahead to the Licking to procure boats and provisions, and to kill buffalo, bear, and deer. They stopped at the

[16] The account of Bowman's expedition which follows in the text is based on several accounts by eyewitnesses: Draper Collection, 12C1-12, 12C15, 12CC65, 4CC89-109; Clark to Mason, James (ed.), *Clark Papers, 1771-1781*, 114-54 (see also lix); Collins, *Kentucky*, II, 180, 426, 483, 613; Marshall, *History of Kentucky*, I, 91-95; Butler, *Commonwealth of Kentucky*, 26 ff., 102 ff., 110; and "Bowman's Campaign of 1779," and "Logan's Campaign, 1786" (copies of two original accounts in the Bedinger and Hall Papers, Draper Collection), in *Ohio State Archeological and Historical Quarterly*, XXII (1913), 502-21.

Big Bone Lick to collect large specimens, which, as always, were irresistible to souvenir hunters.

Will had two keelboats and three canoes ready when the other companies arrived. The leaders brought parched corn which they doled out to the men, "a peck apiece," after which they crossed the river, leaving a few men behind to guard the boats.

Since there were no cabins here, Will ordered the guards to live in the boats, plying up and down to avoid being ambushed.

Finally, the expedition assembled and the men marched along the northern shore of the Ohio to the mouth of the Scioto while the boats followed upstream with the provisions. Two days later they reached the vicinity of Old Chillicothe (Oldtown). Here they halted for the purpose of deploying the men. It was a foggy, dark night, and the soldiers threw their blankets around their shoulders as they crouched in the woods. The three companies under Bowman, Logan, and Harrod were next directed to move closer to the first town and await orders for an attack. Their men stationed, Will and the other two commanders went out to reconnoiter the woods. While they were gone an Indian, apparently returning from a hunt, approached from behind Harrod's men.

This unexpected occurrence presented the troops with a serious problem, since with Will away there was no one to direct action. One of the men, fearful that the tribesman might report the presence of white troops, took it upon himself to shoot the unsuspecting Indian; however, when he ran up to take his scalp another militiaman mistook him for a second Indian and shot him in the side.

Naturally the near-by town was aroused by this "rumpus." The dogs began to bark furiously, while the squaws cried, "Kentucky! Kentuck!" Finding their town surrounded, the women fled in dismay to the large council house near the center of town.

Blackfish, the chieftain who had led the attack on Harrodsburg when James Ray saved the fort from surprise, ran outside the gates to investigate and was killed by the fire, while those trailing him were badly wounded.

The necessary element of surprise having been destroyed, the white men had to remap their plans immediately. Colonel Bowman accordingly called a hurried council with Will Harrod and Ben Logan. It was decided to leave the troops divided into three companies, as they were before the excitement. At a given signal they were to charge from three sides—Logan on the left, Harrod on the right, and Bowman in the middle.

Logan and Harrod waited for Bowman's signal, but it did not come. Four or five hours elapsed, then finally, toward morning, the Indians came out of their huts to give battle. Still there was no signal from Bowman.

Harrod now took matters into his own hands and led his men in a rush on horseback into the town. The other companies followed. It was a desperate move, but, as all agreed later, a fortunate one. They broke the Indian line of battle and forced the savages to flee.[17] But the whites had lost eight or nine men, and their ranks were in complete disorder. Harrod and Logan rode among them, shouting frantically in an effort to bring them into line. Then they dashed after the fleeing tribesmen, followed by most of the men, still in disorder.

The scattered Indians crept through the outlying woods, firing, skulking away to reload, then shooting from another position. On the other hand, whenever the Kentuckians fancied they saw the trembling of some distant cluster of bushes or luxuriant growth of tall grass, they would fire upon the suspected covert. This singular contest, which lasted nine hours, was comparatively bloodless.[18] The last Indian had been swallowed by the woods, doubtless on his way to warn the other towns. Bowman held a council with his captains

[17] John Filson, *The Discovery, Settlement and Present State of Kentucke* (Wilmington, Del., 1784), 71.
[18] Draper Collection, 12C1-12.

WE the Subscribers, inhabitants of Kentucke, and well acquainted with the country from its first settlement, at the request of the author of this book, and map, have carefully revised them, and recommend them to the public, as exceeding good performances, containing as accurate a description of our country as we think can possibly be given; much preferable to any in our knowledge extant; and think it will be of great utility to the publick. Witness our hands this 12th day of May, Anno Domini 1784,

DANIEL BOON,
LEVI TODD,
JAMES HARROD.

FIRST PAGE OF JOHN FILSON, *The Discovery, Settlement and Present State of Kentucke* (WILMINGTON, DEL., 1784). *Library of Congress, Rare Books Division.*

and decided to end the campaign. Their surprise had failed; another engagement against a forewarned, well-armed enemy might bring complete disaster.

When it was all over the men decided to hold a sale of horses and other booty, and then to make an equal division of the profits. Each purchaser was to have a year's credit; the captains were to keep accounts for their respective companies, and when it developed that anyone had bid in property "in excess of the value of his purchase," an adjustment was to be made. "The theory was very pretty," one survivor commented, "and all seemed well pleased with it." Horses identified by their owners present as having been stolen from the settlements were excepted from sale. Some of the finest animals were struck off at fifty or sixty dollars, but generally for much less; while a pound of silver trinkets brought some twenty dollars. Thus went the large droves of horses, the silver ornaments, the clothing, and the other articles.[19]

In spite of the large amount of booty taken from the Indians, the battle was not a fortunate one for the white men. At the very best, said some witnesses, it had been a draw, while Clark declared it a tragic mistake which prevented his using these troops against Detroit and stirred up unnecessary fears among friendly Indians.[20] Others declared it a disgrace, saying that Bowman should have gone on to the next village. James Ray, who had served under Harrod and carried his wounded cousin on his horse during the battle, was, as always, loyal to his superior officer, commending Colonel Bowman for having had the moral courage to return home and not sacrifice his men to false pride by attacking forewarned towns farther north.[21]

There is reason to believe that Bowman was shocked and then confused by the Indians' unexpected discovery of his company. At least one deponent claimed that a Negro woman stole out of town to warn the whites that there were a hun-

[19] *Ibid.*
[20] Clark "Memoir," in Butterfield, *Clark's Conquest*, 208-302.
[21] Draper Collection, 12C15.

dred warriors in the settlement and more on their way from the Pickaway towns. It was this news, according to this version, that had induced Bowman to withhold his signal for an attack.

Will Harrod was never inclined to blame the colonel. He and Jim believed Bowman had been made a scapegoat for the failure to take all the Chillicothe towns by surprise. According to their versions of the incident, had the Monongahelans been as much interested in chasing the Indians as they were in taking plunder, the result might have been different. It is apparently true that Will's men pillaged their section of the town, helping themselves to horses, bolts of cloth, and silver ornaments, and that they had no interest in pursuing the fleeing Indians.[22]

Although most of the companies had been made up in Kentucky, from settlements where volunteers were eager to stop Indian raids as a matter of self-protection, the majority of Will's men expected to return to the Monongahela, and therefore plunder was their chief concern.[23] It is interesting that many of them returned to live at Louisville, Lexington, and other points, in the years following this first settlers' march into the Ohio country.[24]

Will's son claimed that his father killed two Indians in the battle. The Harrods' cousin, Samuel Moore, who had been associated with Jim in the first settlement and had served as a spy for Clark in the Illinois country, lost his life. Strangely, he had dreamed the night before the march that he would either be killed or wounded, but, rather than remain at home and be considered a coward, he had gone along, taking bandages as a precaution.[25]

Clark returned from the Illinois country bitterly disappointed because he had been unable to organize his campaign against Detroit. He was provoked with Colonel Bowman for

[22] *Ibid.*, 12C1-12, 1A20, 9J10-11.
[23] *Ibid.*, 9J10-11.
[24] See Durrett, *Louisville*, Appendixes H,M,N.
[25] Draper Collection, 37J168-74.

failing to meet him as arranged. While the men pointed out that Bowman had expected to join Clark later, the Virginian showed plainly that he considered this explanation unsatisfactory and that he was disgusted by Bowman's expedition as much as by his failure.

Mortified by the poor showing his Monongahelans had made, and by the fact that he had allowed himself to become a party to such an ill-fated adventure, Will resigned his command of the fort at Louisville—against the wishes of Clark, who made him promise to return after a visit in the Monongahela country.[26]

Will's company were restless and eager to go home. Further depreciation of Continental currency partially increased their desire to get back to their farms, a soldier's salary being no longer attractive.

This devaluation of currency also affected campaigns at the forks of the Ohio, where Colonel Daniel Broadhead, the Western commander who had taken Hand's position, was trying to recruit men for an expedition to the Indian country. Not all his difficulty could be traced to devaluation. Broadhead was unpopular with the men because he was pompous, fond of strict discipline, overconscious of rank, and jealous of his position. It was the same old story; Will had heard it a hundred times.[27]

Having received permission to pass Fort McIntosh, twenty miles down the Ohio from Fort Pitt, Harrod's men began to grumble about Broadhead and the possibility of difficulties with him over passports. Would he issue one so that they could proceed to Redstone, or would he force them to enlist at once for his expedition? Being in command, Will knew that he had to see his men through any difficulty that might arise; so, cocky, experienced, wise in the ways of British-trained regulars, he stalked into Broadhead's headquarters,

[26] *Ibid.*, 12C1-12, 4NN76, 46J55, 49J89-90.
[27] Louise P. Kellogg (ed.), *Frontier Retreat on the Upper Ohio, 1779-1781* (Madison, 1917), 32-34.

doffed his big hat, and proclaimed in his booming baritone, "Good morning to your Holiness, Colonel Broadhead, let your name be Broadhead or Narrohead or the Devil's head, I want a pass. If I can get one, well and good. If not, I'll go without it. I'm Colonel Bill Harrod that commands at the falls of the Ohio and here's the old black gun that barked loud at the Illinois . . . falls of the Ohio, Forbes' campaign, Pickaway, and Chillicothe towns and elsewhere. . . ."[28]

Broadhead hastily granted Harrod his pass.

This rather astonishing declaration was reported by two of the regulars present. Each claimed to have overheard the incident.

Broadhead was not able to get enough men together to undertake a campaign. Not long afterward the commander was accused of using his position to further his private interests—a charge which was probably brought on as much by his highhanded methods in dealing with civilians around Fort Pitt as by his accusers' suspicion of his dishonesty or inefficiency.[29]

The commander had received a lesson that either Jim, Will Harrod, or any other experienced captain could have explained to him in advance—had he been inclined to listen: to handle frontier soldiers an officer needed more than a knowledge of military science. Jim knew from his own experience in Dunmore's campaign that any military commander in the West would have to secure the personal loyalty of the frontiersmen whom he wished to command. This they gave most easily to men they trusted from past experience. Jim and Will Harrod were born on the frontier. Their prominence came from demonstrated superiority in common skills, from personal magnetism, from the homely traits so valued and needed in wilderness communities—honesty, bravery, industry, tact, and, above all, patience and insight.

[28] Draper Collection, 6NN74. See *ibid.*, 11E14-16 for a slightly different version of this incident.
[29] Kellogg (ed.), *Frontier Retreat*, 32-34.

It mattered not that the Harrods had little book learning. They could read and write well enough to keep company lists and to make brief reports. They had persuasive powers beyond the average; they were resourceful and never failed their men in an emergency. As with other leaders in the wilderness West, these were the measure of the Harrods' success. It became the foundation of James Harrod's legendary fame.

Chapter XV

THE HARD WINTER
(1779-1780)

"The Inhabitants avered they never knew so severe weather at that season. . . ."[1]

NOTHING was dearer to the hearts of early Kentuckians than military titles. During the winter of 1779 Jim Harrod received a permanent commission as colonel. Several times previously he had held this rank on a temporary basis, and the settlers had continued to address him as "Colonel" in affectionate recognition of his services. Ben Logan, the new county lieutenant, in requesting this promotion for his old friend, took pains to say that it was long overdue. Another honor came Jim's way that year, when he was elected Kentucky County's second representative to the Virginia legislature, to serve with Colonel Richard Calloway. Jim's main contribution was a bill for improvement of the Wilderness Road, which the Assembly passed in October.[2]

The population had been expanding so rapidly since Clark's campaign that Colonel Jim Harrod had little time for concern over militia rank or legislative duties. Following the recent passage of a new land law, prospective settlers had been organizing parties in the Piedmont, far east of the cen-

---

[1] "Journal of Colonel William Fleming" (November 10, 1779—May 27, 1780), in Newton D. Mereness (ed.), *Travels in the American Colonies* (New York, 1916), 624 ff.

[2] Draper Collection, 12C22; Palmer and others (arrs.), *Virginia State Papers*, II, 280-82; *Journal of the Virginia House of Delegates, 1779* (Williamsburg, 1779); Robert Lee Kincaid, *The Wilderness Road* (Indianapolis, 1947), 157.

ters that had furnished the nuclei for the first pioneer settlements.[3] They had been rushing to the new country like cows into a cornfield. Pennsylvanians caught the fever, too, sailing down the Ohio in flatboats from Brownsville (or Redstone Old Fort, as it was often called at that time) on the Monongahela. One old farmer remarked that new settlers bound for Kentucky were as thick as butterflies in July.

The immediate reason for the rush was that hearings on land claims were to begin in October with the arrival of four commissioners from Virginia, and everyone interested in Western land wanted to have some kind of rights established by that time.[4] Then, there were many people who had been in Kentucky earlier but had left their claims under pressure from Indians or for other reasons; these were hurrying back to keep others from taking over their land.

From Jim Harrod's point of view the law was a good one. It provided for two kinds of rights, settlement and preemption, on easy terms. Anyone who had been in the country before January 1, 1778, and had raised a crop of corn on any "waste and unappropriated lands" to which no other had any legal right or claim, was entitled to four hundred acres. Those who had established themselves under these provisions, as most of Jim's company had, could obtain as much as one thousand adjoining acres at the rate of forty pounds per hundred acres in Virginia money, the equivalent of ten shillings per hundred acres in colonial currency. An additional ten shillings was due the clerk.[5]

There was a "catch" in the law, even for Harrod's men,[6] for Virginia had made no provision for supervising the surveys—an omission that led to more actual heartbreak over a long period of years than any amount of Indian trouble. After

---

[3] Marshall, *History of Kentucky*, I, 102-103.
[4] *Ibid.*
[5] George M. Bibb (ed.), Vol. I of *Reports of Cases at Common Law and in Chancery . . . of Kentucky* (Frankfort, 1815), Introduction. Hereinafter this volume will be cited as Bibb (ed.), *Reports*.
[6] Marshall, *History of Kentucky*, I, 98-101.

all, when someone put in a claim to a piece of his land, Jim could not very well shoot it out with him; nor could he settle the controversy through arguments, for it was necessary to bring in witnesses. Most of this legal trouble came later.

For the present, James Harrod was in a good position. Land prices were rising rapidly, and he sold one in-lot and three out-lots in Harrodsburg, with adjoining five hundred acres, for three hundred pounds.[7] Land exchanged at an increasing rate during these months before the commissioners arrived.

The men sent out to settle original land claims were all familiar by name to Jim Harrod.[8] They were good, western Virginia gentlemen, headed by Colonel William Fleming, who had been on the Point Pleasant campaign, where he had fought bravely and suffered severe injury. The commissioners had little to guide them, since the land law required only that settlers furnish the direct location of their claims, "specially and precisely," so that others would be able to determine the boundaries with "certainty." Out of this vague ruling, a half century of appeals were to pass through the courts,[9] while the practice of issuing warrants for a certain number of acres to include the settler's cabin added to the confusion.

The commissioners used well-known or generally located spots as the basis for determination of boundaries, with names such as Harrod's Landing, Harrod's Fort, Chapline's Fork, and particularly Harrod's Creek appearing frequently in the affidavits.[10]

Colonel Jim testified frequently during this session of the land court, several times in behalf of members of his own family. For instance, the certificate book carried a record of Harrod's appearance for his stepson: "James Harrod this day appeared & claimed a right to a settlement & preemption as

[7] Draper Collection, 17J6.
[8] "Certificate Book of the Virginia Land Commissioners," in *Register of the Kentucky State Historical Society*, XXI (1923), 5-7.
[9] Bibb (ed.), *Reports*, Introduction.
[10] Draper Collection, 11CC17.

THE HARD WINTER

Guardian to James McDonald," it began, referring to land on Gilbert's Creek, settled in 1776 by the boy's father, who had died intestate. "The Court are of the opinion that McDonald Heir at Law to the Decedent has a right to a settlement of 400 Acres of Land including the improvement and a preemption of 1000 acres of Land Adjoining and that" a certificate should be issued for it.[11] Jim testified, too, for his wife Ann in her claim of 1,400 acres on the Ohio, 50 miles below the falls.

Harrod was active in behalf of members of his original company; and at least once—in the case of the Pogues, who were claiming land surveyed by Abraham Chapline in 1774— he had to testify against good friends. Jim appeared for his brother Thomas, who claimed settlement and pre-emption rights on land near Sinking Spring, adjoining the claim of James Brown. Thomas' son James asked for land lying in the forks of Bullskin Creek, where he had made a settlement in 1779. On his own behalf, Jim "claimed a right to a settlement and preemption to a tract of Land lying on Harrod's Run at a place known by the name of the Boiling Spring," because of the improvements made in 1774, 1775, and 1776.[12]

With all the argument, conflicting testimony, charges and countercharges, the pioneers seemed to agree that the commissioners were doing the best they could under circumstances made more difficult by inclement weather. Even for men used to the rough Kentucky wilderness, that winter was difficult, and for the commissioners, who had to spend a large part of their time traveling between hearings, it was about the worst they could have chosen.

Severe cold with snow and ice set in early in November and continued without a thaw to the middle of February. Cattle perished; deer, wolves, beavers, otters, and wild turkeys froze to death in the woods. Sometimes the animals, famished for want of water, came up in the clearings to roam

[11] "Certificate Book," *loc. cit.*, 11-12.
[12] *Ibid.*, 19-20, 235-36.

with the tame cattle. Wild fowl, unable to find insects and grain in the heavily frosted ground, died of starvation when they did not freeze on their perches during the long cold nights. Streams froze over, and fish perished; bear and buffalo cried out in the darkness outside the forts, and pigs died in their pens. Such was the scarcity of food, that a single johnnycake would be divided into a dozen portions and distributed among the inhabitants to serve for two meals. Finally even this resource failed, and for weeks there was nothing to live on but emaciated wild game. Some people ate cattle and horses which had perished in the lots. At the first sign of higher temperatures, the men ventured far out into the woods to kill buffalo, but the animals were so "poor" a person could not eat them without becoming sick. Many settlers actually died for want of solid food.[13]

When the hard winter ended, corn was selling at $175 a bushel, Continental money. By planting time Jim Harrod and the other men had made trips to the Falls to buy seed corn brought down from Fort Pitt, paying the equivalent of sixty dollars a bushel—an enormous price even in the depreciated Continental currency. A short time later the price fell to forty dollars.

Nearly everyone was sick. Jim, long considered as healthy a man as ever lived, developed rheumatism—a common complaint among men wearing porous deerskin moccasins and leggings.

Colonel Fleming noted in his journal that it was small wonder there were so many illnesses, particularly fever and dysentery, at Harrodsburg, since the spring below the fort was fed by the overflow ponds above, which washed putrified flesh, dead dogs, horse, cow, and hog excrements into it along with the ashes and sweepings of filthy cabins. Decrying the dirtiness of the people, he noted that they steeped skins and

[13] "Fleming Journal" (1779-80), Mereness (ed.), *Travels*, 624 ff.; Draper Collection, 4CC101-02; "Trabue Journal," Harper (ed.), *Colonial Men and Times*, 19 ff.

washed "every sort of dirty rags and cloths in the spring," thus poisoning the water and making it "the most filthy nauseous potation imaginable."[14]

Certainly not all of this condition could be attributed to the hard winter. Even in later years, long after the pioneer days had passed, Harrodsburg suffered from plagues, which showed plainly that even Colonel Fleming's well-considered criticism was never heeded.

A delightful spring brought relief to the settlers, as fruit trees thrived and vegetable patches flourished; but it also brought Jim Harrod new worries—or at least the same old ones with ever fresh terror. Indians fired on grain boats as they floated down the Ohio. Here were ample reminders that the tribesmen, who had been pocketed in their camps all winter, were at their business of killing again. Reports that three thousand people were ready to come across the mountains or down the Ohio to settle had roused the Indians to new efforts.

On the Cumberland Trace the Cherokee proved so troublesome that Jim made up a company from his and Logan's forts to put a stop to their raids on immigrants. Hearing that most of the trouble in the south came from a party under Chief Moon, Harrod and his men hid near the Warrior's Path to waylay Moon and his followers. When shortly thereafter they appeared, Moon fell to Harrod's first fire, and the other tribesmen fled. The whites returned to Harrodsburg with Moon's scalp and the silver plate fastened to a sash that the chieftain had worn as an ornament. On the plate was a bear design in bold relief. This trophy remained in Jim's family for many years but was finally lost by his grandchildren.[15]

To add to Jim's woes, the horses disappeared at a more alarming rate than usual. Ann saw about twenty or thirty cattle and horses killed by Indians just outside the gate.[16]

[14] "Fleming Journal" (1779-80), Mereness (ed.), *Travels*, 630.
[15] Draper Collection, 12C23.
[16] *Ibid.*

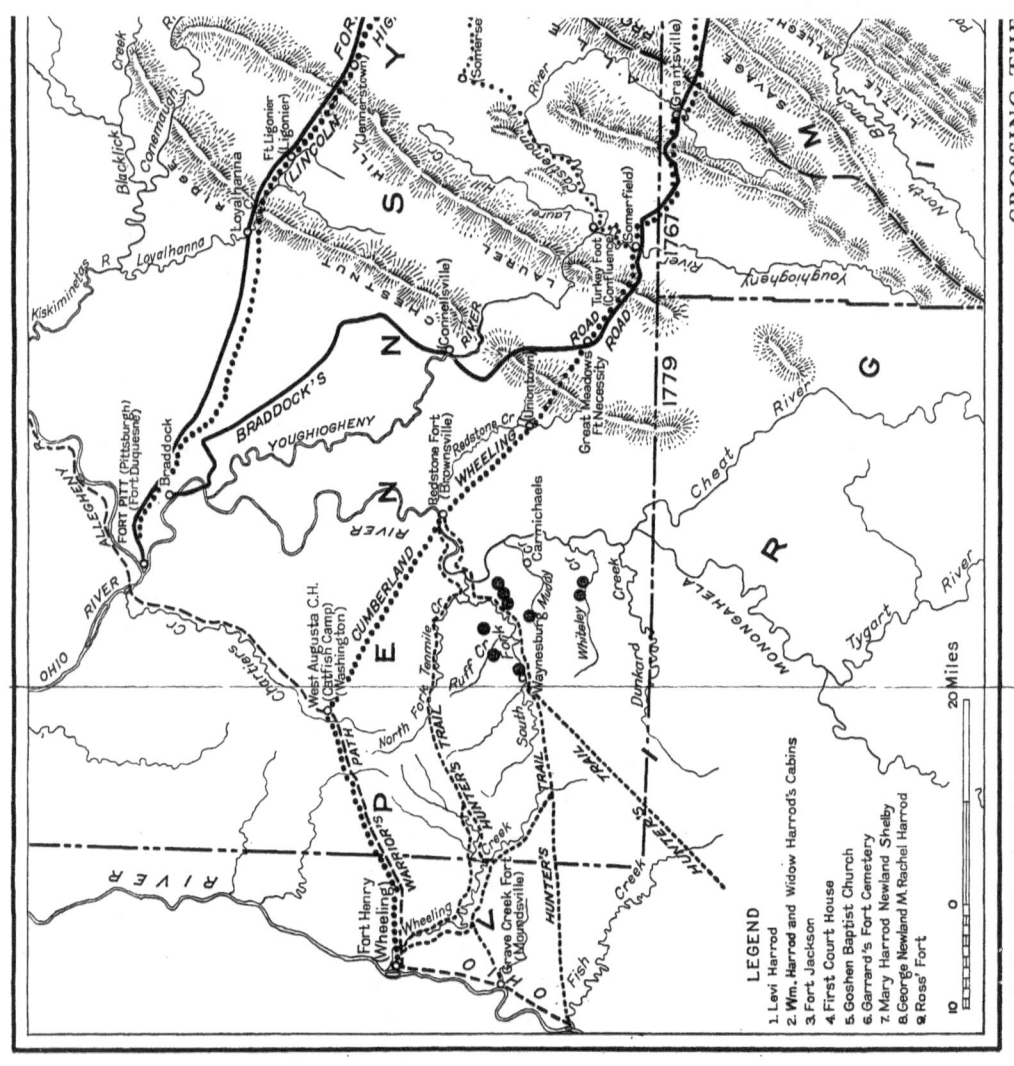

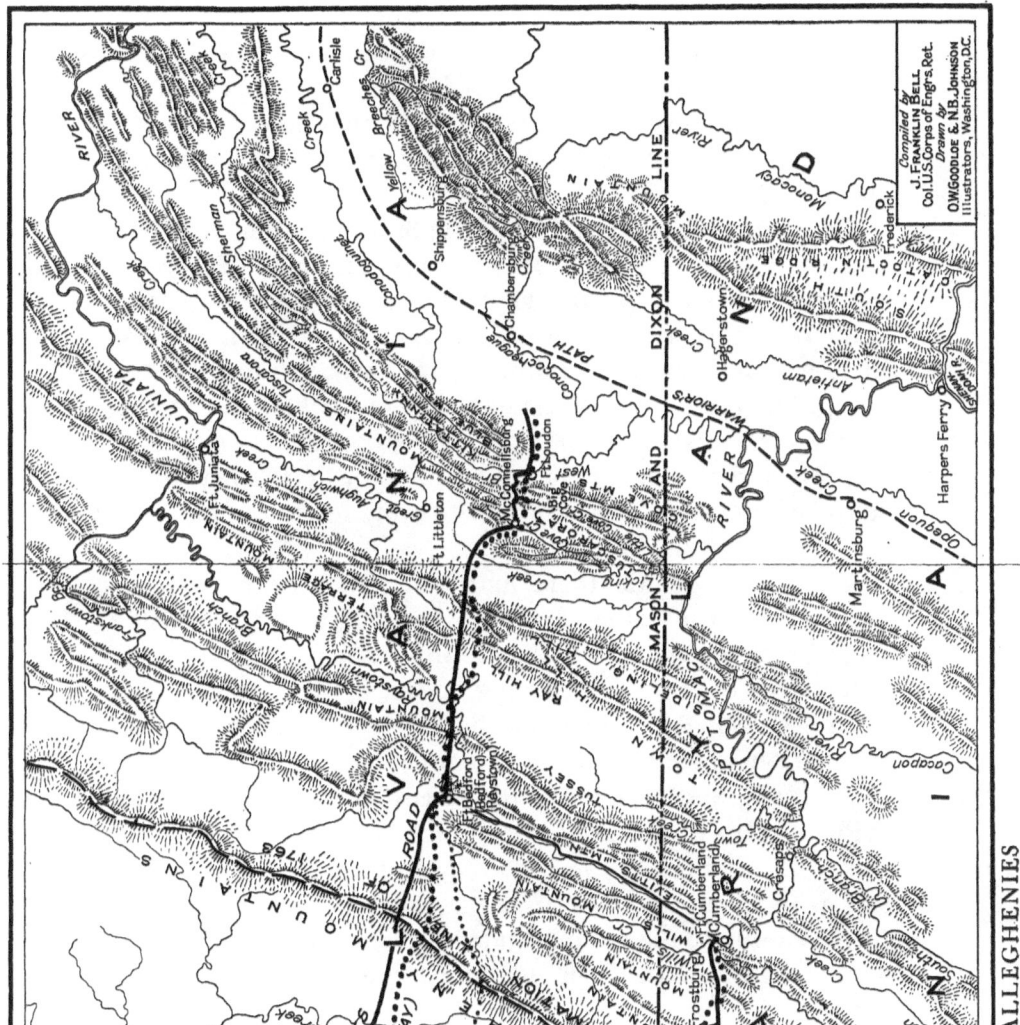

ALLEGHENIES

Not all of these losses could be blamed on Indians, however. Some of them were due to carelessness. While new immigrants were crossing the Pass they usually stopped the horses' bells to keep the tribesmen from hearing them, but after they reached Kentucky they often allowed the animals to run loose with bells unstopped. The noise naturally attracted the attention of red men, who had a great liking for the metal trinkets and killed the horses in order to obtain them.

One party from Harrod's Boiling Spring station went out to hunt for strayed horses and ran into trouble.[17] The men had gone through rich pea vines and cane for some distance from Jim's fort when fresh Indian signs caused them to seek shelter in an abandoned cabin not far away. It was cold and damp, but the settlers determined not to strike a fire in the fireplace for fear of giving away their position. For greater warmth and safety, they climbed into the loft, where they stretched out on the clapboards to wait for nightfall, each man clutching his rifle.

They had not lain there long when they heard Indians approaching the cabin. Six well-armed tribesmen entered, placed their guns and tomahawks in a corner, kindled a fire, and started to powwow, growing noisier by the minute.

One of the white men in the loft could not resist the temptation to see how many Indians were below. He was in the middle, and as soon as his intention to turn over was evident to his companions, each grabbed an arm, attempting to keep him quiet; but in the struggle one of the poles broke, and with a resounding clatter the clapboards and men fell into the midst of the dumbfounded Indians, who, terrified and yelling, fled from the house without stopping to pick up their guns.

The whites, as astounded as the red men, took their trophies and returned to Harrod's station, where they regaled the

---

[17] Story related by James Ray, as retold in J. J. Polk, *Autobiography of J. J. Polk* (Louisville, 1867), 111 ff., and in Collins, *Kentucky*, II, 624.

inhabitants with this story, which ever afterward they called "The Battle of the Boards."

In spite of the severe winter, which affected the Monongahela residents as much as the Kentuckians, Will Harrod remained on militia duty at various forts on the upper Ohio. But in the spring he made plans for conducting a party of immigrants to the Bluegrass country.[18]

Clark had paid him a visit at Ten Mile on his return from Richmond and had persuaded his former captain to resume command at Louisville.[19] Clark had orders from Virginia to erect a fort at the mouth of the Ohio, and it was necessary that he leave the Falls in experienced hands. Will's return to Kentucky was delayed by a tragedy involving one of his men. Adam Rowe had lost his wife and several children through Indian attacks on the river. Upset and thoroughly discouraged, he had hidden his pot metal and plow irons and returned as far as Grave Creek. While there, under Will's command, Rowe lost two more sons. Harrod then persuaded the grief-stricken man to go down to Kentucky where he could start life over.[20]

They were on their way to meet several other boats when they passed the point where Rowe had hidden his belongings. Warning him that fresh Indian signs were visible along the bank, Harrod cautioned against rescuing the irons, but Rowe insisted, taking a man named Perry along with him.

Indians, hidden in a near-by cabin, discovered the two, fired on them, and killed Perry. Rowe escaped to rejoin Will, who led him around backwater to avoid another encounter. This caused considerable delay, and Will feared that the large immigrant party might have gone downstream. Fortunately, however, they were still waiting, with Harrod's keelboat tied where he had left it.

Will's account of the Rowe incident, written to Amelia,

[18] Draper Collection, 37J168-74, 49J89-90, 12C1-12.
[19] *Ibid.*, 37J168-74, 46J55.
[20] *Ibid.*, 4NN79; Kellogg (ed.), *Frontier Retreat*, 160.

concluded: "I intend yet to pursue my Jorney as there has a Number of Boats Arived here on their way to the Falls in which I shal go so no more at present by my kind Love to you and Remains Loving Husband Till Death."[21]

Evidently Will, a man seldom inclined to consider danger, had a few secret misgivings on this occasion. Raids along the Ohio were at that time as serious as on the Trace, since Indians could hide along the banks on the north side and fire almost at pleasure. Usually the boats came down in companies to afford better protection, the large family craft staying inside while a formation of small skiffs and canoes protected the flanks.

When Will and the immigrant party arrived at the Falls, they found a lively community—far different from the small garrison of the year before. The population had increased, but the old feeling of good will was gone. Many of the newcomers were from Virginia and Pennsylvania, and the bitter rivalry that had sunk so deep in the minds of Virginians and Pennsylvanians had begun to show itself in Kentucky, despite the agreement the two states had made to forget the boundary controversy until the end of the war.

It may have been a part of Clark's diplomacy to put Will in charge at the Falls in order to bring about better feeling. The captain was in good standing with Pennsylvania authorities, having served without prejudice under both governments. Whatever the reason for resuming his command, Will remained at the Falls only a few months.[22]

Word came that his brother Sam had been killed by Indians.[23] Sam, the eldest of the widow's sons, had taken a party of men to New Orleans to trade skins for powder. On their return, Sam had left the others at the mouth of the Tennessee in order to go ashore and dig up some tools he had hidden near by. The men waited a long time at a river island, but he did not return. Since they had heard several shots fired

[21] Kellogg (ed.), *Frontier Retreat*, 160.
[22] Draper Collection, 4NN80.
[23] *Ibid.*, 37J168-74.

in the distance, they reported at the Falls that Sam had probably been killed. Will thought that his brother's murderers were Indians hired by resentful Frenchmen whom Will had put in irons at Kaskaskia.[24]

Perhaps to no other of his family could Sam's death have brought more sorrow than to his brothers Will and Jim, to whom he had been both father and brother, teaching them his own skills in trapping, hunting, woodcraft, and dealing with Indians. Although Will had not lived with Sam in the Illinois, Jim had; and much of his success he owed to the patience and interest of his older brother. Will, torn between his own desire to be near Jim and Sam and his wife's insistence on remaining at Ten Mile, had never given up hope that sometime he could persuade Amelia to move to the Falls. Sam had talked of settling there and had signed the petition for the establishment of the town of Louisville only a short time before his fatal journey.[25] With this personal loss, however, Will's interest in the new town he had helped establish began to waver.

Before he was ready to return home, he heard that the British were planning a sweeping offensive into the West. Originally they had hoped to take the Southern outposts, but this plan had been spoiled through Spanish action in taking over British posts on the Mississippi. The English were now hoping to drive down from Mackinac to attack Kentucky in an attempt to divert the Virginians' attention from the upper Mississippi posts, which they could then attack at their discretion.

Clark was already planning a march into the Ohio to prevent this attack. He wrote Will a letter, briefly outlining his intentions and stating that he would be glad to see Will "at the head of a fine Company." He hoped Will would again take over command of the militia at the Falls at the close of the expedition.[26]

[24] *Ibid.;* "Fleming Journal" (1779-80), Mereness (ed.), *Travels,* 643.
[25] Durrett, *Louisville,* 143. (See also Appendix H.)
[26] Draper Collection, 46J55.

There is no record of Will's reaction to this letter, but it is likely that events in western Pennsylvania influenced his decision to return to Ten Mile. A band of Wyandots had attacked forts along the Monongahela, spreading considerable alarm in Kentucky as well as in near-by frontier settlements.

Hastily procuring a couple of keelboats, Will, with six others, gathered his belongings, including bones and tusks from Big Bone Lick, and prepared to go up the Ohio to Redstone.

Before his departure he hurried to Harrodsburg to visit Jim. While there he wrote Amelia:

Loving Wife
I Take this opertunity To Let you no that I am well at present Hoping you are all in the same state. . . . I Entend [going] home as soon as poseble I can Setle my Consarns here You Will have opertunity of hering the situation of this Cuntry by the people that is gon home.
      From your Loving husband,
          Wim Herrod.[27]

The "consarns" to which Will referred were his land interests. These he entrusted to his brother Jim, who kept Will's surveying notes in a box with his own, so that the older brother could return to his wife in perfect confidence that his claims would be as vigorously pressed as Jim's own.

[27] *Ibid.*, 4NN80.

Chapter XVI
THE 1780 CAMPAIGN

"Nothing could excel the few regulars and Kentuckians, that composed this little army, in bravery, and implicit obedience to orders; each company vying with the other who should be the most subordinate."[1]

JIM HARROD and the other first settlers had seen so many small forts fall to the Indians that they accepted news of such setbacks with a kind of philosophical sadness and not a little regret that the unfortunates had chosen remote locations instead of tying their forces to stronger, better-established stations. But when the British and their red allies captured Ruddle's and Martin's stations on the Licking, Jim and his colleagues realized that a new and ominous element had appeared in the frontier wars, one that threatened disaster to all the Kentucky towns.

Although Jim and Clark and others had long known that the British had artillery pieces which they were likely to send out against the settlements, the settlers had thought that they would have some advance warning of their use, enabling them to prepare countermoves. But now the British, equipped with cannon, had struck suddenly on the Licking. Dismay and surprise gripped Kentucky.[2]

---

[1] "Extract of a letter from Col. George Rogers Clark to his Excellency, the Governor, dated Louisville, August 22, 1780," included in "Gen. Clark's Campaign, 1780. Official Letters," *Ohio State Archeological and Historical Quarterly*, XXII (1913), 500-501.

[2] Accounts of the attack may be found in Thwaites (ed.), *Wither's Chronicles*, 294-98; Marshall, *History of Kentucky*, I, 106-109; and Collins, *Kentucky*, II, 328-29. For accounts by participants, including Clark, see James (ed.), *Clark Papers, 1771-1781*, 451-84.

Early in June, 1780, as part of the large operation which the enemy was planning to send against the Illinois country and Kentucky, the commander at Detroit dispatched 100 Indians and 150 whites under Captain Henry Bird to take the Falls of the Ohio. On their march down the Miami, Bird's men recruited a large party of Indians, making a total force of seven hundred tribesmen. Instead of going directly to the Falls, they first made two quick stabs at the small Licking forts, Ruddle's and Martin's. How the British managed to surprise the settlers is a mystery, because they had moved slowly, hacking out their own crude trail as they went. The unexpected appearance of the enemy shocked Captain Ruddle into capitulation.

The Indians rushed through the wide-swung gates, grabbed a man, woman, or child each, and proceeded to strip the people and their cabins of every possession. Soon they were entirely beyond Bird's control.

From there the invaders rushed to Martin's station, about five miles distant, and captured it. Here Bird managed to keep his prisoners in his own hands, although he allowed the Indians to divide the spoils among themselves. Then he ordered a retreat.

It had all been so easy that Bird had difficulty in dissuading the Indians from moving against Lexington and Bryan's station. What Jim Harrod, Clark, and the others were never able to understand was why Bird wanted to stop at this point, since the evident purpose of the expedition was to hand out a deathblow to Kentucky's defenses in the north.[3]

There are several logical explanations for the sudden retreat. The waters of the Licking were falling,[4] and low water would endanger the return with artillery. The Indians had slaughtered all the captured cattle, also, and there was danger of famine among the forces. Another explanation offered

---

[3] James (ed.), *Clark Papers, 1771-1781*, cxxix.
[4] See Capt. Henry Bird's account, "Capt. Henry Bird to Major Arent S. De Peyster," in the "Haldimand Papers," *Michigan Pioneer and Historical Collections*, 38 vols. (Lansing, 1874-1912), XIX (1892), 527 ff.

by early historians, but one which the pioneers including Jim Harrod would have rejected indignantly, was that the British commander was too humane to allow this almost uncontrollable army of revenge-seeking Indians to go farther.[5]

For weeks after the news of the tragedy had reached Harrodsburg, Jim's settlers lived in daily terror of further assaults, fully aware that their stout pickets would break off like cane under the impact of the dreaded cannon balls. Abraham Chapline, who had been captured by Indians and taken to Detroit the year before, had managed to escape about this time to Harrodsburg, where he had added to Captain Jim's apprehensions with the report that the British were alarmed by the great number of settlers arriving in Kentucky and were determined to dislodge them from the West—once and for all.[6]

The steady arrival of these new recruits served to allay the Kentuckians' fears, however, and as the summer passed and they heard no more of new British expeditions on the way, the people almost forgot that they were in serious danger.[7] Land speculators swarmed around the surveyor's office at Fort Harrod, flashing Virginia treasury and pre-emption warrants in the faces of early settlers who lacked either the means or the knowledge to prove their prior rights and consequently looked on this kind of threat as more real and pressing than possible Indian attacks.

These speculators sat on Jim's front porch or gathered around the big wooden table in his large living room to draw plat maps of their new surveys, unaware or unconcerned about the indignation they were causing among Harrod's old followers.[8] Always hospitable to visitors, Jim welcomed them, but he knew that his friends disapproved of his hobnobbing

---

[5] Draper Collection, 17CC24.

[6] Clark to John Todd, Jr., March, 1780, James (ed.), *Clark Papers, 1771-1781*, 404-406.

[7] Temple Bodley, *History of Kentucky Before . . . 1803* (Vol. I of *History of Kentucky*, 4 vols. [Chicago and Louisville, 1928]), 285-86.

[8] Draper Collection, 12C23.

with speculators.⁹ Finally, alarmed by the national government's apparent indifference to Kentucky's uncertain political status and by the physical dangers threatening the area, Harrod joined the older settlers in drawing up a petition to the Continental Congress, calling attention to the situation in Kentucky, where "on every side" Indians were murdering wives and children. "We are Situate from Six Hundred to one Thousand Miles from our Present Seite of Government," they pointed out, "Whereby Criminals are Suffered to Escape with impunity, Great numbers who war Ocationaly absent are Deprived of an Opertunity of their Just Rights and Emprovements . . . ," while at the same time they were unable to determine whether the "Contry Out of right out to belong to the United States or the State of Virginia. They have by another late act required of us to Sware alegiance to the State of Virginia in Particular Notwithstanding we have aredy taken the Oath of Alegance to the United States." After dilating on their accumulated grievances the pioneers asked "that the Continental Congress . . . Take Proper Methods to form us into a Separate State or grant us Such Rules and regulations as they in their Wisdoms shall think most Proper, During the Continuance of the Present War. . . ."¹⁰

Then followed a list of 640 names, including those of Colonel James Harrod, his nephew-namesake, and a large number of early as well as recent arrivals—particularly from the Monongahela country, where sentiment against Virginia was strong because of the state's compromising stand on the Virginia-Pennsylvania boundary crisis.

The influence of the Monongahelans on the general temper of the population was increasing, for three hundred boats and at least three thousand immigrants had come down the Ohio that year.¹¹ Most of these were poor people, easily influenced

[9] *Ibid.*, 46J59; Butler, *Commonwealth of Kentucky*, 117.
[10] "Memorials from Illinois, Kentucky" (1780-1788), Vol. 48 of Papers of the Continental Congress, Library of Congress.
[11] Bodley, *Kentucky Before 1803*, 279.

THE 1780 CAMPAIGN

by arguments of the land jobbers who were tied up with companies antagonistic to Virginia's Kentucky claims and would have been glad to see the old scramble for land begin all over again to their subsequent advantage.

Jim Harrod's position in the land dispute appears to have been contradictory. In the struggle against Transylvania, the issue had been clear cut—a clash between the individual and proprietary land interests. But this new struggle was more complex, involving many individuals with opposing claims: the wealthy Virginia speculators, among whom were the holders of the despised treasury warrants; the Monongahelans and the Pennsylvania jobbers who would dispute Virginia's right to grant land and who were looking to men like Tom Paine and ultimately the national government for support; and finally the men who, like Jim, had settled in Kentucky without financial backing, basing their hopes on old Virginia settlement law and the Treaty of Fort Stanwix.[12] Jim apparently wanted to be friends with all of these, and, being one of the largest land claimants in Kentucky, he had a natural affinity with the large speculators. Still, he was not the kind of man who would desert old friends who had placed their confidence in him and supported his early efforts. Nor did he bring himself to speak out openly against the extremists from the western Pennsylvania settlements. Harrod had no understanding of nor interest in the legal or political implications. Kentucky needed more people; she needed law and order. Numbers meant security and prosperity. Somehow the quarreling factions would be reconciled. Justice would be done.

Virginia was doing little to correct the situation. Even Jim's oldest settlers were grumbling. The division of the area into three counties, with the establishment of Kentucky district, did not appease them.[13] They complained about the Monongahelans and the Tidewater Virginians who were pouring into Kentucky. They even criticised George Rogers

[12] Draper Collection, 28CC61.   [13] See next chapter.

Clark for his new Fort Jefferson at the mouth of the Ohio.[14] They could see no reason for adding another garrison when they were having so much trouble supplying their own older establishments. But they need not have shown so much concern. Within a short time Clark, plagued by supply difficulties and Indian opposition, abandoned Fort Jefferson.[15]

When Clark learned of the attack on Ruddle's and Martin's stations, he proceeded at once to Harrodsburg to plan with Jim and the other militiamen for a counterattack against the Ohio country and Detroit.[16] Upon his arrival Clark expressed his amazement to Jim over the people's indifference to the danger threatening Kentucky. They were talking of nothing but land and milling around the land office like bees around a hive. Harrod would never have had the nerve to do what George Rogers Clark did that day. First, he ordered a detachment of men to the Crab Orchard, at the foot of the Cumberlands, to stop and to disarm if necessary any who might want to return to Virginia; then, elbowing his way into the land office, he told the surveyor that he was through doing business for the time being. Assuring the surveyor that he, Clark, would take the entire blame and responsibility for the action, he closed the place, posting a notice that it would not be reopened until after the expedition against the Indians.[17]

This sudden action brought the populace to its senses, and when Jim Harrod, Ben Logan, and Hugh McGary began calling for volunteers, more than a thousand Kentuckians enrolled.[18]

Among the first to sign their names to Harrod's list was Simon Kenton, a man who knew from personal experience

---

[14] Five miles below the mouth of the Ohio. James (ed.), *Clark Papers, 1771-1781*, cxxi-iv.

[15] *Ibid.;* Palmer and others (arrs.), *Virginia State Papers*, II, 313-15.

[16] James (ed.), *Clark Papers, 1771-1781*, cxxxvii-viii.

[17] *Ibid.;* Butler, *Commonwealth of Kentucky*, 117.

[18] James, *Clark Papers, 1771-1781*, cxxxvii-viii; Butler, *Commonwealth of Kentucky*, 117.

how cruel the Indians could be, for only a short time before he had escaped to Harrodsburg after months of captivity among the Shawnee. Strangely, these Indians seemed to think at first that they had captured Harrod, or "Black Beard," as they referred to him.[19] Eager to retaliate against Jim for bringing so many white men into the Indian hunting grounds, they beat Kenton unmercifully, made him ride through the forest naked and strapped flat to a horse's back, and inflicted other tortures on him until a man named Simon Girty told them that they were punishing Kenton and not Harrod.[20]

Most of the Kentuckians were as eager to have a hand in the expedition as was Kenton. Enrollment went so well that there was danger of the forts being completely unmanned; therefore, the leaders worked out a plan whereby every fifth gun should stand guard at the forts while the others went on the proposed expedition to the Piqua towns and Detroit.

Time being short, Jim had to organize his regiment in a hurry. He ordered every man to furnish his own provisions and every six men to form a mess equipped with pack horse to carry blankets, cook kettle, ax, parched corn meal, and salt. Each volunteer was to take his own supply of bread for the first few days.[21]

Harrod and Logan had orders from Clark to rendezvous at the mouth of the Licking. Knowing that their men were eager to march, and that with volunteers enthusiasm soon spends its force, Harrod left as soon as his regiment was organized, not even waiting to put in a supply of jerked meat. He and his men went straight to the Falls, where they were to join Clark and the volunteers from that section; but when they arrived they found that there were not enough boats ready to carry the men to the Licking. Since a delay would mean a crisis for the commissary, Harrod gave his men permission to go on a two days' hunt. The task of finding food

[19] Draper Collection, 12C23, 12C24.
[20] *Ibid.*
[21] The following account, as it relates to Harrod, is based largely on Draper Collection, 9J21.

proved harder than many had anticipated, however, for while in early days game had been plentiful along the Ohio backwaters, the recent heavy influx of people had frightened much of it away. The men killed but two buffalo and seven deer, scarcely enough to supply their own immediate needs.[22]

To make up for the deficiency, Hugh McGary from Harrodsburg suggested to Jim that he be allowed to take his company of thirty men across to the Indian side of the river to hunt along the shore as they marched toward the place of rendezvous. Although Harrod realized that the plan was risky he did not oppose it, knowing well that McGary's hot temper was very likely to start an argument.[23]

However, when General Clark discovered what McGary was doing, he immediately ordered him back to the Kentucky side. Before the order could be carried out, McGary's company routed a large number of Indians from their camp upon the bank of the river. As the white men were picking up their booty, including some half-grained deerskins and jerked meat, the Indians, in an effort to cut off their retreat, ran out of the bushes and fired, killing or wounding nine of them.

As one of Harrod's men summed up the incident, "This little check put a stop to hunting on shore."[24]

Provisions soon ran so low that the men almost despaired of continuing the campaign. Fortunately, near the mouth of the Licking, they found a flatboat loaded with corn on the way to the Falls for marketing. This they impressed, dividing the grain among the men. Since it was not ground and ready for use, the army had to stop while it was being prepared.[25]

Jim arranged for each man to pound, parch, or bake his share, according to his own tastes. And since many of the volunteers had trouble with their teeth, most of them elected to grind the corn. Jim therefore ordered them to bring the big ax from his pack horse and chop down an eight-inch oak sapling, then square it off at one end and shave it to a point

[22] *Ibid.*
[23] *Ibid.*
[24] *Ibid.*, 11CC54-66.
[25] *Ibid.*, 9J21.

THE 1780 CAMPAIGN 189

at the other. This done, the men next drove their hominy block into the ground and made a wooden pestle about three feet long. Then, taking a piece of deerskin from the Indian camp, they wound it around the top of the block, extending it some eight or ten inches above the top. After making it fast with a rawhide string, they poured in their corn, a pint at a time, and ground it. As soon as one man tired, another took over, and as they powdered the grain several others who had prepared fires and heated salt water poured in the meal for the mess.[26]

While some of the men cooked the corn in this way or parched it, others raised a cabin on the Indian side of the river, to provide a place for guards who were to keep their boats ready to go across to the Kentucky side in case of hasty retreat. In later years, survivors of Harrod's regiment proudly claimed that they had erected the first cabin on the site of Cincinnati.[27]

The march up the valley of the Little Miami was quick and uneventful. When the main force arrived at a point within five miles of Old Chillicothe their spies returned with the surprising news that the Indians were deserting the town. In order to get there as soon as possible, the army "kept up a good smart trot," but when they reached the town at midday, they discovered that they were too late. The Indians had burned the buildings and disappeared into the forest, leaving blazing fires; on spits over these hung pots in which green corn and snap beans were cooking.[28] Some of the hungry troops dropped their guns and began feasting on the Shawnee's meal; others rushed into the fields to gather more food. One of the men later maintained that he had eaten fifteen roasting ears before he stopped to cook any, or even left the field.

While the men satisfied their appetites, Harrod and the other officers wondered who could have tipped off the Indians about their approach. From what they could discover, it was

[26] *Ibid.*, 11CC54-66.　　　[27] *Ibid.*　　　[28] *Ibid.*, 9J21.

likely that one of their own men, or at least one of the Kentucky settlers, had played Tory. This was a startling but realistic thought, for they had learned to expect treachery. With the experience at the Falls two years earlier unforgotten, it was logical now to suspect one of their own men. Who could have slipped out to warn the Indians of their arrival?

Jim preferred to believe that it was a newcomer. His brother had told him about new arrivals in his section who ran away from colonial service and sifted into the backwoods.[29] Crossing the mountains into Kentucky, they easily lost themselves in the crowd of speculators.

To be sure, Jim and the other officers had recruited their men as quietly as possible, being careful to say as little about their destination as necessary. But the enthusiasm which had run so high had spoiled any attempt to make this look like a routine operation. Even the Tories had found themselves under pressure to join the expedition. One of them had managed to avoid service by swallowing a "chew of tobacco."[30] Now it was as plain as hominy to Harrod that one of this group of reluctant soldiers had warned the Indians. This surmise appeared to be justified when a man from Bryan's fort told of a deserter who had stolen a horse and disappeared before the expedition started.[31] It was likely that others had joined him.

There was nothing the party could do about it now but move on to their next objective. The men cut down the remaining corn, excepting five or six acres to use on their return, then marched on up the Miami to the Piqua town, which they reached about eight the next morning. Having crossed the river, only knee-deep at this point, they had to pass through a dense nettle patch, from which they emerged to face a body of Indians crouched behind a brush fence surrounding a patch of woods.

There followed a short skirmish with little apparent damage to either side. Finally the Indians ran into the woods.

[29] *Ibid.*, 11CC54-66. [30] *Ibid.*, 9J21. [31] *Ibid.*, 11CC54-66.

The troops then halted to take stock of the situation. Harrod moved off to the side with a company of men, to hide in the woods and protect the flanks while Clark marched up an adjacent hill to attack the retreating tribesmen. This was a hazardous position for Jim's men, and one belonging to Logan's regiment remarked later that he had been "mightily pleased" that the orders had not included his company.[32] Everyone suspected that the Indians were taking cover in the woods preparatory to more fighting.

Jim's party had reached only the edge of the woods when an Indian fired, killing one of the men. This was the signal for a general fire from many directions. The Indians had the advantage because they controlled an area full of ridges. But Harrod ordered his men to advance. As soon as they climbed up one ridge, the Indians would fire briefly and retreat to the next, with the range so close at times that bullet fire singed the warriors' eyebrows. Harrod's men drove the Indians from tree to tree, and "stand to stand, first in one direction two miles from town, and then in another one," until finally, about three o'clock in the afternoon, the red men retreated to their fort, a triangular stockade, covering perhaps half an acre in the lower part of the town. It was evident to Jim that the fort was a new one—erected in expectation of this attack.[33] Harrod and the other leaders—excepting Logan, who crossed the river to prevent the Indians' escape in that direction—formed a hollow square, while a detachment rushed to the rear to bring up an old brass six-pounder that the Illinois regiment had taken at Vincennes. They loaded the cannon with balls and fired a dozen times into the fort.

The stockade shivered and split when the balls struck. Then suddenly everything was quiet.

As Clark, Harrod, and their men waited for signs of surrender, the Indians attacked from the rear, breaking up the formation and forcing the white men "to tree."

---

[32] *Ibid.*, 9J21.   [33] *Ibid.*

Logan, quickly recrossing the river with his party, rushed to Clark's aid.

At this juncture all the Indians fled.

It was now dark. The Kentuckians camped around the fort, nearly half of them on guard duty to prevent more surprise attacks. A tabulation of their losses showed that twenty white men had been killed and forty wounded, while they had taken seventy-three Indian scalps. The only plunder was twenty horses.[34]

In the morning Harrod and the other officers conferred with Clark on their next move. The wounded needed attention; they could not be taken any farther, nor could they be left behind without sufficient guard for protection. To the small army this would mean a serious loss of fighting power. Also, provisions were scarce, since the Indians had left little behind. The weather was hot, sticky, exhausting. So, with their real objective, Detroit, still out of range, the officers ordered the men to destroy the town and crops and return to Kentucky.

Sadly the men spent two days burying their dead and carrying out the orders for destruction; then they started home. On the return trip their greatest foe was scarcity of food. Some of them said later that during the trip they had thought they would all starve.

One of the most seriously wounded fighters was Captain William McAfee, Harrod's old friend of 1774. His men carried him to the mouth of the Licking on a litter, but he grew weaker by the hour. Instead of continuing with the other companies, they took him by water to friends at Beargrass, where his wife reached him two days before he died.[35]

The death of this loyal friend was hard on early settlers like Jim Harrod, who in the years that followed saw many others die in the long-drawn-out and bitter struggle which, regardless of increasing population, was still theirs to win.

[34] James (ed.), *Clark Papers, 1771-1781*, 451-84.
[35] Draper Collection, 9J21.

The speculators and fine gentlemen from east of the mountains could talk all they wanted of beautiful cities, of colleges, of fancy clothes and luxury—the need for more physical security remained the immediate problem in Kentucky. The pioneers who had cleared the first fields, who had cut the stout oaks for Harrod's, Boone's, Bryan's, and Logan's forts, would continue to carry the burden.

Chapter XVII
CROSSROADS
(1781-1782)

"Harrodsburg was a central point and called the fort. The country was very much annoyed this year."[1]

WHILE Jim Harrod and his friends struggled to maintain their wilderness homes, the name of the land that had inspired and beckoned them to this frontier was almost lost. In recognition of the growing population and of the consequent need for better military protection, Virginia abolished Kentucky, the county, setting up instead three new counties—Lincoln, with Harrodsburg as its center, Fayette in the northeast, around Boonesborough, and Jefferson in the middle-northwestern part near the Falls, with the newly chartered town of Louisville as its seat of government.[2]

The government of these three counties in military matters was, according to Virginia law, entrusted to the county lieutenants, Ben Logan for Lincoln, John Todd for Fayette, and John Floyd for Jefferson. Their title derived from the old English shire system, which the emigrants had adapted to the needs of Virginia's government. In early days people had called this official the Commander of Plantations, and he was, according to custom, a man of substance and a gentleman. His position as head of the civil government was executive rather than judical, with power to order out the militia and call court-martials.[3]

[1] Statement of Gen. Robert B. McAfee, Draper Collection, 4CC102.
[2] For boundaries, see Marshall, *History of Kentucky*, I, 111.
[3] Palmer and others (arrs.), *Virginia State Papers*, I, xxi-iii; James (ed.), *Clark Papers, 1771-1781*, 83-86. Governor Henry summarized these duties in a letter to John Todd, county lieutenant of Illinois.

The governor appointed members of the county court. In the early days they, like the lieutenant, were customarily men of substance and were often referred to as "conservators of the peace." They appointed their own clerk.

The name clerk was pronounced "clark" then, and even today in some rural districts of the East and Middlewest old folk frequently say "clark," much to the embarrassment of their city relatives who are happily ignorant of the fact that the country cousins are using the traditional English pronunciation.

Since there was an "unprecedented invasion by females" of Kentucky during 1781, historians have claimed that the first process issued by county clerks was a license to marry.[4]

The county courts had only limited civil and criminal jurisdiction, holding quarterly sessions, trying and punishing misdemeanors and felonies, and adjudicating at common-law and equity cases. They transacted the remainder of the judicial business at monthly sessions, either individually or as a group; but they had no power to try capital cases, for these had to be taken to Richmond—a fact that James Harrod and his neighbors had decried in the opening remarks of their 1780 petition to the Continental Congress.

In the second meeting of the 1781 Lincoln county court consideration was given to the matter of a permanent meeting place, since a blockhouse or the Fort Harrod enclosure could obviously be no more than a temporary haven. Ben Logan, who was a business-minded frontiersman as well as a good public servant, saw the need early and made a handsome offer of ten acres of his own land, including the Buffalo Spring, for building a courthouse and other necessary public buildings. He also offered the county an additional fifty acres one mile southeast of the Spring.[5] The Court accepted the proposal, but it is not certain how soon the buildings were ready, since the justices met at Harrodsburg for at least a year. The Buffalo

[4] Marshall, *History of Kentucky*, I, 122.
[5] Many of the items mentioned here may be found in an account by W. W. Stephenson, "The Old Courthouse and Courts and Bar of Mercer County,

Spring location later became the present city of Stanford.

For the most part, the first justices were preoccupied with orders for locating roads between the various stations, with setting the price of "spiritous liquors," and, strangely, in view of later history, in trying cases for horse racing and betting. They fined Hugh McGary, "Gentleman," who was a member of the court, for betting on a mare worth twelve pounds, but as soon as they had pronounced sentence, McGary resumed his seat on the bench and continued hearing cases. The justices fined several other settlers also, for retailing whiskey without licenses and for betting at the races.

John Cowan caused a little confusion when he refused to take the oath of allegiance to Virginia, saying he had already taken the oath to the United States; but he thought about it overnight, changed his mind, and the next day took his seat as a justice of Lincoln County.[6]

During these first court meetings, Will Harrod came out to Kentucky to hunt and to look after his land rights in Clark's new Illinois grant, which Virginia had offered as compensation to the officers and men who had served in Clark's regiment.[7]

The feeling of cohesion among the settlers which Will had found so pronounced in the seventies had been strained by the recent arrival of more Monongahela and eastern Pennsylvania settlers, as well as by land disputes, the stress of continued Indian warfare, and the arguments concerning possible independence from Virginia. With the establishment of the new three-county government, other loyalties were born. For example, the "Lincolnites" felt no responsibility for communities along the Ohio and, almost to a man, refused to con-

---

Kentucky," in *Register of the Kentucky State Historical Society*, VII (1909), 31-35.

[6] Draper Collection, 12C24.

[7] Palmer and others (arrs.), *Virginia State Papers*, II, 313. See also *Journal of the House of Delegates of Virginia* (Richmond, 1833), December 2, 1833, Doc. 32, pp. 3-8, for a report by J. H. Smith on the "validity of the Illinois claims." This sets forth exhaustively the laws and precedents bearing on the status of Clark's "Illinois Regiment."

tribute the necessary support for Clark's regiment at the Falls, believing that they had enough trouble financing and recruiting men for their own county government. The residents of the other two counties agreed. There was some justification for their stand, in that although Clark was the highest ranking military officer in Kentucky, he had no regular jurisdiction over the county militia, because his unit was a part of the state organization.[8]

During the summer of 1782 Indian raids grew more and more frequent and serious. Spies brought back news that formidable expeditions might be launched under British pressure. McAfee's station, only seven miles from Fort Harrod, received a sudden attack. And had it not been a still morning with a gentle breeze from the north and all sounds easily audible, the Indians might have taken the garrison with little difficulty.

Jim Harrod was not in town at the time, but Hugh McGary was, and his sharp ears heard firing in the distance. Quickly he gathered a party of hatless, saddleless riflemen, who raced through the narrow trace from Harrodsburg to McAfee's, yelling and whooping louder than Indians.

It worked out just as McGary had hoped. Hearing this impressive approach, the Indians scurried away, no doubt expecting to be counterattacked by at least a hundred men. The men, women and children in this small Salt River settlement were overjoyed at this unexpected deliverance, and they never forgot it.[9]

This thrust was only the start of more trouble. Indians also attacked Ben Logan's fort, and that brave, able leader nearly died of wounds he received in saving one of his men.

So serious and frequent were the assaults that even the boys had little time for idleness, and several of the older ones joined a company that went to the assistance of Bryan's sta-

[8] Marshall, *History of Kentucky*, I, 114-18.
[9] *Ibid.*, I, 117.

tion, which was under siege. Jim Harrod and the other leaders, fearing that Bryan's would be unable to withstand the formidable attack being made upon it, sent out companies from all the older stations. Daniel Boone led one from his fort, and Logan, recovered sufficiently to travel, also led a party to Bryan's. McGary was at the head of the Harrodsburg company.

Jim Harrod did not go because of lumbago, which confined him to the house, but he fitted out one of his men to substitute for him, giving him his fine English mare, buffalo robe, rifle, saddlebags, and even some clothing for the expedition.[10]

The thought of defeat had not entered anyone's mind, least of all Jim's. With 150 or more of Kentucky's prime riflemen, including most of the experienced Indian fighters in the country, why should anyone expect defeat? Certainly he did not. Therefore, when the scouts raced back to the fort to tell him that the Indians had won a great victory in a surprise attack near the lower Blue Licks, Harrod and all the other settlers were thunderstruck. The tribesmen had killed more than sixty whites, including John Todd and many other able and much-needed men, with a loss of a mere half dozen of their own!

At the time, the survivors were so confused that none of them could satisfactorily explain the unexpected outcome of this most tragic of Kentucky's battles. Many of them blamed Major McGary. The evening before the battle he had advised a delay in operations, only to be accused of cowardice. Perhaps smarting under the accusation, he had led the vanguard in pursuit of the tribesmen when his men discovered them near the lower Blue Licks. Most of the levelheaded and experienced fighters had agreed earlier that it would be best to

[10] Draper Collection, 12C23, 12C24. For accounts of this battle, see all early Kentucky histories. The account which follows in the text is based largely on Draper Collection, 27CC31 ff., 12CC135-37, 12C17-19, and on James Alton James (ed.), *George Rogers Clark Papers, 1781-1784*, Vol. XIX of Illinois Historical Collections (Springfield, 1926), 89-109.

wait for Logan's reinforcements before facing the Indians, but when McGary dared every man who was not a coward to follow him, these hot-blooded, sensitive woodsmen rushed ahead pell-mell into the Licking River to death and disaster. The next day Colonel Logan arrived at the scene of battle with 450 men—but too late to do more than bury the mangled dead.[11]

The effect on Kentucky settlements was immediate and violent. One man recalled that the panic was so great that even old-timers declared their intention of returning to their former homes. One settler, he said, offered his father the entire 1,400 acres of his pre-emption for one little black horse to carry his family back to Virginia.[12]

Aside from the loss of many of their best men, the greatest tragedy of this battle was the aftermath of accusations against the participants. Todd and McGary received a large share of the blame—Todd, now dead, for an alleged anxiety to prove his military skill, and McGary, still alive, for his rashness in leading the vanguard to ruin. McGary now became the most-hated man in Kentucky, and all his years of devotion to the general good—his willingness to serve day after day in court or to head the file whenever danger threatened—were forgotten largely because of that one tragic blunder.

Jim Harrod often said that had he been along he believed he could have stopped Hugh before it was too late.[13] Perhaps Jim could have, had there been time to argue. But McGary's brash call, "All who are not cowards follow me!" no doubt voiced the impetuosity which lay deep in many a frontiersman's heart when he saw a chance to avenge the many costly Indian attacks.

Clark took immediate action.[14] Having received added au-

[11] Draper Collection, 12C23, 12C24, 27CC31 ff., 12CC135-37, 12C17-19; James (ed.), *Clark Papers, 1781-1784*, 89-109.
[12] Draper Collection, 12CC50.
[13] *Ibid.*, 12CC24.
[14] This account of Clark's campaign of 1782 is based on Butler, *Commonwealth of Kentucky*, 130-31; James (ed.), *Clark Papers, 1781-1784*, 140-82;

thority from the governor to prepare a large offensive expedition in Kentucky, he called a meeting of the superior militia officers, including Harrod, Logan, Floyd, and many other experienced men, to sit in on a council to draft plans for a retaliatory attack. Although a few of those present feared that the disaster at Blue Licks might make a draft necessary in order to obtain enough recruits, others disagreed, advocating instead that Clark call for volunteers.

How well this last group knew their friends and neighbors was apparent in late September when over a thousand men under Harrod, Logan, Floyd, and others assembled on the banks of the Ohio at the mouth of the Licking, where they were to meet Clark for the march to the North and—they hoped—to Detroit.

Clark took every precaution to make sure that this time his expedition would not fail because of advance warning. He issued detailed plans for the march, giving strict orders for the maintenance of discipline. Harrod, Logan, and indeed all the superior officers received orders to keep their men in line and allow no exceptions; there was to be no confusion regarding prisoners, no freehanded looting or grabbing of booty, and no breaking of ranks.

The officers did their work well, maintaining a rigid discipline throughout the six-day march along their hastily cut path. Just before they arrived at Old Chillicothe a vanguard went ahead to surprise the town by a swift attack. But the Indians, as a result of hysterical warnings sent out from Detroit, had been on an almost constant alert. They had learned of the white army's approach and scurried northward as the vanguard came within gunshot. The Kentuckians managed to capture seven prisoners, take ten scalps, and liberate two whites.

Once more the Kentuckians had failed in their efforts to

Draper Collection, 11CC2, 12CC136-37, 12C15, 11CC6-7, 11CC143-44, 9J21, 9J65; and Pension Records of various participants.

stage a major assault. But they wasted no tears. Several parties rushed to neighboring towns up the Miami where they destroyed or captured everything of value. The men camped in a hollow square for the night, hoping that the Indians would return for an engagement.

The next morning a Captain McCracken, a member of Harrod's regiment, started out to find his horse, which had disappeared during the short engagement. He approached the sentry, calling, "Have any of you seen my horse?" A white man popped up out of the bushes near by and answered, "Yes, here he is."

McCracken looked up, somewhat startled, then started walking toward the stranger. There was a quick flash, and a bullet whizzed through McCracken's arm and into his body.

The sentries dashed out, several of them trying to locate the assailant, who had apparently darted away through the brush.

Harrod and a couple of others ran up to McCracken and carried him into the enclosure. Jim knelt down beside the wounded man, trying to stop the blood with slippery-elm bark.

McCracken grew weaker and weaker, but Jim stayed with his friend during the three days they camped there.[15]

Meanwhile the officers took stock of their situation. While no Indians returned to challenge them the white men had fared well. They had destroyed 10,000 bushels of corn and other provisions which the red men had laid aside for their winter sustenance. Supplies such as blankets, kettles, guns, and the like were gathered together to be sold later at auction.

One of the soldiers later told of finding some corn and bean dumplings, steaming and laid out on a tray ready to eat. Unfortunately they proved most unpalatable because they had been made without salt. But jerked meat, parched corn, and garden greens made up for this little disappointment.

With considerable reluctance the officers passed on orders

[15] Draper Collection, 12CC136-37.

for the return march. The season was too far advanced and the weather too threatening to go on to Detroit.

Jim Harrod and the others who had been attending McCracken put him in a horse sling and started back toward the site of Cincinnati, where the wounded man died. Harrod buried him beside the cabin that his men had built and, after burning a log heap over the grave to keep it secret, moved on across the river.

Only a short distance beyond, the soldiers came upon another lonely cabin. Suddenly the regiments heard a loud "Hallooooo!" in a powerful voice that rose to a crescendo on the trailing notes and was repeated several times, as the army halted awaiting orders.

Clark shouted angrily to the hidden caller: "Bring all the Indians in Hell, we are ready for you!,"[16] as he directed the officers to bring up the six-pounder cannon and train it on the cabin door. The ball missed the target, however, passing through the logs at one side and out the other end, as clean as a chisel.

After waiting a few minutes, and hearing no more from the cabin, the men resumed march without making an investigation. In the words of one of them, "This ended the conversation."[17]

While Detroit was still not theirs, this seemingly inconsequential expedition had accomplished more than many Kentuckians dared hope. The Indians were now panic-stricken. Winter supplies were gone. The British, with exaggerated ideas of their opponent's army, believed the Long Knives were about to march on their headquarters with as many as four thousand men. The British were already reducing their support of their Indian allies. Sickness was widespread among their regulars, and little could be expected from the tribesmen, who at last were beginning to realize the hopelessness of their struggle against the Kentuckians.

The confidence which the Kentuckians had lost as a result

[16] *Ibid.* [17] *Ibid.*

of the Blue Licks defeat was now restored. In taking stock of their situation Jim discovered that, in spite of a tragic year, his people had gained many new recruits who had come to the Blue Grass country as to a land of promise. When in the spring Virginia restored the magic name, creating Kentucky district and setting up a higher court system which for the first time had power to handle capital prosecutions, the inhabitants knew that their faith had been justified.[18]

Jim Harrod would have been even better satisfied with the progress his country was making had he read a confidential letter that George Rogers Clark received from James Monroe. It was not every day that a member of the Council of Virginia talked of moving to Kentucky:

Richmond June 26, 1782
Sir, I take ye liberty tho' a stranger to address a few lines to you to make an offer of a correspondence. . . . I wish to correspond with you upon the gen^l affairs of that country as well the means of supporting ye operations there, a detail of ye operations themselves with the principles & motives w^h severally lead to each, as the progress of society, ye increase of settlements, ye ability of ye people to protect themselves, ye resources of ye country in every degree of produce or trade & the prospect they have of attaining ye rank at a future day of independence to w^h all generous & enterprising people aspire. As I have a particular respect for ye exertions of these people & admire & esteem them for that spirit of enterprise w^h has so eminently distinguish'd them during ye progress & operations of things under you in that quarter & sho^d be happy to render any service w^h my situation in ye councils of ye state may put in my power. . . . I have been educated to ye law & my interest & connections are at present in this part of ye country but have some thoughts of turning my attention toward y^r quarter & perhaps sometime hence removing thither myself. I wish our correspondence to be private & as it shall be on my part conducted with intire confidence in you. . . .
I am with great respect & esteem y^r
very humble servant
Ja^s Monroe.[19]

[18] James (ed.), *Clark Papers, 1781-1784*, lvi-lix.
[19] Draper Collection, 52J23.

Chapter XVIII

COLONEL JIM—KENTUCKY CITIZEN
(1783-1784)

"In this situation the people became politicians from necessity, not from choice. . . ."[1]

FOR THE first time since Jim Harrod had come to Kentucky his settlers enjoyed an era of comparative peace. During the two years following Clark's 1782 campaign only scattered raiding parties ventured onto the dark and bloody ground. This meant that families could leave Fort Harrod and return to their clearings to fence in more land, repair their neglected plows, and put up new cabins to house their growing families; children might roam almost at will through the settlements, picking flowers and berries in the woods, shooting at marks, and hunting and fishing with their fathers. Wives were free to venture alone from the clearings to gather rotted nettle for weaving with buffalo wool, or to help with sugar making at the camps near the Shawnee springs, where maple trees grew in great abundance. To be sure, all of these activities had continued in a restricted way during the early years, but until now there had always been a sense of uneasiness which allowed only brief periods of carefree work and play.

There were signs of renewed civil activity, too, and increasing demands for more self-government. But for the present, Jim Harrod turned his attention to family matters, preferring, as usual, to leave controversial subjects to others. Al-

[1] William Littell, *Political Transactions in and Concerning Kentucky*, Filson Club Publication, No. 31 (reprint, Louisville, 1927), 11.

though he had made frequent hurried trips across the mountains, usually he had done so under conditions of great personal risk which precluded any hope of taking Ann to the Yadkin and Catawba settlements for a visit.

It was natural that Ann should be homesick for old friends and relatives down in North Carolina. Her son James was almost nine years old now, and it was only human that she should want to show him off to the homefolk. All the well-wishers at her wedding with Harrod had not charmed the gods into sending her other babies to fill the empty cradle, but everyone admitted that Jim could not have loved his own child more than he did this handsome stepson.

Harrod was happiest when he had children around him. Bill Harrod, Jr., and Thomas' son James had been living at Boiling Spring for several years now, and Tom, son of Colonel Jim's half-brother, John, Jr., had joined his cousins in Kentucky. Since the death of Tom's father a few days after Christmas, 1781, the boy's mother had been sending messages, trying to induce Colonel Jim to bring her son home. Reluctantly Harrod agreed to take his twenty-year-old nephew back to Bedford so that he could "look after his mother and the girls."[2]

John Harrod, Jr., had crowded a great amount of living into his forty-five years.[3] He had an impressive military career, beginning with Colonel Washington's march to Fort Necessity and continuing under Braddock and Forbes and later at Montreal. In the Revolution he served under Baron De Kalb, a German officer who helped infix discipline into the American army. John was in the battles of White Plains, Princeton, Trenton, Yorktown, and Monmouth and during this last engagement was wounded and later honorably discharged, having attained a rank of brigade major, the equivalent today of brigadier general. Only a year after that John Harrod died,

[2] Revolutionary Pension Office, S 16398, National Archives; Darling Papers.
[3] The Darling Papers form the basis of the estimates of his career which follow in the text.

leaving his widow Rachel with five girls and four boys, of whom Tom was the eldest.

While Ann was visiting in the Yadkin country, Jim and Tom went to Bedford. Harrod stayed long enough to help Rachel straighten out her affairs, then went back to Carolina.

On their way out in the spring the Harrods stopped for a day and two nights at Belmont, Colonel William Fleming's plantation in the western part of Virginia, beyond New River. In this comfortable frontier home they exchanged news with Mrs. Fleming and agreed to deliver letters and messages to her husband, who had gone out to Kentucky as one of the commissioners to settle Virginia's western military accounts.[4]

After a short visit at Ten Mile, Jim, Ann, and young James set out by boat with others bound for Kentucky. When they reached the Licking River they left the craft and continued by land to the Falls, where they rested, exchanged more gossip, and prepared for the trip to Harrodsburg.

Colonel Fleming and the other commissioners had been away from home for more than two months and were eager for news. Fleming was happy and relieved to hear that his family were well, but he had other things on his mind. He admitted to Harrod that conditions at the Falls were worsening rapidly. Part of the trouble was due to too much liquor. Two thousand gallons had been brought down from Fort Pitt while Harrod was there and most of the men were "in liquor." Their morale was low, partly because they received pay in depreciated currency and partly because they had little to do.

Probably they reflected Clark's own sense of discouragement, for the commander had offered his resignation after he heard of charges that he had misused state funds. He had advanced large sums for purchasing militia supplies and for erecting fortifications. He had done this under stress at a time when the Western frontier was in constant peril and confusion. Little of the money could be accounted for now. For instance, Clark was at a loss to explain what had happened to

[4] "Fleming Journal" (1783), Mereness (ed.), *Travels*, 661-64.

a number of horses sent to him by the Virginia government. Apparently only half of them ever reached Louisville. But Fleming and the other commissioners refused to be stampeded into filing charges. They were in and out of Harrodsburg, Lexington, Louisville, and Boiling Spring many times during their hearings.[5] The militiamen, eager to receive recompense for their service and personal outlays, searched low and high for records, pulling out loose rocks from chimneys, looking through battered wood chests, or rushing from one settlement to another in their effort to find witnesses to early transactions. Harrod did not have vouchers or sufficient evidence to support all his claims for reimbursement, any more than did most of the Kentuckians, but he managed to account for more than $1,400 he had paid out of his own pocket. In Clark's Illinois accounts alone Harrod received credit for fifteen bushels of salt, more than a hundred pounds of gunpowder, a large amount of lead, numerous casks of whiskey, livestock, and money spent for boat repairs.[6]

Under Colonel Fleming's diplomatic guidance, the charges of fraud and misuse of funds gradually died down. Even Clark was vindicated, if not compensated, when the Virginia Assembly awarded him a handsome sword engraved with his name and bearing a tribute to the commander for his services in the West.[7]

As soon as the hearings had ended, Jim Harrod turned his thoughts to duties of another nature. The establishment of the new district court brought him a seat on its grand jury, where he heard cases prosecuted on such varied charges as selling spiritous liquors without a license, adultery, fornication, and irregularity on the part of the Lincoln county clerk. The first court met at Harrodsburg, but since there was no adequate building, the justices authorized one to be erected at Crow's station, not far from the Boiling Spring and near the

[5] *Ibid.;* Palmer and others (arrs.), *Virginia State Papers,* II, 598.
[6] James (ed.), *Clark Papers, 1781-1784,* 266, 363, 411; Draper Collection, 12C24.
[7] Text of presentation published in Butterfield, *Clark's Conquest,* 782.

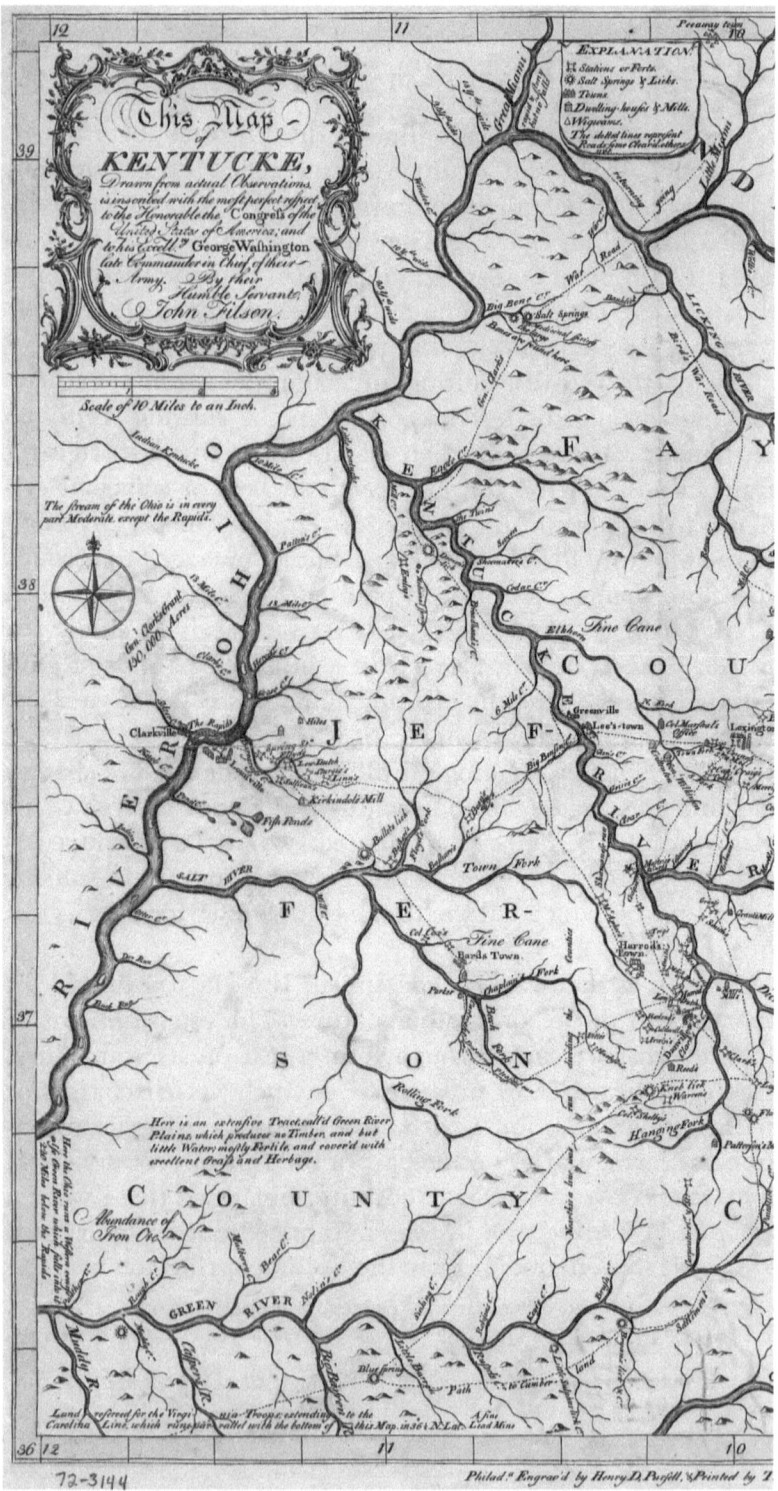

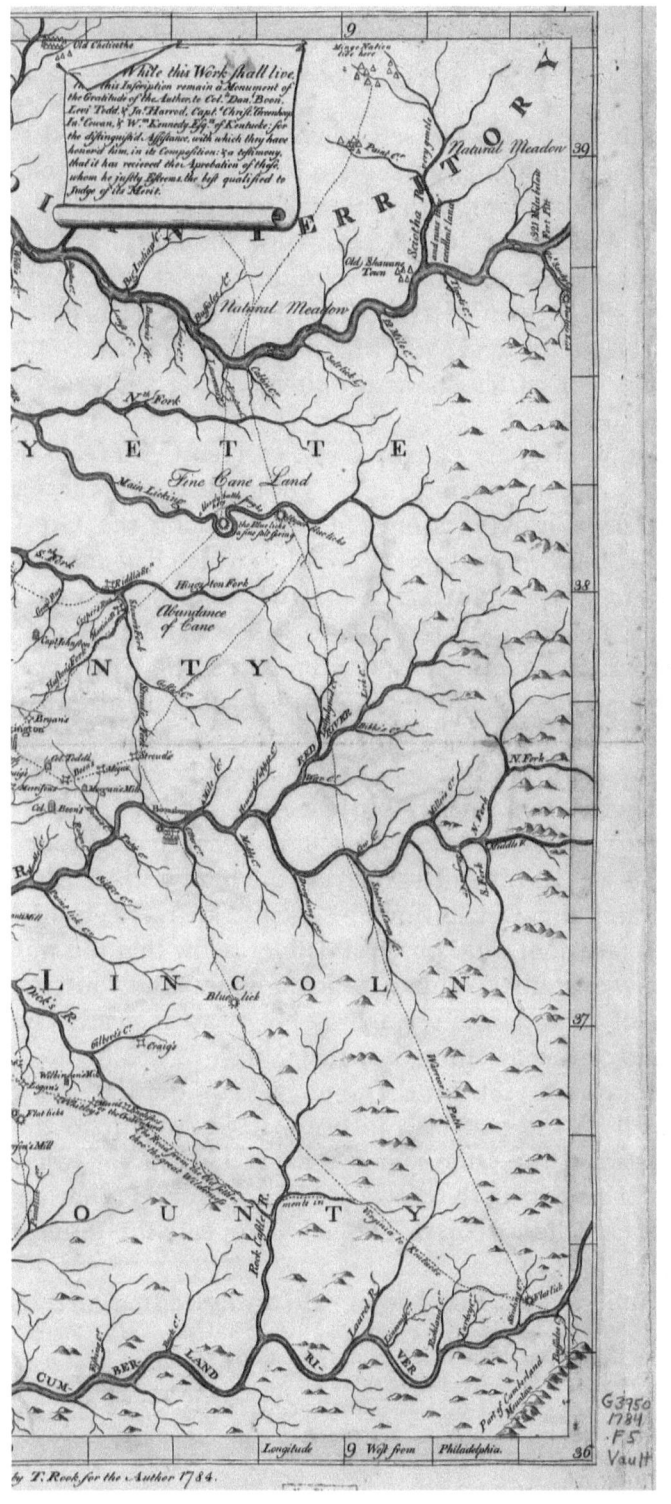

John Filson's
Map of
Kentucky
1784

Wilderness Road to the old settlements. They specified that there be a log building large enough for a courtroom in one end, and two jury rooms in the other. They also authorized a prison of hewed, sawed logs at least nine inches thick.[8]

The effects of this decision to move the district court were far-reaching. The town of Danville, which arose as a result of the court activity, grew at a surprising rate and later outdistanced the first settlement as a political center and trading city.

Like most Westerners Harrod had expected the Treaty of Paris to end Indian fighting in the West, since by its terms Great Britain would relinquish her posts along the Great Lakes and withdraw the source of supplies which had enabled the Indians to carry on warfare. But ratification was slow, and the red men, finding their old friends still at hand and eager to retain their fur-trade monopoly, bargained for assistance. Gradually the Indians resumed their old tactics. While they could no longer make mass attacks against Kentucky, they had the power to make sharp stabs at the weakly fortified and inadequately manned smaller settlements.[9]

The recurrence of Indian troubles damaged Kentucky spiritually as well as physically. During the hard years of early settlement and the Revolution the Kentucky pioneers had expected to face continual physical danger. Now that the war was officially over they wanted peace and security, but the realization of their hopes seemed as far away as ever. The worst aspect of the situation was that Virginia was loath to authorize forays into the Indian country, since she was about to relinquish to the national government her claim to the territory between the Ohio and the Great Lakes. Nor could the Kentuckians expect to receive permission for an offensive from Congress, whose delegates hoped to appease the Indians temporarily.

In November, 1784, Ben Logan called the leading men of

[8] Stephenson, "Old Courts of Mercer County," *loc. cit.*, 31 ff.
[9] Butler, *Commonwealth of Kentucky*, 143.

his county to meet at Danville to see what could be done about their difficulties. Spies from the south had warned him that the Cherokee and Chickamaugas were on the warpath and about to send out a large force to attack Kentucky.[10]

Logan stressed immediate physical dangers in his opening remarks to the meeting, but fundamental defects in Kentucky's political organization soon entered the discussion. The assembly discovered that it had no legal basis for calling out militia to be used in offensive operations; nor was there any magazine to provide powder and bullets for an expedition.[11] This being officially a time of peace, the Kentuckians could no longer impress private supplies for the common good. Although news came that the feared invasion by southern Indians had been either a false alarm or at least a project abandoned for the time being, the meeting in effect focused attention on Kentucky's weak position.

The war was over, to be sure, but as far as Jim Harrod, Ben Logan, and the other early leaders were concerned, the Indian dangers were almost as great as during the Revolution. The delegates decided to call a formal convention to meet the next month, when representatives of each militia company were to consider their problems in more detail.[12]

The convention met two days after Christmas, elected a president and a clerk, and proceeded at once to transact its business, with much decorum. Regardless of the immediate grievances, the temper of the inhabitants, or the urgency of the situation, these early frontiersmen attempted to carry out their legislative business according to the accepted legal pattern.[13]

Here in the first formal Danville convention all the old grievances and some new ones received an airing. Complaints reminiscent of the early petitions to which Jim Harrod had

[10] Draper Collection, 11J37-38.
[11] Thomas P. Abernethy, "First Kentucky Convention, Dec. 27, 1784-Jan. 5, 1785," in *Journal of Southern History* (Baton Rouge), I (1935), 67.
[12] *Ibid.*, 67-68.
[13] Butler, *Commonwealth of Kentucky*, 145.

affixed his signature were listed by the delegates: unequal taxation, inefficient administration of justice, lack of provision for calling out the militia, the drainage of currency to the east, the double allegiance to Virginia and the national government. They recorded their vote on only one resolution—a complaint against a special tax which had been levied on estates of 1,400 acres or more. It was carried by a vote of 20 to 10, with James Harrod voting "aye," along with large land speculators. Ben Logan and Isaac Shelby stood with the civil and military officials in opposing the resolution.

The delegates handled the question of separate statehood openly but gingerly.[14] After all, Virginia had been their only dependence up to this point. On the other hand, as some of the bolder members of the convention pointed out, why should they continue to be loyal to a far-off government that went on issuing land warrants to aristocratic Easterners who were only too willing to take advantage of the pioneers' imperfect titles? These settlers who had fought and suffered to hold Kentucky listened sympathetically to this argument, largely unaware that behind it lay sinister forces which wanted to take Kentucky out of the Union altogether. Spain had her conspirators in the West, and they were only too eager to sound out separatist tendencies.[15] But pioneers like Jim Harrod were "cagey." His western land had cost too much in blood and toil to let it become a pawn in national or international politics. He listened and would even go part way in registering protests, but when it came to declaring outright independence of any government, here was a horse of a different color. Nor was he in favor of a sudden break with Virginia, though, like most Kentuckians, he was convinced that the pioneers' best interests lay ultimately in separation from Virginia. While Jim wanted statehood, he was in no hurry. Up to now the scout, the woodsman, the Indian fighter, and the home-

---

[14] Abernethy, "First Convention," *loc. cit.*, 67-68.

[15] Abernethy, *Western Lands*, 297-300; Butler, *Commonwealth of Kentucky*, 149-50; Marshall, *History of Kentucky*, I, 155-99.

maker had ruled in this wilderness. They were the earlycomers who had taken up land under pre-emption or military warrants which had been handed out as reward for service in the French and Indian War or in the Revolution. Their respect for tradition, their tenuous but plainly visible attachment to the commonwealth that had fostered their early efforts, acted as a brake on the headlong impatience of the large speculators. So far as the record shows, Ben Logan, Jim Harrod, and Daniel Boone's brother Squire, who represented Daniel's company, remained silent throughout most of the discussion. Powerful as the speculator clique was, it was unable to obtain a vote for separate statehood. Instead, the convention called for another meeting to take place the following April, when this matter could be discussed at greater length.[16]

Jim Harrod was not a candidate for election to this next assembly, which undoubtedly would concern itself more and more with political matters. In his simple, fumbling, largely inarticulate way he had done what he could to help Kentucky shape her own future. The problems of this country to which he had given his best efforts were no longer his to solve. They required more than a woodsman's skill, a frontier education, and native diplomacy. From now on Kentucky needed men trained and experienced in the ways of law. James Harrod was not fitted for this role, and he, modest and level-headed, knew it.

But Jim's role as Kentucky civic leader was not finished. He had one more job to do. He and his neighbors at Harrodsburg had decided to petition the Virginia legislature to establish the town legally. One hundred and forty townspeople joined him in signing the petition.[17] They were of the opinion that the survey of 640 acres of land which the honorable House of Delegates had formerly reserved for the use of the

[16] Abernethy, "First Convention," *loc. cit.*, 67-68.
[17] Charleston, *Oldest Town*, 13-14.

garrison and town of Harrodsburg was the most convenient and suitable in the county.

That autumn the legislature passed an act establishing Harrodsburg and providing for the survey and purchase of lots and for setting up a governing body of trustees, including James Harrod, Abraham Chapline, Benjamin Logan, and nine others.

The trustees met the following March according to advertisement. They first defined boundaries for the public lands, allowing persons already resident thereon until the first of December next to give his or her note or bond for the amount of any lands he or she proposed to occupy at the rate of ten shillings per acre, with the reservation that if the purchasers chose they should have the liberty of sowing grain "at any time after the first of November next."[18]

[18] William Littell (comp.), *Statute Law of Kentucky* (Frankfort, 1809-11), III, 552.

Chapter XIX

FAMILY BUSINESS
(1785-1786)

"Ten years have produced a difference in the population and comforts of this country, which to be pourtrayed in just colours would appear marvellous. . . ."[1]

KENTUCKY'S situation might seem precarious to men like Jim Harrod, but in the East an opposite view prevailed. There the end of the Revolution, the creation of the new district court, and the division of Kentucky into three counties served to give the wilderness country an aspect of stability and promise it had hitherto lacked. It was now "respectable" to move to the new frontier.

Nearly all the early immigration had come from Virginia, Maryland, North Carolina, and Pennsylvania, but now new families from more-distant places—New England and even Europe—began to sift into the pioneer settlements. Of course, as before, many of the newcomers were mere adventurers or speculators or perhaps traveling journalists, eager to exploit the colorful backwoodsmen and their hair-raising experiences; but there was a predominance of actual settlers among them, and many who came to look remained to live. Young girls in particular arrived in large numbers—the first time this had happened in Kentucky. Surely, here was a certain indication that the wilderness West was no longer beyond the periphery of civilization.

Another sign, equally important, was the opening of a

[1] Gilbert Imlay, *A Topographical Description of the Western Territory of North America* (Dublin, 1793), 136-37.

"real, honest-to-goodness" dry-goods store in Louisville, where new arrivals as well as old citizenry could stock up on almost forgotten luxuries and actual necessities.[2] Dan Broadhead, son of Will Harrod's old commander at Fort Pitt, was the proprietor of the imposing establishment—a double log cabin with board roof and puncheon floor. Here he displayed silks, satins, broadcloths, and many other items which had been saddle-packed across the mountains from faraway, romantic Philadelphia to Fort Pitt and shipped from there in flatboats to Louisville.

Before 1790, however, most of the goods were coming west in Conestoga wagons, piloted by hard-heeled, tobacco-chewing drivers, who lashed and swore and coaxed their reluctant teams through ravine and mire across the perilous ridge to Fort Pitt.

Ann Harrod and her equally eager neighbors found any excuse they could to visit Dan Broadhead's new store. Those who lacked money with which to buy pewter, imported dimity, fine silk stockings, or parasols brought home-woven linen, linsey, new maple sugar, tobacco, corn, pork, or cured skins with which to barter. Here Ann bought her husband his first silver buckles and silk waistcoat—items which he donned in quiet recognition of his own economic progress, although he probably longed secretly for his hunting shirt, jeans, and dilapidated beaver hat. Like other husbands, Harrod good-naturedly stopped in at Dan's on his way home from a long hunt or surveying trip to pick up a jacket pattern or a bit of lace his wife could not do without. Bothea tea, candle molds, and silver spoons and candlesticks found their places in Ann's corner cupboard.[3] It was all great fun, even for Harrod, who took pride in acquiring these trappings of civilization even though he seldom used them.

Now that his station had become a regular stopping place for the Virginia land speculators, it was good to have a few

[2] Collins, *Kentucky*, I, 20; Durrett, *Louisville*, 70-72.
[3] Inventory of James Harrod's estate, Mercer County Will Book 1, February 5, 1794, pp. 146-49.

refinements. The first shingle house in the district was something to boast about.[4] Its furnishings were simple, to be sure, but they included more than a dozen books and a few pieces of queen's ware and Delftware. No longer did Jim have to go up to Fort Pitt to buy his rifles, for good gunsmiths had set up business at Louisville and Harrodsburg.[5]

New articles of food were always in demand on the frontier, where the monotonous diet of hog and hominy was irksome. The pioneers had a particular craving for sweets and would go to considerable trouble in order to satisfy this. In 1786 or thereabouts Harrod made a trip to the Ten Mile country to get a bee gum (a hive in a section of a hollow gum-tree trunk).[6] While bees had always been plentiful in central Ohio and to a lesser degree in the Monongahela country, they were never present in quantity in Kentucky. Before he left the Ten Mile country Jim told the settlers there that he intended to "steal" a bee gum just for good luck; but if they would look, he added significantly, they might find something in its place. Afterwards one of the settlers recalled that Harrod had left two dollars for the owner before he loaded the gum in his canoe for the trip down the river. The news of this new delicacy traveled fast, and settlers came from all sections of the Bluegrass country to buy honey at Jim's station.[7] Later, someone said that Isaac Shelby, the Tennessee-country pioneer who became Kentucky's first governor, paid Jim "a cow and a calf, for a gum."

More than any of the other signs of civilization, the increasing number of babies being born in Kentucky gave an air of permanence to the settlements. Ann and Jim Harrod had been married seven years now but had no children. To be sure, James McDaniel, Jr., had arrived as promptly after Ann's first marriage as any young wife could have hoped, but it was not until September of 1785 that Ann's second child— the only child of her second marriage—was born.

There is considerable mystery surrounding the paternity

[4] Draper Collection, 12C23, 12C25.
[6] Draper Collection, 17CC207.
[5] Dillon, *Kentucky Rifle*, 13 ff.
[7] *Ibid.*

of this baby, Margaret, and some slight evidence to show that she was not Harrod's daughter at all, but the child of a man named Mahon, the manager of Harrod's farm, who was often seen around the house. When the Reverend John Shane made his trip through Kentucky, gathering recollections of the early pioneer days, several long-memoried folk told him flatly that the daughter whom Harrod acknowledged as his was really Mahon's, and that they believed they could prove it too. Mahon had red hair; so had Margaret. Jim Harrod's hair was jet black. One old pioneer, Colonel Nat Hart, whose reminiscences were voluminous and decidedly personal, recalled that Mrs. Harrod had acknowledged Mahon as the father of her second child. "Col. Harrod gave Mahon 200 acres of land, in which Mrs. Harrod afterwards claimed her dower," he said, "which was thought rascally, after her acknowledgement of their intercourse."[8]

Such frailties as age, envy, and carelessness may cast doubt on the authenticity of the story, but evidence of Harrod's disputed paternity is not limited to a few recollections. In a day when families were large, with intervals of seldom more than two years between births, it is indeed strange that in their thirteen years of marriage Ann and Jim had but one child. Further, the records of Mercer County do show a land transfer to Mahon.[9]

On the other side, it should be recalled that James acknowledged Margaret as his daughter,[10] and he was as devoted and generous a father to her as to his stepson.

While Ann Harrod was very attractive as a young woman, and her contemporaries accused her of being flirtatious, there is no evidence to show that she and Jim were unhappily married. He appears to have been appreciative of her attrac-

---

[8] *Ibid.*, 17CC192; Harrod to Mahon, Mercer County Deed Book 6, November 1787. According to Mrs. Swainson, no person claiming descent from James Harrod has applied for membership in the Daughters of the American Revolution. See also Draper Collection, 12CC112.
[9] Draper Collection, 17CC192, 12CC112.
[10] See his will, Mercer County Will Book 1, pp. 144-45.

tions to other men, but not jealous. Shortly after Margaret's birth, Harrod opened at his house a Latin school, said by one pioneer to have been the first in Kentucky. Schools had been held in the forts almost from the beginning, but it was not until this later period that education went beyond the three R's. The teacher at Harrod's was a man named Worley, and according to the gossip, he brought a young teacher from Lexington who came to Jim's house, sat beside Mrs. Harrod, and during a three-day revival meeting held her hand while she whispered in his ear. "Harrod was polite and attentive to him and never seemed to take any offence at his wife's conduct," the storyteller recalled.[11]

Harrod was essentially a man's man. He had not married until he was about thirty-four—far beyond the average age for men to marry in those days. He went on long hunting trips for months at a time, leaving his pretty, vivacious wife to entertain herself. It is not surprising, then, that in a country where men outnumbered women more than three to one Ann received her share of attention.

When the evidence has been brought out in the open and carefully weighed it is apparent that a positive statement as to Margaret's paternity cannot be made. All that was important at the time was that Jim Harrod acknowledged her as his daughter and that he loved her and treated her as if she were his own. Without her, Harrod would have had no child to inherit his vast estate, for, during the summer vacation only a year after the Latin school opened, the stepson James wandered out into the woods one day and ran into hostile Indians.[12] The red men, apparently drunk or on the warpath, tied the handsome lad to a stake and burned him—to the everlasting grief of his family and friends. The boy's schoolmates recalled sadly how Harrod mourned him and how, unwilling to bear the torture of other boys' prattle about the house, Jim closed the Latin school.[13]

Among these schoolmates was one John Fauntleroy, the son

[11] Draper Collection, 12CC112.   [12] *Ibid.*, 17CC192.   [13] *Ibid.*, 12C24.

of a widow who was living in the new town of Danville. The Fauntleroys came from a prominent Chesapeake Bay family who had settled in Maryland and migrated to Kentucky but a few years earlier. John was only eight when Harrod's Latin school closed, but his mother was so eager for him to have a good education that she sent him all the way to Lexington—much to the amusement of the people around Harrodsburg and Danville. "Why send boys way off there to learn Latin?" they inquired. "Better teach them Indian."[14]

Mrs. Fauntleroy had reason to return their derisive laughter some fifteen years later when this same John Fauntleroy returned to the Boiling Spring settlement to marry the richest and most sought-after young heiress in central Kentucky.[15]

Folks whispered then, and the echoes can still be heard in Harrodsburg, that when Margaret Harrod married John Fauntleroy at the greatest celebration of its kind this green country had ever seen she wore the most beautiful lace drawers in Kentucky.

Shortly after Margaret's birth, Ann "got religion."[16] There had been a number of preachers in Kentucky—men who came, preached a sermon or two, looked for bargains in land, and departed, never to be heard from again.[17] Even in the earliest days, at the first Transylvania Assembly meeting, there had been an Episcopal minister, the Reverend John Lythe, who held the first religious service in Kentucky, only to be killed by Indians a few years later. But his loss was not keenly felt from the religious angle, for there was little sympathy among backwoodsmen for rigid types of worship. Too many of them had unpleasant memories of early Virginia, where the State church had discouraged dissenters if it did not bar them outright.

One of the most successful preachers in Harrodsburg was "Father" David Rice, a tall, portly Presbyterian who prob-

---

[14] *Ibid.*
[15] May 2, 1802; Draper Collection, 12C24.
[16] *Ibid.*, 12C25.
[17] *Ibid.*, 12CC111-12; Collins, *Kentucky*, I, 416.

ably married more couples than any minister in early Kentucky and who could pray and chew tobacco with equal vigor, sending a fine brown spray through the open doorway without soiling a bonnet.[18] It took a stout character to hold the interest of the restless frontiersmen.

Another preacher who was equal to the task was the Reverend John Poytress. According to the story he prayed with his eyes open—to keep the attention of all his listeners.[19]

Many ministers in the East were probably deterred from moving to Kentucky by reports of the coldness to religion shown by the people. There were factors which served to offset this religious indifference of the West, however, for even a preacher could become prosperous in Kentucky. And even though such manifestation of wealth as a fine barn and beautifully plowed farm could prove embarrassing at times—particularly when a devotee of the gospel came up for election before a congregation, only to find himself criticized for the fineness of his coat—a man with the proper amount of humility soon learned to pass off such criticism. For if there was a certain lack of religious fervor on the frontier there was a corresponding tolerance for worldly behaviour.[20]

Like many of the frontiersmen who had spent their lives away from organized religion, Jim Harrod adhered to no particular sect. His ancestors had been dissenters, but he early recognized the importance of establishing churches of any sort in his community. The Reverend Shane, who reported the slighting remarks about Ann, said that Colonel Harrod was a kind, friendly man, and though no "professor of Religion," yet held his house open to public worship.[21]

Religious interest was high in later years, when the tempo of living became more even and the large influx of Easterners brought an insistent demand for religious teaching. Harrod's house continued to serve as the chapel during these first years,

---
[18] Draper Collection, 12CC111-12.
[19] *Ibid.*
[20] Sweet, *The Story of Religion in America*, 312, 324-26.
[21] Draper Collection, 12CC111-12.

it being large enough to accommodate with comfort a worshipping assembly.

The first quarterly conference of the Methodist circuit was held at Harrod's station in 1786 and, according to Ann, had sixty-five worshippers gathered around the hearth. There were many converts—including Ann, who became a devout and influential member of the Methodist congregation.[22]

Some of the early Protestants shuttled from one denomination to another. One pioneer recalled that his brother who had belonged to the New Lights—an early evangelistic sect—left to join the Shakers when they started their colony near Harrodsburg. When this brother came to his house to ask why he had been criticized by the New Light preacher for this change of heart, the storyteller told him to dismount and eat his breakfast, that he could easily see that he would no doubt leave the Shakers in due time and join the Presbyterians.[23]

As in all communities, religion was promoted chiefly by the women, whose responsibility in raising the children made them more conscious of the need for moral training, while the men, perhaps equally conscious of their responsibilities as providers for large and growing families, devoted most of their efforts to economic pursuits.

Jim Harrod, although his family had now been reduced to two by the murder of his stepson, nevertheless wanted a large landed estate for his heirs as a matter of personal satisfaction. The possession of broad acres was a symbol of his pride in his pioneering efforts. It was not so much a financial inducement with Jim; money itself meant little to him. He was generous with his goods, and, according to his son-in-law, "he was very careless of his papers."[24] As it was, Harrod owned 1,300 acres of fine farming land surrounding his home and representing his settlement and pre-emption.

In that one section of the state Jim made numerous entries including 1,400 in Lincoln County, 18,000 in Jefferson, and

[22] *Ibid.*, 12C25.   [23] *Ibid.*, 11CC8.   [24] *Ibid.*, 12C23.

700 in Mercer. In addition, he had surveyed a vast quantity of land in the Green River country, 200,000 or 300,000 acres according to his son-in-law, but most of this he never recorded —largely because of inadequate evidence. This land was included in the "consolation grant" in the Henderson holdings, handed over by the Virginia legislature. Other well-known pioneers also lost much of their land because of "inadequate paper evidence," but Jim could still boast of large, undisputed acreages of the finest soil in the state.[25]

The Harrods were good judges of land. Along the Monongahela, for instance, they arrived early and chose the richest, the best-watered, the best-located land available.

But interest was already beginning to shift to the Ohio River tracts opposite the Falls, where Jim's brother Will was active in securing land under Clark's Illinois grant. Following a resolution passed at the time that Virginia ceded her Ohio lands to the national government, an exception had been made in favor of the officers and soldiers of the Illinois regiment, who were to receive 150,000 acres in reward for their services. This tract was located opposite Louisville, on the "Indian side of the River Ohio," beginning at the Silver Hills below the mouth of Silver Creek—land now constituting a portion of Clark, Floyd, and Scott counties, Indiana.[26]

A sliding scale beginning with the rank of brigadier general entitled William Harrod, as captain in the Illinois Regiment, to three thousand acres.

William Clark, one of the commissioners and a cousin of George Rogers Clark, was to lay off one thousand acres opposite the Falls for the town of Clarksville. Because Will had a right to lots there but was unable to appear in his own behalf, Jim wrote Clark the following letter:

Dr Sir—As Opportunity will not admit of my attending to the

[25] Willard R. Jillson (ed.), *Old Kentucky Entries and Deeds,* Filson Club Publication, No. 34 (Frankfort, 1926), 38, 217, 419, 498, 562.

[26] William W. Hening (ed.), *The Statutes at Large . . . of Virginia, 1619-1792* (Richmond, 1819-21), X, 565. See James (ed.), *Clark Papers, 1781-1784,* for details concerning the disposition of the grant.

Clame of *Wm Harrod*—I hope you will oblige me So Fare as to quit Out his Surtificate & If there is a Lottery be kind anuf to attend his Drafts   I Expect my Brother will be at the falls Every Day and if he—Should be Disapointed from Comming I will pay you for aney Expence that may arise from it
Pray oblige your Hble Servant

          (signed) James Harrod[27]

Aprile 25, 85

 Other members of the family who held acreages in this grant included James Francis Moore, a first cousin to the Harrods, who served as Illinois land commissioner for many years and bought enormous acreages from other grantees.[28]

 The grant which William Harrod drew contained fine bottom land. North of it is the now vanishing town of Harrodsburg, Indiana—named after Will, a fact that all the inhabitants save one seem to have forgotten.[29]

 Jim had other duties to keep him tied to civilization and away from his favorite hunting ground during these years. He served on the jury and acted as arbitrator and witness in countless court proceedings in Lincoln and Mercer counties.

 Many of the first pioneers, including Harrod, had to prove their prior claims against later arrivals largely through the testimony of their fellow settlers, because few of them had any documentary evidence. Frequently these cases went to the court of appeals or to the supreme court. Sometimes the firstcomers faced one another at the bar. Logan and Harrod appeared as codefendants as well as opponents in land-title cases, while Harrod and Squire Boone were on opposite sides in one instance. Daniel Boone's suit against James Harrod, instituted in September, 1788, went through twenty-five continuations before its dismissal in 1893.[30]

[27] Draper Collection, IM109.
[28] James (ed.), *Clark Papers, 1781-1784*, 280. (For further references, see index.)
[29] Investigation by the writer in the summer of 1944.
[30] See Mercer County Order Books, office of the clerk, Harrodsburg, Ky.; Packet D, I, Docket Book of Circuit Court, Harrodsburg, Ky., and Lincoln County Order Book I, Stanford, Ky.

Sir As Oppertunity will not admit of my Attending to the Cabins of Mr. Hoover. I hope you will Oblige me So fare as to quit Out his Mortificate & if there is a Lottery to hire any the attenders His Draft, I Expect my Brother will be at the falls Every Day and if he Should be Disposed from Coming I will pay you for any Expence that ma arife from it. Pray Oblige your Humble Servant

James Harrod

April 25 – 85.

Col. Jas. Harrod
Apl. 20 1785.
To H. Wm Clark Jnr.

William Clarke
Heard by
Mr Lewis (at the falls of Ohio)

LETTER FROM JAMES HARROD TO WILLIAM CLARK, APRIL 25, 1785, DRAPER COLLECTION, 1M109 (ONLY KNOWN EXISTING LETTER WRITTEN BY HARROD). *Wisconsin Historical Society.*

Thomas Harrod, the eldest brother, had taken up large acreages in Kentucky during his frequent and prolonged trips to the new country. These too were finally subject to prolonged and bitter litigation between the heirs of the two brothers.[31]

It was the case of Harrod v. Crow, however, which was the most spectacular of these suits.[32] Jim's heirs sued William Crow, whose station near Danville had housed Transylvania, the first college in the West. Although Crow had been in the wilderness with Harrod's men in 1775, he had taken land, including the town, which Jim's heirs claimed was contained in Harrod's first surveys. The case dragged through the courts for years before it was finally settled in favor of the plaintiff. Margaret thus gained title to large, valuable tracts of Danville land, which she sold at nominal prices to the settlers there.

Jim's experiences were typical of, if a little more extensive than, those of his fellow pioneers, many of whom lost nearly all their holdings. Fortunately, although Harrod had to withdraw from certain tracts, he had developed well-paying farms which paid the taxes and provided him and his heirs with a comfortable income.

All during the fall of 1785 and through 1786 the move for statehood gained adherents in Kentucky. Although the radical element that was pushing for complete and immediate independence from the Union won new adherents the majority of the inhabitants continued to look eastward for authority. The third Danville convention sent a petition to Virginia in the spring of 1786 and made provisions for still another meeting in the late summer. At that time the delegates resolved unanimously that it was the indispensable duty of the convention to make application to the General Assembly at

[31] Harrod's Heirs v. Harrod's Heirs, in court records of Mercer County. See also Draper Collection, 37J225.
[32] For a digest of this case, see Benjamin Monroe (ed.), *Reports of Cases at Common Law and in Equity Decided in the Court of Appeals of Kentucky*, 18 vols. (2d ed.; Cincinnati, 1909), V, 136-41.

the ensuing session for an act to separate the district from the parent government forever, on terms honorable to both and injurious to neither.[33]

At the next meeting of the Assembly, Virginia passed an act setting certain conditions for statehood, the most important being that Congress should first assent to Kentucky's admission into the Confederation.[34]

The slowness of communication from the mother state, together with delays in Congress, caused impatience in Kentucky, where tempers rose high over rumors that in order to protect Eastern trade the Senate would approve a treaty with Spain closing the Mississippi River to commerce for twenty years. The Kentuckians, eager to protect their own commerce, were in a furor over these negotiations. There were strong-minded people in the district who argued that secession was the only answer. Others felt that if Kentucky were a state and had her own representatives in Congress Western commercial rights would be assured a fair hearing. But there were strong reasons for counseling patience—as Jim Harrod and his neighbors well knew. The people in Tennessee, cut loose prematurely by North Carolina, had set up what they hoped would be a new state, only to find themselves embroiled in a conflict of authority, a repeal of the act of cession, and consequent turmoil and loss of population in the region. So, patiently, year after year, the Kentuckians, in spite of blunders and misunderstandings, of intrigue and glowing promises, adhered to legal processes—a fact that indicates a degree of self-discipline on the part of frontiersmen not often credited to them.[35]

[33] Butler, *Commonwealth of Kentucky*, 148-49.
[34] Francis N. Thorpe (comp.), *The Federal and State Constitutions . . .* , 7 vols. (Washington, 1909), III, 1264.
[35] N. S. Shaler, *Kentucky, A Pioneer Commonwealth* (Boston, 1885), 97-98; Frederick Jackson Turner, "Western State-Making in the Revolutionary Era," in *American Historical Review*, I (1895-1896), 70-87.

Chapter XX

TRAGEDY AND MYSTERY
(1786-1792)

*" 'Tis hard to say where we have the
greatest number of enemies."*[1]

ORDERLY processes of statemaking continued, but they were interrupted time and again by recurrent Indian warfare. Although these attacks were never on a large scale, nor as widespread as they had been in early years, they brought death and destruction and a depressed morale in Kentucky. The settlers asked whether, after all their years of hard labor and bloodshed, they were not at last entitled to a little peace and security. The people were bitter over the new national government's failure to oust the British from their fortified posts within America's borders, and they could not understand why this same national government's treaties with the Indians never succeeded in winning peace.[2]

The weakness of federal military power was evident to British and Indians alike, and naturally the tribesmen broke their agreements freely. Sometimes wandering bands of white men used Indians as fair game for their restless triggers; then the red men retaliated—and the first to suffer were the settlements below the Ohio. Just as the white men blamed the Shawnee for most of their trouble—regardless of the fact that nearly all of the marauders came from country farther north and only passed through the Shawnee territory—so the In-

---

[1] Col. Levi Todd to Gov. Patrick Henry, July 12, 1786, Palmer and others (arrs.), *Virginia State Papers*, IV, 155.
[2] Shaler, *A Pioneer Commonwealth*, 97-98.

dians, seeing the white men crossing the Ohio from Kentucky and taking up land on the northern bank, thought that they had all migrated from the old hunting ground.[3] They did not know or care that these settlers were for the most part Easterners who merely traveled along the southern bank for safety and then crossed over near the Falls to take up land in what is now lower Ohio and Indiana.

The central Kentucky leaders, as well as those farther north, knew that drastic measures would have to be taken. Kentucky's chief militia officer wrote Governor Henry in July of 1786 that within the three weeks past small raiding parties had struck the whole of the north and west frontier of the district. "Much Kentucky Blood I fear will be spilt," he cautioned, "tho' I hope that Vigorous Operations the ensuing Fall will make much in our favour. The Wabash Indians have repeatedly said that the Kentucky people dare not march to the Wabash. . . ."[4]

In the spring the Lincoln militiamen had been reluctant to go on an expedition for the protection of their neighbors along the Ohio, but their leaders now believed such an expedition was necessary for the common good. Their chief concern was how to organize it, for Congress had forbidden any punitive measures, and Virginia, while agreeing that the Kentuckians were justified in doing anything essential to their protection, would not go so far as to say that militiamen could be drafted and sent out of the district against their will.

Early in August the field officers, determined to take matters into their own hands, met at Jim's fort with Colonel Benjamin Logan presiding. They decided to call out one half of the militia to assemble at Clarksville, where George Rogers Clark would take command.[5] Since the local leaders were still opposed to a draft, only 1,200 men—about half the number needed—showed up at the place of rendezvous.

[3] *Ibid.*
[4] Palmer and others (arrs.), *Virginia State Papers*, IV, 155.
[5] Marshall, *History of Kentucky*, I, 246, 247.

Clark held a council with Logan and the other officers. They decided that the commander should take the men to Vincennes while Logan returned to Lincoln to marshal more men to attack the Shawnee towns as a diversionary tactic. In the meantime Clark was to move against the Wabash confederation.[6]

Logan and Harrod, who came to Clark's assistance, managed to recruit a large number of men, since the Kentuckians were more willing to go out against their special enemies, the Shawnee. As in previous campaigns, however, difficulties of supply plagued their undertaking. For example, the officers had trouble finding sufficient salt and flour. Those who had these precious commodities were reluctant to part with them for an expedition which appeared to be illegal and which would in all likelihood have no financial backing. However, there was more than one way to obtain necessities. On one proprietor's refusal to give up his supply of salt an officer ordered the guards to open the door and seize it as public property. When the owner drew a pistol to stop them he was arrested and accused of insult.

With Logan at the head and Harrod and McGary next in command, the army of about eight hundred men marched to the Ohio, crossing at the Three Islands not far from the mouth of the Licking, moving into the Indian country "with great expedition," and heading directly for the Shawnee towns.

Harrod commanded one party for an attack on the upper village while McGary took another party to a lower town.

The Indians—only those left behind after the others had marched to meet Clark's expedition—were taken by complete surprise. The encounter was brief, with Jim taking prisoner about ten men and a few dozen women and their children.

[6] Sources for this account are chiefly: Palmer and others (arrs.), *Virginia State Papers*, IV, 204, 212; Draper Collection, 17CC197, 27CC33-35, 17S118-19, 12C15, 32J78; Leonard C. Helderman, "The Northwest Expedition of George Rogers Clark, 1786-1787," in *Mississippi Valley Historical Review*, XXV (1943-1944), 317-34.

McGary, brandishing a long knife, slashing right and left, caused a wild scampering fright, killed two men, and took thirty squaws and a host of papooses as prisoners. Then, at the head of this weird procession of volunteer militia and Indian captives, McGary led the way to the upper town to congratulate Harrod on his success.

When it was all over, Harrod's, McGary's, and Logan's men together had burned two hundred houses and destroyed the winter supply of corn, amounting to 15,000 bushels. They had killed ten Indians and taken thirty-four prisoners, including two chiefs.[7]

Harrod captured the aged Shawnee chieftain Moluntha (the victor at Blue Licks), who had his horse packed ready for flight. When Moluntha surrendered, he was shielding himself with an American flag and holding up the recent treaty between his tribe and the Federal government. Wearing a cocked hat at a jaunty angle and professing his friendship for the whites, the old Indian chief made a pathetic figure.

As McGary's men, returning from their own foray, rode into the Indian town, a crowd of men pressed close to see the famous chief. McGary dismounted and started over toward Moluntha. Logan, having just ordered the men to place the prisoners in the houses under heavy guard, reined his horse as he caught sight of McGary. "You must not molest these prisoners," he warned.

"I will see to that," replied McGary, waving the crowd aside and forcing his way to the center. "Were you at the defeat of the Blue Licks?" he asked the smiling old chieftain.[8]

The Indian, unaware of the hostile feeling behind this question, answered, "Yes."[9]

Instantly McGary seized an ax from the hands of a squaw and raised it high above his head. The men who were standing beside him threw up their arms to ward off the blow.

[7] James, *Clark*, 357.   [8] Draper Collection, 4B83-84, 12CC34-36, 2M7.
[9] *Ibid.*, 27CC34-35.

TRAGEDY AND MYSTERY   229

The ax handle struck one of them in the left wrist as it descended. The blade sank deep into Moluntha's head, and he fell lifeless at McGary's feet.

Harrod and the other witnesses to this barbaric attack were speechless with indignation. Then a torrent of angry words poured forth from the crowd. McGary had committed a dastardly, cruel trick that would undoubtedly lead to more Indian trouble, they charged. Moluntha had surrendered willingly; he was a prisoner of war, and as such, entitled to protection. A number of the men demanded that Logan and Harrod hold a court-martial right then and there.[10]

Realizing that the feeling against McGary for his rash act was too intense to permit a hearing at the moment, the leaders wisely put off the proceeding, with a promise to hold it promptly on their return to Kentucky.

Courts-martial were common in those days, with many of the most prominent, well-meaning, and able men in the country as instigators. This time, interest was particularly high. The court charged McGary with disobedience to orders (which had called for sparing all prisoners), with behaving in a disorderly manner, with insulting and abusing other officers, with declaring he would chop down any man who attempted to hinder him from killing Indian prisoners at any time, and with conduct generally "unbecoming the character of a gentleman and an officer."[11]

When the court-martial met, James Harrod was not present, no doubt out of choice, for he had had his share of "run-ins" with McGary. After hearing dozens of witnesses, the court-martial decided that Colonel McGary was guilty of murdering Moluntha, "the Indian King," and that his conduct in general was unbecoming the character of an officer and a gentleman, and suspended him from active service for one year.[12]

[10] *Ibid.*
[11] Palmer and others (arrs.), *Virginia State Papers*, IV, 258-60.
[12] *Ibid.*

In counterattack, McGary brought charges against other Fayette-county officers, accusing them of impressing and drinking a barrel of rum, of having twenty beeves shot down without orders, and of delaying the army. The result was a series of courts-martial calling forth a string of witnesses, all of whom naturally tried to clear their own records. The bitterness which arose caused lasting enmities.

The expedition under Clark met with failure. The soldiers, uneasy about the lack of proper authorization for the campaign, had not been eager to join in the first place, and they seized the opportunity afforded by the absence of Logan, their commander, to desert or delay the advance. They circulated a report that the supplies would be exhausted before the troops reached the Wabash villages. Clark was unable to proceed under these conditions and reluctantly led his troops back to Vincennes, where he established a garrison and started negotiations for a treaty.

James Ray and most of the other Harrodsburg men who later tried to explain the failure of the campaign attributed no blame to Clark, who according to reports was in tears over the outcome of his plans.[13] Others claimed that the commander had been drunk most of the time—a charge which appears to present-day historians to be unwarranted at that particular period, although, like other frontiersmen, Clark was fond of alcohol and later in life became a heavy drinker.

In the years that followed, charges of excessive drinking were leveled against Jim Harrod too.[14] One pioneer recalled that Harrod used to get drunk while gambling and lose as much as five thousand dollars at one sitting. In 1786, drinking was the accepted practice. "Every man was obliged to keep a kind of grog shop in his home, for his neighbours, acquaintances, and hangers on," a settler recalled, "or be esteemed a niggard."[15] At corn-huskings or house-raisings, the green-glass whiskey bottle was handed to every man or

---

[13] Draper Collection, 12C15, 32J78.   [14] *Ibid.*, 17CC192.
[15] Daniel Drake, *Pioneer Life in Kentucky* (Cincinnati, 1870), 163-84.

TRAGEDY AND MYSTERY

boy as he arrived. Pioneers looked on liquor as an incentive to labor, and its use was never considered a crime until later years—when religious organizations had a firmer hold.

This 1786 campaign held up proceedings in Danville, where plans toward statehood were still the center of attention. By now, nearly everyone in the country was eager for separation from Virginia.[16] While a growing segment of the populace proposed a radical separation—perhaps even without statehood, which a reluctant Congress would still not assure—representatives of the old-timers at Danville believed in following the written law with great care.[17] They plodded along, calling convention after convention, confident that orderly action would ensure their interests and the welfare of Kentucky to better advantage. Virginia, they knew, was eager to grant their freedom—as soon as Congress would agree to take over the territory and assure statehood.

While others sweated and swore, schemed and quarreled, Jim was most likely to slip out on a hunting or trapping excursion. Central Kentucky was full of people now. Game was as scarce as silver. The old hunters had to go long distances to get away from settlements, to places where only the sound of wind and leaves and the occasional call of a bird or forest animal disturbed the deep silence that they loved and longed for.

Jim had grown to manhood in the quiet wilderness. Although he was less than fifty, he was too old for the confinement of towns and civilized ways. When court hearings were over for the season, he liked to strike out for the woods, either alone or with an old friend or two and his horse and hound. On these trips he wore a broad-brimmed beaver hat, jeans, and a hunting shirt made of linen and trimmed with fine, initialed silver buttons. He would frequently be gone for months. Perhaps before his return he might cross the

---

[16] See Abernethy, *Western Lands*, 304-24, for a discussion of these moves toward statehood.
[17] Turner, "Western State-Making," *loc. cit.*, 70-87.

divide to visit a brother or sister, or call on the Indians in the Illinois country where he had spent so much time as a boy. He was happy there.[18]

It may have been this love of wilderness adventure which overruled his caution when Jim went on his final hunting and trapping journey in the winter of 1792.[19]

All of the pioneers had heard of Swift's Silver Mine, reported to have been worked by the Indians for many years and rediscovered by a white hunter named Swift. Although its exact location was and still is a mystery, and there is considerable doubt among geologists about its actual existence, the tradition persists to this day.

A man named Bridges, who had a hankering for easy money, determined to locate this mine and tried to coax Harrod into going there with him. Ann and many of Harrod's close friends expressed concern over Bridges' proposal, calling attention to the fact that since Bridges and Harrod were involved in a land suit over which the two had said harsh words, the proposal might prove to be a trap. At first Jim hesitated.

Meanwhile, Bridges went out alone for a few weeks. On his return he rode over to Harrod's plantation to talk with him. "Colonel," he said, "I have found Swift's mine, and though we have been at outs, I have confidence in you and prefer you as a partner to any man in Kentucky, and you have the means to work the mine."[20]

Jim promised to think over the proposal. He never held a grudge for long, and as far as he was concerned he was willing to let bygones by bygones.[21] Besides there was good trapping up the three forks of the Kentucky River, where Bridges said he had located the mine.

When Ann heard about the proposed trip, she begged Jim not to go, insisting that it was merely a plan to murder him.[22]

---

[18] Draper Collection, 12C22, 97J35-37.
[19] Principal sources for this narrative are Draper Collection, 12C22, 12C23, 12CC48, 9J35-37, 9J228-29; and Collins, *Kentucky*, II, 414-15, 614-15.
[20] Collins, *Kentucky*, II, 614-15.   [21] Draper Collection, 12C23, 12CC48.
[22] *Ibid.*, 12CC48.

But this reaction only seemed to make her husband more determined. Ann had struck a pioneer's most sensitive spot. Jim answered that he was "not afraid of any man living."[23] Finally, however, Ann persuaded him to take a third man along, and Jim asked his old hunting companion Michael Stoner to accompany them. Then, apparently fearing that Ann's judgment might be correct, he made his will.

The party went up the Kentucky River, trapping beaver and hunting. Bridges seemed unable to find the mine. At one point the three men separated, each taking a fork of the river. Jim went up the south fork of Little Sandy, where he found much more abundant signs of beaver than the others had reported. He therefore proposed that they move the camp to his location.

After a few weeks the men had so many skins that they expressed a desire to go home, but Jim asked them to wait three or four days while he took a few traps further upstream.

To this the others agreed.

The men had made a rule to take turns in getting meals. One morning, while Harrod and Bridges were inspecting their traps, Stoner was preparing breakfast. Bridges rushed into camp declaring that he had heard a shot in the distance in the direction which Harrod had taken that morning. Apparently the colonel had killed a deer. After the men had waited for some time, expecting Jim to come in for breakfast, Bridges offered to go out to investigate. When he returned he appeared startled. Instead of the colonel, he had found fresh Indian signs and was positive that Harrod had been killed.

Stoner proposed that they look for their companion, but Bridges said this would be dangerous because the signs indicated that there were a great many Indians. He believed they should go back to the settlement and bring a larger party. After some delay and misgiving, Stoner agreed.

The searchers who returned later could find no trace of

[23] Collins, *Kentucky*, II, 614.

Harrod. Whether Bridges had told the truth no one ever knew. At several court hearings it was charged that Bridges had murdered Jim, but the accusation was never proved.

Some folk claimed that Harrod had not died at all but had gone to Greenbriar to live with his sister.[24] There is one deposition in the Draper Collection that claims his sister acknowledged this as a fact when she came to Kentucky on a visit a few years later.

There is also a tradition to the effect that Jim Harrod had actually been married in Pennsylvania before he founded the first settlement in Kentucky, and that he merely returned to his first wife and children.[25]

But these stories have no evidence, either circumstantial or direct, to support them. There is no good reason to believe that Jim ever had more than one wife. He was but forty-eight years of age at the time of his disappearance and too well known along the Virginia-Kentucky frontier to remain anonymous in any community. Travel between Harrodsburg and the old settlements was frequent, and had Jim been in any of these some of the Kentuckians would certainly have heard of it.

The accepted theory concerning his mysterious disappearance is that he was murdered by Bridges. Two statements of contemporaries, in addition to Ann's own deposition, support this belief.[26]

It appears that Bridges took some furs and skins to Lexington not long after this fatal journey. With the peltry he sold a pair of silver sleeve buttons with the letter H engraved on them.

The case had created wide interest, naturally; and when these buttons appeared on the counter, the purchaser took them to Ann. She at once declared that they had belonged to her husband and were from the hunting shirt he had worn on the expedition.[27]

---

[24] Draper Collection, 9J35-37.
[25] Collection of H. L. Leckey.
[26] Draper Collection, 12C22, 9J35-37.
[27] *Ibid.*, 12C22.

This incident started another search for the lost leader by a party of men who went immediately to the three forks. In an abandoned limestone cave, they found a skeleton, picked bare by wild animals, but still tightly wrapped in the sedge grass which had apparently been used as a sling to carry the heavy body to its hiding place. Whether this was Harrod's remains no one knew. It could have been the skeleton of an Indian or of one of the numerous trappers who had gone out alone never to return.

There is one other tradition suggesting that Jim went to live among the Indians. Two pioneers who were in captivity at an Indian camp opposite Detroit claimed that among a party of surveyors who arrived there one day was a tall, black-haired, dark-skinned person, erect and manly, whom his companions addressed as "Colonel Harrod." The captives, who were from Kentucky, asserted that they had recognized their old acquaintance. Harrod had seemed glad to meet them, they said, and had made some inquiry about his family; he had said that he intended to return but had not said when.

Upon hearing of this story, Mrs. Harrod offered the men a thousand dollars if they would conduct her to Colonel Harrod, but they deemed this too dangerous and hazardous an undertaking at that time.

About ten years after Jim's disappearance, Ann married again.[28] A short time later, however, this marriage was dissolved by the state legislature at Ann's request, on her declaration that her marriage to the second man was illegal since she had reason to think that Harrod was still living.[29]

There is nothing in her own recollections taken by General McAfee or those of her son-in-law to indicate that she believed this for long. It is more likely that she used this plea as a convenient method for getting out of an incompatible arrangement.

It is extremely improbable that a man of Harrod's tem-

[28] *Ibid.*, 12C22, 9J35-37; Mercer County Marriage Register, I, 96.
[29] Littell, *Law of Kentucky*, III, 196; Draper Collection, 12C22.

perament would have remained away from family and friends for many years. Of all the widow's sons, he had always been the most devoted to his family. Furthermore, Jim would not have been happy in hiding. To a person of his forthright temper self-concealment would have been positively distasteful. He had nothing to gain through anonymity. Why should a man give up all his life's gain at the age of forty-eight for a mere whim? One account had it that Jim was "miffed" by Ann's interest in other men, yet the teller of this story, like others before him, recalled that Jim never appeared jealous nor seemed to object to attentions his handsome wife received from other men.

Whatever the pioneers said about Jim, they always closed their statements with some high tribute. "Col. Harrod, besides possessing remarkable executive talent and other qualities of a great leader," wrote one of them, "was a man of the tenderest sympathy and a stranger to fear." [30] Another wrote, "Colo. Harrod was beloved—honorable—no seeker after fame; he served his country & race. He was a good soldier. . . ." [31] Jim could have asked no better epitaph than these words, typical judgments of his copioneers.[32]

[30] Collins, *Kentucky*, II, 615. See also Chap. XIX of this study.
[31] Draper Collection, 12C24.
[32] See also *ibid.*, 17CC192, 12CC45, 12CC112, 9J35 ff., 12C22-23, 4CC85, 4CC69, 48J10-11; James T. Morehead, *Address in Commemoration of the First Settlement of Kentucky* (Frankfort, 1840).

EPILOGUE

JIM HARROD had gone on so many long hunting and trapping expeditions that for months after his disappearance most of his friends and relatives half expected him to come strolling into town safe and happy with a fresh load of furs, branded and ready for trade at the Falls. Ann and her seven-year-old daughter Margaret waited a year before they gave up hope.[1]

During this period, one of mingled anxiety and hope for Harrod's family, significant changes came to Kentucky. Old Virginia cut her apron strings at last, and on June 1, 1792, the new commonwealth was admitted to the Union as the fifteenth state.[2] Preparatory to admission, the tenth and final one of the historic Danville conventions met to draw up a constitution.[3] The nature of the constitution had been thoroughly discussed in newspapers like the *Kentucky Gazette* and by organizations like the Political Club of Danville.[4] One group, favoring slavery and property rights, pitted itself strongly against the "radicals" from Pennsylvania and North Carolina who advocated a one-house legislature and voting by ballot and opposed a bill of rights which would protect private property and slavery. The result was a compromise—an odd combination of "progressive democracy and staid conservatism,"[5] with a strong kinship to the new Con-

[1] He made his will on November 28, 1791; it was probated in December, 1793. See Mercer County Will Book 1, p. 15.
[2] Thorpe (comp.), *Federal and State Constitutions*, III, 1264-77.
[3] April, 1792; Butler, *Commonwealth of Kentucky*, 206, speaks of it as the eighth.
[4] See Thomas Speed, *The Political Club of Danville*, Filson Club Publication, No. 2 (Louisville, 1894).
[5] E. Merton Coulter, "Early Frontier Democracy in the First Kentucky Constitution," in *Political Science Quarterly* (New York), XXXIX (1924), 665-77.

stitution of the United States. For the first time in this country a state granted suffrage to all free male citizens over twenty-one years of age.[6] This was a fortunate provision as well as a democratic one because, as one writer has observed, "land claims in Kentucky overlapped each other like shingles on a roof. . . ."[7] Representation was to be based on population rather than on territorial units as in Virginia, and elections were to be held annually. The constitution guaranteed freedom of religion.

Eighteen years had passed since Jim Harrod founded the first Kentucky settlement. A rough census showed that the population was about 100,000 in 1792.[8] Jim would have been proud of the growth of the frontier state.

When Harrod's will was probated a year later, everything was in order. He willed his entire estate, which was large and solvent, to Ann and Margaret. The mother was to serve as executrix and guardian.[9] An inventory showed personal items valued at more than four hundred pounds—considerably above the average appraisement for that year, when only a few Kentucky estates had property valued at more than two hundred pounds.[10]

Ann had numerous agreements and an assortment of small debts to attend to, and it was natural that she should call on Will Harrod to assist her in these complicated matters. Will had visited his brother just before the fatal expedition[11] and knew and understood Ann far better than the other Harrods ever did. He called in his own son-in-law, who was a good lawyer, to help her straighten out the tangles.[12]

Between court appearances Will went hunting and trap-

[6] *Ibid.*; Shaler, *A Pioneer Commonwealth*, 122.
[7] Abernethy, *Three Virginia Frontiers*, 76.
[8] Shaler, *A Pioneer Commonwealth*, 108.
[9] Mercer County Will Book 1, p. 37.
[10] Records of the Kentucky State Historical Society, Frankfort.
[11] Draper Collection, 12C24.
[12] Court records of Mercer and Lincoln counties. See also Draper Collection, 27C18. His name was Isaac Miranda, and he was a member of an old trading family of Lancaster, Philadelphia, and Caracas, Venezuela.

EPILOGUE 239

ping in Kentucky or returned to militia service in his own Pennsylvania county, where he held a colonel's commission.[13] Sometimes he was stationed far out on the frontier, substituting for one of his men who found duty inconvenient at the time, or organizing commissaries and calling elections for minor offices.[14] He found time to vote in civil elections, too, and with his brother Levi once signed a petition to the governor of Pennsylvania, protesting a fraudulent election.[15]

Now and then he went over to the Muddy Creek store to buy supplies. One account shows a purchase of two yards of calico and a silk handkerchief. At another time he signed a note for his son William who bought a velvet-jacket pattern, one stick of mohair, a skein of silk, two yards of black ribbon, a handkerchief, and four flints. Will finally invested in a pair of spectacles for himself.[16]

But Will still had a hankering for Kentucky, and when his beloved Amelia died soon after Jim's estate was settled, he sold his home, "Drowl," and moved to Kentucky to live with his son William, near old friends and neighbors from the Ten Mile area. He had been high up on Fish Creek when news of Amelia's death came, and his self-reproach over not having been at her deathbed was such that he could no longer bring himself to call Ten Mile home. For the next eight years, until his death in 1801, Will roamed the Kentucky woods, hunting, trapping, and fishing, occasionally expressing his opinion on some political question, but for the most part living quietly with his children.[17]

Thomas, the eldest of the Harrods, had moved west into Tennessee, although his son James was still living in Kentucky. One day while Tom was plowing on the large farm

[13] Draper Collection, 4NN83.
[14] *Ibid.*
[15] T. L. Montgomery (comp.), *Pennsylvania Archives*, Ser. 6 (Harrisburg, 1907), 41.
[16] Muddy Creek Ledger, original, in collection of H. L. Leckey.
[17] Draper Collection, 37J168-74. The William Harrod Papers, Draper Collection, Ser. 4NN, contain several political tracts.

which he had bought close to the frontier, an Indian crept up to the clearing and killed him.[18]

There was consequently only one of the widow's sons living now: Levi Harrod, Sr., the youngest and proudest of them all, had stayed on in the Monongahela country, moving easily from strenuous military service in the Continental line and the Virginia and Pennsylvania militias, to the position of first justice of the vast Washington County, where he read marriage and burial services and served in court for thirty years. Levi was the only one of the Harrod boys who became an active religious leader. In the records of the Goshen Baptist Church from 1781 to 1811, Brother Levi Harrod and his wife, Rachel, continuously appear among the faithful. Levi served as trustee; he was on a committee to judge whether one of the members was a "lyer" and on another "to exclude a sister for swearing and drinking to excess." Brother Harrod reported "that a Difficulty had arose betwixt Sister Jane Rose and Mary Jones and In order to accomodate the matter the Church" had appointed him to head a committee to straighten it out and report. Levi settled his church dues in cash, too, while most of the others paid in grain. He served as treasurer, moderator, and messenger, and on one occasion chose a pastor.[19]

Finally, when most of their children were well settled in the new Ohio country northeast of present-day Columbus, Rachel and Levi became restive. It was hard for an old woman to be away from her children and grandchildren, especially when they wrote glowing letters about their fine farms and growing prosperity. Levi, too, declared he could stand the Monongahela country no longer. Neighbors as thick as bees in molasses made a country civilized, but they also made for very poor hunting. So Levi asked the Goshen Baptist Church for letters of "dismition," explaining that he

---

[18] Swainson records.
[19] Record Book of Goshen Baptist Church, copy typed from the original by Mrs. Howard L. Leckey, Waynesburg, Pa., in collection of H. L. Leckey.

EPILOGUE

would live no longer in a country where he could not get his "fresh b'ar meat."[20]

Levi, the substantial citizen, man of property, civil and religious leader, returned to his own kind.

One of the pioneers who went out to this part of Ohio with Levi was Abraham Thomas. In his reminiscences Thomas evaluated life as he knew it on the Ohio and Pennsylvania frontiers, and it is unlikely that a single one of the Widow Harrod's sons would have disagreed with what he said. "We were again," he wrote, "in the midst of Indians, who daily visited our cabins; but I felt no other sentiment towards them, than pity for subdued and dejected foes. We lived harmoniously together until they followed the game to remote forests. In our new residence, fat turkeys everywhere abounded, and at all seasons of the year, venison and bear meat, were for a long time our common fare.

"We raised houses full of healthy children; our stock gave us no trouble. We enjoyed the best state of social intercourse with our neighbors, and newcomers. We knew none happier than ourselves; and I have yet to learn, of any higher state of substantial comfort, than [that of] the frontier backwoodsman."[21]

The Harrods were always seeking good land. Farming and land speculation offered the best opportunity for young men in a predominantly agricultural country. Although originally they had aspired to become gentlemen farmer-planters like their rich relatives back in Virginia and Maryland, this first generation of Ohio Valley Harrods were forced to spend most of their time in Indian fighting and in locating and clearing land. Each of the widow's sons achieved a measure of success beyond the average for his time. But it was James, the founder of Kentucky's first settlement, who became the traditional hero of the family, and his name was passed on to

---

[20] Papers of the late Hiram Hiller, excerpts made by Bernice L. Swainson, *ca.* 1938, at Waynesburg, Pa.
[21] Draper Collection, 27CC33.

succeeding generations of Harrod pioneers. While the contributions of his brothers merged with those of thousands of other frontiersmen to form the warp in the ever-widening fabric of frontier civilization, Jim Harrod's became part of the pattern threads. The town that he founded remained the center of pioneer activity during the early years; and today it is a busy trading and tourist center, where a memorial park, a national monument, a reconstructed fort, as well as a number of fine examples of southern architecture, perpetuate his fame.

The story of this first settlement and its founder is also the history of a vital period in the life of the frontier and the nation. Jim Harrod's early occupation, apparently without financial or political backers of any sort, of a region hundreds of miles from older, well-established frontiers, was an achievement of heroic proportions. But the credit for this achievement does not belong to him alone; there were other resourceful, equally brave leaders who left the comparative safety of old frontiers for the excitement and promise of the distant Kentucky wilderness.

In spite of their physical isolation, Jim Harrod and the other Western pioneer leaders managed to keep in touch with their families, friends, and, to a lesser degree, with governmental authorities in the older settlements. These vital contacts formed a reservoir of strength, matched only by their own community of efforts. Kentucky owes her beginnings to no royal or colonial charter, to no one speculative group, to no individual, but to the efforts of "many men and many companies of men," whose talents and primitive resources merged to form one of the most exciting chapters in the nation's history.

APPENDIX

Original members of James Harrod's Company, 1774.

Blackford, Joseph [1,2], Pa.
Blair, James [3,4], Pa.
Brown, James [1,2,3,4], Pa.
Brown, John [1], Pa.
Campbell, Arthur [1], Va.
Campbell, Wm. [1,2], Va.
Chapline, Abraham [1,2,3,4], Va.
Clark, John [1,2,3,4], Va.
Cowan, Jared [2,3,4], Pa.
Cowan, John [1,2,3,4], Pa.
Crawford, John [3,4], Pa.
Crow, John [1,2,3,4], Va.
Crow, William [1,2], Va.
Davis, Azariah (Annanias) [1,2,3,4], Va.
Davis, James [1,2,10], Va.
Doran, Patrick [1,2], Va.
Dugan, Henry [1,2]
Fields, Wm. [1,2,3], Va.
Garrett, Wm. [1,2], Va.
Glenn, David [1,2,3,4], Pa.
Glenn, Thomas [3,4], Pa.
Harlan, Elijah [1,2], Va.
Harlan, James [3,4], Va.
Harlan, Silas [1,2,3,4], Va.
Harmon, John Valentine [4], Va.
Harrod, Levi [4], Pa.
Harrod, Thomas [3,4], N. C.
Henton, Evan (John?) [3,4], Va.
Hite, Abraham [3], Va.
Hogan, Henry [2], Va.
Kerr, James [1,2], Pa.
Martin, Wm. [2], Pa.
Mortimer, Wm. [1,2]
Myers, Wm. [1,2]
Ooley, Peter [9]
Poage, Geo. [3,6], Va.
Quirk, Thos. [4,5], Va.
Rees, Azor (Azaria?) [1,2,3,4]
Sanders, James [1,2], Va.
Shelp, John [1,2,3,4], Va.
Smith, John [1,2], Va.
Sodousky, James [3,7], Va.
Stull, Martin [1,2], Va.
Venable, Wm. [1,2]
Wiley, James [1,2,3,4], Va.
Williams, David [1,2], Va.
Wilson, John [3,4,8]
Zane, Andrew [4], Va.

F. P. Strickler, M.D., of Louisville, Kentucky, in a conversation with the author, August 17, 1949, asserted that he had seen

[1] Draper Collection, 12C24, letter of John Fauntleroy, son-in-law of James Harrod. The list is, according to Fauntleroy, incomplete. Harrod's Company Book was in his possession.

[2] Ibid., 14J128, Robert B. McAfee, who had copied names from Harrod's Company Book.

[3] Collins, *Kentucky*, II, 517, 422, 750.

[4] Lucien Beckner, "James Harrod's Company," *Register of the Kentucky State Historical Society* (Frankfort), XX (1922), 280-82.

[5] Draper Collection, 36J23-28.   [6] Ibid., 4CC113-14.   [7] Ibid., 4CC69.
[8] Ibid., 7ZZ8-22.   [9] Ibid., 12CC146.   [10] Ibid., 3QQ61.

records stating that James Francis Moore was also a member of the company.

The places of residence for members of the company prior to the settlement in Kentucky do not necessarily indicate the states of their birth. The frequent assertion that most of Harrod's men came from the Monongahela country is clearly in error. The majority of them came from southwest Virginia, in the vicinity of Roanoke. Nor are most of the men "related by blood or marriage," as stated by Richard Henderson and others. So far as the records show, Thomas Quirk, a native of Ireland, was the only member of the company not born in this country. James Sodousky and George Poage are often listed as members of Isaac Hite's company that came into Kentucky soon after Harrod. It is possible that the Hite company had earlier agreed to join Harrod. There is also reason to believe that not all the men who had signed the Company Book came down the Ohio with Harrod. In his narrative, Abraham Chapline says that the captain waited for others to join him, but left before they arrived.

Names of men who joined Harrod's company at Harrodstown, summer of 1774:

Isaac Hite's Company, including

Gilbert, Robert[4]	McColloch, James[4]	Sodousky (Sandusky),
Hamilton, James[4]	Petrey, Alexander[4]	James[4]
Hite, Isaac[4]	[Poage, George][3]	Tutt, Benjamin[4]
Knox, James[4]	Sandusky, Jacob[4]	Williams, David[4]

Additional names of men who located land or built cabins in vicinity of Harrodstown in summer of 1774:

Batson, Mordecai[2]	Floyd, John[2]	Nash, William[2]
Boone, Daniel[1]	Hamilton, James[2]	Taylor, Hancock[2]
Cowan, James[2]	Hanson, Thomas[2]	Taylor, Richard[2,3]
Douglas, James[2]	McCra, Roderick[2]	

[1] Bakeless, *Daniel Boone*, 78-79.

[2] Draper Collection, 14J58-84, Hanson Journal, published in *Dunmore's War*, 110-33.

[3] Draper Collection, 12CC113-14; Reminiscences of General John Poague. It is not clear whether George Poage was originally a member of Hite's or Harrod's company.

[4] Collins, *Kentucky*, II, 517.

CRITICAL ESSAY ON AUTHORITIES

Manuscripts and Manuscript Collections

Records of the Harrod family are widely scattered. Of the numerous sources used in the preparation of this study, the Draper Collection at the Wisconsin Historical Society in Madison is the most important. Since most of the documents pertaining to the Harrods had been collected only incidentally, it was necessary to examine more than three hundred volumes in this collection. The William Harrod Papers, Series 4NN, comprising nearly one hundred original documents, are in the Pittsburgh and Northwest Virginia Series of the Draper Collection and furnish some of the most reliable data on the family. Many William and James Harrod manuscripts are in the George Rogers Clark J Series, containing sixty-four volumes. For James Harrod, the Kentucky CC Series of thirty-two volumes was also a valuable source, while the Boone C Series was particularly helpful for data on William. Most of James Harrod's papers were lost when his house burned in the early 1800's, but a few of them were saved and are now in Series CC of the Draper Collection. There are a surprising number of contemporary Harrod records at Madison; but because some of the most interesting of these are in the form of recollections, they had to be used with caution and checked against known historical facts. Frequently it was possible to verify these recollections through the Pension Records in the National Archives, Washington. These records include sworn statements of eighty-three Kentucky, western Pennsylvania, Virginia, and Maryland Revolutionary soldiers. The applications of sons, cousins, and nephews of the Harrods were particularly helpful, as were those of men who had served with them in various campaigns. Although the Durrett Collection of personal and family records at the University of Chicago is also a rich source, much of the Harrod material there duplicates that in the Draper Collection.

The twenty-four county courthouses visited in Kentucky, Virginia, Maryland, Pennsylvania, and Ohio contained numerous source materials, such as wills, estate settlements, court orders, and depositions. Also used extensively were the collections of state records in Richmond, Philadelphia, Frankfort, and Annapolis. The miscellaneous collections of town, church, Bible, and family records of the historical societies of these states were all helpful.

Numerous private collections were made available to the author, the most important of these being the records in the possession of Bernice Lewis Swainson, of Piedmont, California, and Howard L. Leckey, of Waynesburg, Pennsylvania. These collections contain family, military, court, church, and other records, many of them taken from scattered manuscript and rare printed sources. Mr. Leckey's original Muddy Creek Ledger manuscript is interesting for its numerous items on the Harrods and related families, while Mrs. Swainson's organizational work on the voluminous records in her possession was especially helpful in tracing blood relationships. Judge Albert Cole of Peru, Indiana, is owner of the manuscript record, Rachel Henton's Book, a brief compilation of data mainly on John Harrod, and John, Jr. The Benjamin Van Cleve Memorandum, now in the possession of Mr. Lloyd Waddell Smith, of Madison, New Jersey, contains the only known contemporary sketch and detailed specifications of Harrod's fort.

Travel Accounts

Accounts by early travelers have been long recognized as rich sources for the historian. Among those that have appeared in book form are A. G. Bradley (ed.), *The Journal of Nicholas Cresswell* (New York, 1928); William M. Darlington (ed.), *Christopher Gist's Journals* (Pittsburgh, 1893); the charming account by a boy traveler, the "Journal of Colonel Daniel Trabue," as published in Lillie DuPuy Harper (ed.), *Colonial Men and Times* (Philadelphia, 1916); the Walker and Gist journals edited by J. Johnston, *First Explorations of Kentucky*, Filson Club Publication, No. 13 (Louisville, 1898); James Smith, *Life and Travels of Colonel James Smith* (Philadelphia, 1834), which is one of the important items on the French and Indian War; J. F. D. Smyth, *A Tour in the United States of America*, 2 vols. (Dublin, 1784); Gilbert Imlay, *A Topographical Description of the Western Terri-*

tory of North America (New York, 1793); and Joseph Doddridge, *Notes on the Settlement and Indian Wars of Virginia and Pennsylvania from 1763-1783* (Wellsburg, Va., 1824). John Filson, *The Discovery, Settlement and Present State of Kentucke* (Wilmington, Del., 1784), is of particular interest because it was published in James Harrod's lifetime, and its author consulted with Harrod, Daniel Boone, and Levi Todd while preparing his famous map of Kentucky. Filson dedicated his book to these men and included in it a statement from them, certifying to the accuracy of his information. Reuben G. Thwaites (ed.), *Early Western Travels*, 32 vols. (Cleveland, 1904), one of the better-known collections, was referred to frequently, as were Neander M. Woods (ed.), *The Woods-McAfee Memorial* (Louisville, 1905), containing the journals of the McAfee brothers for the year 1773, and John Bradford, *Notes on Kentucky* [reprint] (San Francisco, 1932).

Published Correspondence

The Harrod brothers can be traced through the maze of border warfare preceding the settlement of Kentucky in such sources as Lewis Burd Walker (ed.), *The Burd Papers*, 2 vols. (Pottsville, Pa., 1899); Alfred P. James (ed.), *The Writings of General John Forbes* (Menasha, Wis., 1938); and Clarence E. Carter (ed.), *The Correspondence of General Thomas Gage with the Secretaries of State, 1763-1775*, 2 vols. (New Haven, 1931-33).

Several volumes of the Northwestern Pennsylvania Historical Series have been of great value in this respect also, particularly those containing the correspondence of Col. Bouquet: Sylvester K. Stevens and Donald H. Kent (eds.), *The Papers of Col. Henry Bouquet*, Northwestern Pennsylvania Historical Series 21631-[21660] (mimeographed, Harrisburg, Pa., 1940——). Of the approximately twenty-nine projected volumes of these papers, only the first eight had been published when this study was in process of preparation: N.W. Pa. Hist. Ser. 21634, 21652, 21653, 21654, 21643, 21644, 21645, and 21631-21632, respectively. Of these, Vols. III, IV, V, VI, and VII (21653, 21654, 21643, 21644, and 21645, respectively) were most helpful.

Published Records

The most ambitious presentation of Harrod records is contained in Susan W. Atkins (comp.), *Hereward Records and Papers, 1620-1940* (Greenfield, Ind., 1940), which served as a guidepost in the early portion of the study. But the many inaccuracies resulting from the compiler's illness, as well as her imperfect knowledge of related history, made it necessary to check all pertinent records. Unfortunately Mrs. Atkins proceeded on the erroneous assumption that John Harrod was really John Harwood, since this spelling of the name appears frequently in official records. Eli Biggs (ed.), *A Short History of the Harrod and Biggs Families* (Mt. Vernon, Ohio, 1931) is important to descendants of Levi Harrod, although it too contains many errors and confusing statements.

The various volumes of the *Illinois Historical Collections* were of great value, particularly Vol. VIII, James Alton James (ed.), *George Rogers Clark Papers, 1771-1781* (Springfield, 1912), and Vol. XIX, James Alton James (ed.), *George Rogers Clark Papers, 1781-1784* (Springfield, 1926). The publications of the Wisconsin Historical Society were also used extensively, especially Reuben G. Thwaites and Louise P. Kellogg (eds.), *A Documentary History of Dunmore's War, 1774* (Madison, 1905), *The Revolution on the Upper Ohio, 1775-1777* (Madison, 1908), and *Frontier Defense on the Upper Ohio, 1777-1778* (Madison, 1912); and Louise P. Kellogg (ed.), *Frontier Advance on the Upper Ohio, 1778-1779* (Madison, 1916), and *Frontier Retreat on the Upper Ohio, 1779-1781* (Madison, 1917).

Willard Rouse Jillson has edited a number of important documents including: *The Kentuckie Country* (Washington, 1931), *Tales of the Dark and Bloody Ground* (Louisville, 1930), and *Old Kentucky Entries and Deeds,* Filson Club Publication, No. 34 (Frankfort, 1926). Equally valuable for early Harrodsburg history is Mrs. Harry E. McAdams (ed.), *Kentucky Pioneer and Court Records* (Lexington, 1929); James R. Robertson (ed.), *Petitions of the Early Inhabitants of Kentucky to the General Assembly of Virginia, 1769-1792,* Filson Club Publication, No. 27 (Louisville, 1914); Philip P. Taylor (comp.), *Calendar of Warrants for Land in Kentucky for Service in the French and Indian Wars* (Frankfort, 1917); and Peter Force (ed.), *American Archives,* Ser. 4, 6 vols. (Washington, 1837-1846).

Two compilations by William Littell, *Political Transactions in*

CRITICAL ESSAY

and Concerning Kentucky, Filson Club Publication, No. 31, (reprint, Louisville, 1927), and *Statute Law of Kentucky*, 3 vols. (Frankfort, 1809-1811), were invaluable in tracing social and political developments and the involved legal tangles that enmeshed the early pioneers.

Valuable material was found in such publications as Samuel Hazard (comp.), *Pennsylvania Archives*, Ser. 1, 12 vols. (Philadelphia, 1852-1856); T. L. Montgomery (comp.), *Pennsylvania Archives*, Ser. 6, 15 vols. (Harrisburg, 1907); Samuel Hazard (ed.), *Minutes of the Provincial Council of Pennsylvania . . . March 10, 1683—September 27, 1775*, 10 vols. (Philadelphia, 1851-1852), part of the *Pennsylvania Colonial Records*, 16 vols. (Philadelphia and Harrisburg, 1851-1853); W. L. Saunders (ed.), *The Colonial Records of North Carolina*, 10 vols. (Raleigh, 1886-1890); Walter Clark (ed.), *The State Records of North Carolina*, 12 vols. (Raleigh, 1895); William H. Browne (ed.), *Archives of Maryland . . .*, First 29 vols. (Baltimore, 1883-1912); and Harry W. Newman (ed.), *Maryland Revolutionary Records* (Washington, 1938).

For Virginia the most valuable sources of material were William W. Hening (ed.), *The Statutes at Large; Being a Collection of All the Laws of Virginia, from the First Session of the Legislature, in the Year 1619 . . . 1792*, 13 vols. (Richmond, 1810-1823); and W. P. Palmer and others (arrs.), *Calendar of Virginia State Papers and Other Manuscripts . . . Preserved in the Capitol at Richmond . . .*, 11 vols. (Richmond, 1875-1893), of which Vols. I-IV were used. Also of value were H. R. McIllwaine (ed.), *Executive Journals of the Council of Colonial Virginia*, 4 vols. (Richmond, 1925-1930), and *Legislative Journals of the Council of Colonial Virginia*, 3 vols. (Richmond, 1918-1919); and J. P. Kennedy and H. R. McIllwaine (eds.), *Journals of the House of Burgesses of Virginia, 1619-1776* [title varies], 13 vols. (Richmond, 1905-1915). These three works were used only as a general guide, however, while most footnote references throughout the text are to the original editions of the various journals of the Virginia legislature *(Journal of the House of Burgesses, Journal of the Virginia Convention, Journals of the Council of Virginia, Journal of the Senate of Virginia, Journal of the Virginia House of Delegates*, etc.), which were printed immediately following the close of each session of the respective bodies and are now located in the Library of Congress Rare Book Division. The three above-mentioned works are more generally available and are therefore cited here instead of the rare editions.

Biographies

Among the biographies used extensively were John Bakeless, *Daniel Boone* (New York, 1939), a recent study of the popular American hero based on manuscript sources and following closely Lyman Draper's manuscript biography of Boone; Reuben G. Thwaites, *Daniel Boone* (New York, 1902), based on manuscripts in the Draper Collection; Max Savelle, *George Morgan, Colony Builder* (New York, 1932); Lily Lee Nixon, *James Burd, Frontier Defender* (Philadelphia, 1941); Hubertus M. Cummings, *Richard Peters, Provincial Secretary* (Philadelphia, 1944); Albert T. Volwiler, *George Croghan and the Westward Movement, 1741-1782* (Cleveland, 1926); Howard H. Peckham, *Pontiac and the Indian Uprising* (Princeton, 1947); and Edna Kenton, *Simon Kenton* (New York, 1930). Since George Rogers Clark played a role of considerable importance in Harrodsburg history, all the biographies of this prominent figure were studied in detail. The standard work is James Alton James, *George Rogers Clark* (Chicago, 1928), but since this biographer made little use of the vast sources in Richmond, it was necessary to refer to an earlier, almost forgotten biography by Consul W. Butterfield, *A History of Lieutenant Colonel George Rogers Clark's Conquest of the Illinois* . . . (Washington, 1904). William Hayden English, who—unlike Butterfield—was an uncritical admirer of Clark, gives useful information on William Harrod and the other officers who served under Clark in the Virginia Regiment, and prints—as does Butterfield—the colonel's "Memoir," the letter to Mason, Clark's diary at Harrodsburg, and other Clark papers, in his *Conquest of the Country Northwest of the River Ohio; and Life of Gen. George Rogers Clark*, 2 vols. (Indianapolis, 1895).

County and State Histories

Among the histories of the Western frontiers, there are several that have become standard for any student of the period. For the first chapter on the Harrods in the Shenandoah Valley, local color was furnished by Samuel Kercheval, *A History of the Valley of*

Virginia (4th ed.; Strasburg, Va., 1925). For the central and western Pennsylvania period, material was drawn from Israel D. Rupp, *The History and Topography of Dauphin, Cumberland, Franklin, Bedford . . . Counties* (Lancaster, Pa., 1848); and John Fiske, *Old Virginia and Her Neighbors*, 2 vols. (New York, 1897). Additional Pennsylvania material is in Boyd Crumrine (ed.), *History of Washington County, Pennsylvania* (Philadelphia, 1882); Earle R. Forrest, *Washington County*, 2 vols. (Washington, Pa., 1940); F. G. Hoenstine (ed.), U. J. Jones, *History of the Early Settlement of the Juniata Valley* (reprint, Harrisburg, 1940); William H. Koontz (ed.), *History of Bedford and Somerset Counties, Pennsylvania . . .*, 3 vols. (New York, 1906); James Veech, *The Monongahela of Old; or Historical Sketches of Southwestern Pennsylvania to the Year 1800* (Pittsburgh, 1858-92; reissue, 1910); Andrew J. Waycoff, *Local History*, No. 145 (Waynesburg, Pa., n.d.), published by the Waynesburg *Democrat Messenger*.

Few county histories in the Kentucky field were used, but a number of state studies were helpful: Mann Butler, *A History of the Commonwealth of Kentucky* (Cincinnati, 1834); Lewis and Richard H. Collins, *History of Kentucky*, 2 vols. (rev. ed.; Covington, Ky., 1878); R. S. Cotterill, *History of Pioneer Kentucky* (Cincinnati, 1917); Robert M. McElroy, *Kentucky in the Nation's History* (New York, 1909); Humphrey Marshall, *History of Kentucky*, 2 vols. (Frankfort, 1824); N. S. Shaler, *Kentucky, A Pioneer Commonwealth* (Boston, 1885); and *History of Kentucky*, 4 vols. (Chicago and Louisville, 1928), a multivolumed work without a general editor, of which the first two volumes were used, Temple Bodley, *History of Kentucky Before the Louisiana Purchase in 1803*, Vol. I, and Samuel M. Wilson, *History of Kentucky from 1803 to 1928*, Vol. II.

Monographs

Numerous monographs were helpful: Thomas P. Abernethy, *Three Virginia Frontiers* (University, La., 1940), and *Western Lands and the American Revolution* (New York, 1937); G. H. Alden, *New Governments West of the Alleghanies Before 1780* (Madison, 1897); John R. Alden, *John Stuart and the Southern Colonial Frontier* (Ann Arbor, 1944); Clarence W. Alvord, *The Mississippi Valley in British Politics*, 2 vols. (Cleveland, 1917);

Kenneth P. Bailey, *The Ohio Company of Virginia and the Westward Movement, 1748-1792* (Glendale, Calif., 1939); Solon J. and Elizabeth H. Buck, *The Planting of Civilization in Western Pennsylvania* (Pittsburgh, 1939); Clarence E. Carter, *Great Britain and the Illinois Country, 1763-1774* (Washington, 1910); Merle Curti, *The Growth of American Thought* (New York, 1943); Reuben T. Durrett, *The Centenary of Louisville*, Filson Club Publication, No. 8 (Louisville, 1893); Dixon R. Fox, *Sources of Culture in the Middle West* (New York, 1934); Lawrence H. Gipson, *The British Empire Before the American Revolution . . .* , 6 vols. (Vols. I-III, Caldwell, Ind., 1936; Vols. IV-VI, New York, 1939-1946), of which Vol. IV, *Zones of International Friction; North America South of the Great Lakes Region, 1748-1754*, and Vol. VI, *The Great War for the Empire; The Years of Defeat*, were used; James Hall, *Legends of the West* (Cincinnati, 1832), *Romance of Western History* (Cincinnati, 1857), and *Sketches of History, Life and Manners in the West*, 2 vols. (Philadelphia, 1834); Charles A. Hanna, *The Scotch-Irish in . . . North America* (New York, 1902); Archibald Henderson, *Conquest of the Old Southwest* (New York, 1920); Benjamin Hibbard, *A History of the Public Land Policies* (New York, 1939); Archer B. Hulbert, *Boone's Wilderness Road* (Cleveland, 1903); William S. Lester, *The Transylvania Colony* (Spencer, Ind., 1935); T. L. McKenney and James Hall, *History of Indian Tribes of North America*, 3 vols. (Philadelphia, 1836-44); Allan Nevins, *The American States During and After the Revolution* (New York, 1924); Frederick A. Ogg, *The Opening of the Mississippi* (New York, 1904); Frederick L. Paxson, *History of the American Frontier, 1763-1893* (New York, 1924); Max Savelle, *The Foundations of American Civilization* (New York, 1942); William W. Sweet, *The Story of Religion in America* (New York, 1939); Frederick J. Turner, *The Frontier in American History* (New York, 1920); and Justin Winsor, *The Mississippi Basin* (Boston, 1895), and *The Westward Movement* (Boston, 1899).

Newspapers and Periodicals

A popular title for Virginia newspapers of this period was *Virginia Gazette*. Five firms in Williamsburg published papers bearing this title between the years 1736 and 1780, and a sixth

CRITICAL ESSAY 253

firm in Richmond issued a *Virginia Gazette* from 1780-1781. There were eight Richmond papers published between 1781 and 1809 which bore the name *Virginia Gazette* in combination with another name, such as *Virginia Gazette, and General Advertiser, Virginia Gazette and Independent Chronicle, Virginia Gazette and Weekly Advertiser,* etc. Several of these papers overlap in date of issue; others are continuations of one another in date and number. The files of these various papers and of the Lexington *Kentucky Gazette* (1787-1820) furnished good contemporary material for the period between 1736 and 1795. Also used were the files of the Philadelphia *Pennsylvania Gazette* (1728-1815), the Baltimore *Maryland Journal* (1773-1797), and the Baltimore *Maryland Gazette* (1778-1779, 1783-1791).

Valuable material was located in the files of two short-lived monthly publications, *The Olden Time: A Monthly Publication, Devoted to the Preservation of Documents and Other Authentic Information in Relation to the Early Explorations, and the Settlement and Improvement of the Country Around the Head of the Ohio* (Pittsburgh), I-II (1846-1847); and *The Cincinnati Miscellany; or, Antiquities of the West,* I-II (1844-1846). Many of the contemporary letters, official reports, and other materials found in these monthlies are unavailable elsewhere.

Much source material no longer available in the original form is to be found in articles in recent periodicals. Of these, the following were most helpful in the preparation of this study: St. George L. Sioussat, "The Breakdown of the Royal Management of Lands in the Southern Provinces, 1773-1775," in *Agricultural History* (Chicago), III (1929), 68-98; Stanley Pargellis, "Braddock's Defeat," in *American Historical Review* (New York), XLI (1935-1936), 253-69; Frederick Jackson Turner, "Western State-Making in the Revolutionary Era," *ibid.,* I (1895-1896), 70-87; Thomas D. Clark, "Salt, a Factor in the Settlement of Kentucky," in *Filson Club History Quarterly* (Louisville), XII (1938), 42-52; Thomas P. Abernethy (ed.), "Journal of the First Kentucky Convention, Dec. 27, 1784-Jan. 5, 1785," in *Journal of Southern History* (Baton Rouge), I (1935), 67-78; Archibald Henderson, "Richard Henderson and the Occupation of Kentucky, 1775," in *Mississippi Valley Historical Review* (Cedar Rapids, Iowa), I (1914-1915), 341-63; Leonard C. Helderman, "The Northwest Expedition of George

Rogers Clark, 1786-1787," *ibid.,* XXV (1943-1944), 317-34; Wilbur H. Siebert, "The Tory Proprietors of Kentucky Lands," in *Ohio State Archeological and Historical Quarterly* (Columbus), XXVIII (1919), 48-71; "Gen. Clark's Campaign, 1780. Official Letters," "Bowman's Campaign of 1779," and "Logan's Campaign—1786," *ibid.,* XXII (1913), 500-501, 502-19, and 520-21, respectively; E. Merton Coulter, "Early Frontier Democracy in the First Kentucky Constitution," in *Political Science Quarterly* (New York), XXXIX (1924), 665-77; John Redd, "Reminiscences of Western Virginia, 1770-1790," in *Virginia Magazine of History and Biography* (Richmond), VI (1898-1899), 337-44; VII (1899-1900), 1-16; "Deposition of John Gibson in Regard to Delaware Indians," *ibid.,* XIII (1905-1906), 423-24; Clarence W. Alvord, "The Daniel Boone Myth," in *Journal of the Illinois Historical Society* (Springfield), XIX (1926), 16-29; W. W. Stephenson, "The Old Courthouse and Courts and Bar of Mercer County, Kentucky," in *Register of the Kentucky State Historical Society* (Frankfort), VII (1909), 31-35; *id.,* "The Old Fort at Harrodsburg," *ibid.,* VIII (1910), 47-50; and Lucien Beckner, "History of the County Court of Lincoln County, Kentucky," *ibid.,* XX (1922), 170-90.

INDEX

Allegheny River, 19, 24
Ammunition, supplied by proprietors, 84; brought in by J. Harrod, 102-103, 127-28
Arms. *See* Kentucky rifles
Armstrong, John, 18

Backwoodsmen. *See* Pioneers
Baptists. *See* Goshen Baptist Church
Batson, Mordecai, 244
Battle of the Boards, 176-77
Beall, Alexander, company of, 17, 20
Bedford, road to, 15. *See also* Harrod, James
Belmont, is visited by J. Harrod, 206
Big Bone Lick, description of, 39-40, 163
Bird, Henry, campaign of 182-83
Blackford, Joseph, 243
Blair, James, 244
Blue Licks, 49; battle of, 198-99
Boiling Spring settlement, is founded by J. Harrod, 48; land is cleared at, 84; isolation of, 147; claims near, 173; men from, in battle, 176-77; Latin school at, is founded by J. Harrod, 217-18
Books, scarcity of, 215
Boone, Daniel, meets J. Harrod, 31; son of, is killed, 42; on mission, 51; builds cabin at Harrodsburg, 51; founds town, 77; as road builder, 77-78; in Transylvania Assembly, 84; is awarded land, 87; surveys at Louisville, 87; leads families, 87-88; carries defense burden, 110; life of, is saved, 153; at Bryant's Fort, 198; in battle of Blue Licks, 198; suit of, against J. Harrod, 222
Boone, Squire, at Danville convention, 211
Boone's Fort, unfinished, 110; defenses of, are co-ordinated by John Bowman, 125

Boonesborough, is founded, 76-77; food shortage in, 85; defense burden of, 193
Booty, sale of, 165. *See also* Pioneers
Boston Tea Party, news of, 65
Boundary disputes. *See* Land, Maryland, Pennsylvania, Virginia, and names of individual pioneers
Bounty lands, 33. *See also* Pioneers and Harrod, James
Bouquet, Col. Henry, campaign of, 21-29. *See also* Harrod, James; and Forbes, John
Bowman, John, serves as county lieutenant, 124; co-ordinates defenses, 125; at Corn Island, 138; Ohio expedition of, 162 n., 163-66
Bowman, Joseph, is consulted, 126; serves as captain under Clark, 136
Braddock, Gen. Edward, campaign of, 13-16, 14 n., 15-20, 31; death of, 15
Braddock Mountain, 3
Braddock's Road, 14, 15, 22
Bradstreet, John, 27
Branle (dance), 159
Bridges, ———, sues J. Harrod, 232; is suspected of murdering him, 232-34
British. *See* Great Britain
Broadhead, Col. Daniel, grants pass, 167-68
Broadhead, Daniel, Jr., store of, 214
Brown, James, land claim of, 173; original member of Harrod's company, 243
Brown, John, 243
Brown, Sarah. *See* Harrod, Sarah
Bryant's Fort, 162; sends men to John Bowman, 162; is threatened, 182; is attacked, 198
Buffalo Spring, 195-96. *See also* St. Asaph
Bullitt, Thomas, survey of, 35-41; his men join J. Harrod, 71-72; sees im-

INDEX

Bullitt, Thomas, *continued*
portance of Louisville, 87. *See also* Preston, Col. William
Bullskin Creek, 173
Burd, James, as road builder, 14-15, 22-23
Burns, Patrick, 11
Bushy Run, battle of, 26
Butler, Simon. *See* Kenton, Simon

Cabins. *See* Pioneers
Cahokia, is captured, 141-42
Calloway, Richard, 161; in Va. Assembly, 170
Camp Union. *See* Union, Camp
Campaigns. *See* names of individual commanders
Campbell, Arthur, 243
Campbell, John, lands claims of, 157-58
Campbell, William, 243
Catawba Indians, 6, 20
Catawba River, 32. *See also* McAfee brothers
Cato (Negro fiddler), 159
Census, in Ky., 129. *See also* Population
Chambersburg, 15
Chapline, Abraham, joins J. Harrod, 44; finds branch of Salt River, 47; builds cabin for Levi Harrod, 48; land claims of, 173; escape of, 183; serves as trustee of Harrodsburg, 212; in Ky., 243, 244
Chapline's Fork, 47, 172
Cherokee Indians, 20, 152, 209; Chief Moon of, is killed by J. Harrod, 175
Chickamauga Indians, 209
Chillicothe towns, 62; forewarned, 166; deserted, 189. *See also* Bowman, John; and Clark, George Rogers, 1780 campaign of
Cincinnati, J. Harrod's discovery claim at, 46
Clark, George Rogers, on Ten Mile Creek, 50; at Fort Gower, 92; characteristics of, 92-93, 93 n., 126, 178; in Ky., 92-96; represents Ky., 97-98; sends letter to Harrodsburg, 98; conveys powder, 101-102; defends Fort Harrod, 117-18; sends spies to Ill., 125-26; consults with Harrods, 126; revisits Patrick Henry, 129; Ill. expedition (1778) of, 130-42; holds celebration, 158-59; captures Gov. Hamilton, 159-60; plans of, upset, 162, 165-67; erects fort on Ohio River, 177; visits William Harrod, 177; is criticized, 185-86; 1780 campaign of, 186-92; Ill. grant of, 196, 221-22; 1782 campaign of, 197-203; letter to, from James Monroe, 203; is discouraged, 206; is vindicated, 207; 1786 campaign of, 226-27, 230. *See also* Bowman, John
Clark, John, 243
Clark, William, commissioner, 221; receives letter from J. Harrod, 221-22
Clarksville, 221
Clinch River. *See* Boone, Daniel; Harrod, James; and Russell, William
Coburn, Sam, family of, 32, 143; moves to Ky., 143-44; is killed, 148. *See also* Harrod, Ann (Coburn)
Commander of Plantations, title of, 194
Company Book, J. Harrod's, 244
Conestoga wagons, 214
Connallways, 10
Connally, John, 34-35; lands of, 49; as loyalist, 138, 157-58
Conococheague, valley of, 9
Continental Congress, 65
Continental money, 152, 167
Coomes, Mrs., teaches school, 112-13
Coomes, William, escapes, 114-16
Corn Island, is fortified, 137, 167; volunteers at, 138; is abandoned, 156-57
Cornstalk, Chief. *See* Shawnee Indians
County clerks, powers of, 195
Court, first meeting of, 128-29; system of, 195; of Mercer County, 222; of Lincoln County, 222. *See also* names of individual pioneers
Cowan, James, 244
Cowan, Jared, 243
Cowan, John, 196, 243
Cowardice. *See* Pioneers, disregard for dangers of
Crab Orchard, 186

INDEX 257

Crawford, John, 243
Cresap, Michael, 55
Crow, John, 243
Crow, William, 243
Crow vs. Harrod (lawsuit) 223
Crow's Station, 207
Cumberland Trace (road), 124, 127-28
Currency. *See* Continental money

Danville, political conventions at, 208-10, 223-24, 231, 237; Harrod holdings in, 223; Political Club of, 237
Davis, Azariah (Annanias), 243
Davis, James, 243
De Kalb, Baron, 205
Delaware Indians, 4, 11, 18; at Fort Necessity, 4; move west, 6; Chief Shingas of, 11, 37; attempts to placate, 20; unrest of, 25; treaty with, 27; friendliness of, 31-32, 95-96, 131, 150; spread rumors, 103; in Ill. with J. Harrod, 149-60
Deserters. *See* Pioneers
Detroit. *See* Clark, George Rogers
Dick's River, 88
Dinwiddie, Gov. Robert, 2, 3
Discipline. *See* Pioneers and Braddock, Gen. Edward
Doran, Patrick, 243
Douglas, James, 244
Drake, Dr. Daniel, quoted, 230
Dugan, Henry, 243
Dunmore, Gov., relations of, with Connally, 34-35. *See* Dunmore's War
Dunmore's War, 53-67; Fort Gower meeting and resolutions, 65-67; effect of, on settlement of Ky., 66-67

England. *See* Great Britain
Episcopalians, 218

Fairfax, Lord. *See* Land, Fairfax grant
Falls of the Ohio. *See* Louisville, surveys at
Fauntleroy, John, 217-18; remarks of, on J. Harrod, 220
Fields, William, 243
Fincastle County, 35, 43, 93

Fish Creek, fort at, reinforced, 131. *See also* Harrod, William
Fleming, Col. William, commissioner, 172; comments of, on Harrodsburg, 174-75; is visited by the Harrods at his home, Belmont, 206; at Louisville, 206; conducts hearings, 207
Floyd, John, seeks land, 49-50; settles in Ky., 81, 244; relation of, to Transylvania, 86-87; is made a county lieutenant, 194; in 1782 campaign, 200
Floyd County, 221
Forbes, John C., campaign of, 19-24; death of, 24
Foreman, William, defeat of, 132-33
Forks of the Ohio. *See* Fort Duquesne and Pittsburgh
Fort building, 110-11, 113, 116-17
Fort Cumberland, 13
Fort Duquesne, is visited by George Washington, 2; is reinforced, 3; march to, 14-15; is captured, 23-24
Fort Frederick, 17
Fort Gower. *See* Dunmore's War
Fort Harrod, building of, 110-13; siege of, 110-20; first site of, 111. *See also* names of individual pioneers
Fort Jefferson, 186
Fort Juniata, company of men from, under Will Harrod attack Indians, 18
Fort Lexington, is threatened, 182
Fort Littleton, 11-12, 14, 18
Fort McIntosh, 167
Fort Necessity, 3, 4
Fort Pitt. *See* Pittsburgh
Fort Randolph, 118, 130, 136
Fort Stanwix. *See* Treaty, of Fort Stanwix
French, at Kaskaskia, 140-41. *See also* Braddock, Gen. Edward; Forbes, John C.; Washington, George; and Harrod, James
French and Indian War, 13-29, 14 n. *See also* Harrod, James; Harrod, William; Harrod, Samuel; Harrod, John, Jr.; Braddock, Gen. Edward; and Forbes, John C.

INDEX

Frontiersmen. *See* Pioneers
Fur trade, French, 30-31. *See also* Harrod, James

Game animals, 49, 173-76. *See also* Pioneers
Games. *See* Pioneers
Garrett, William, 243
Gay, Frances. *See* Harrod, Sarah
Gilbert, Robert, 244
Gilbert's Creek, fort on, 144; land at, 173
Gist, Christopher, 3, 28
Gist, Thomas, 28, 29
Glenn, David, 243
Glenn, Thomas, 243
Goshen Baptist Church, 240-41
Gossip. *See* Pioneers
Grant, Maj. James, 22
Grave Creek fort 104, 131
Great Britain, Proclamation of 1763 by, 28; allegiance of settlers to, 65-66; plans offensive, 179; sends regiment against Kentucky, 181-82; alarm of, 183; reduces support of Indians, 202. *See also* Forbes, John C.; Braddock, Gen. Edward; Treaties; and specific names of colonies
Great Kanawha River, 35; fort on, 130. *See also* Dunmore's War
Great Meadow. *See* Fort Necessity
Green River, tract on, allotted, 154-55
Greenbriar River, settlements on, 136. *See also* Dunmore's War and Harrod, James
Gunpowder River, 5

Hamilton, Lord, plans attack, 125-26; capture of, 159-60; in Ky., 160-61
Hamilton, James, 244
Hand, Gen. Edward, 110
Hannastown, 34
Hanson, Thomas, 244
Hard winter, 173-75
Harlan, Elijah, 243
Harlan, James, 243
Harmon, John V., 243
Harris' Ferry (Harrisburg), 5
Harrod, spelling of name, 2 n.
Harrod, Amelia (Stevens), marries William Harrod, 27; refuses to move to Ky., 69, 158, 179; death of, 239. *See also* Harrod, William, letters of, to wife
Harrod, Ann (Coburn), moves to Ky., 143; is widowed, 144; marriage of, to J. Harrod, 144; superstitions of, 147-48; as marksman, 148-49; land claims of, 173; visits Yadkin country, 205; obtains luxuries, 214-15; gossip about, 215-18; religion of, 218-20; fears of, for safety of J. Harrod, 232-33; deposition of, 234; remarriage of, 235; attempts of, to resolve mystery of J. Harrod's disappearance, 235-37
Harrod, Hannah, wife of Thomas Harrod, 69, 158
Harrod, James, birth, parentage, and first years, 1, 6, 7-11; under Burd, 22; under Shelby, 22; under Bouquet, 26; skills of, 26, 31, 32, 36-37, 149, 153, 187, 214-15; in the Illinois, 30; character of, 30-31, 45, 46, 82, 155, 216-17; simplicity of tastes of, 30-32, 214-15, 220; in Tenn., 31; first visits of, to Ky., New Orleans, and N. C., 31-32; in Ten Mile country, 31-32; relations of, with family, 31-32, 71, 155, 204-206, 216-17; appearance of, 32, 144; surveys in Ky., 35-41; under Piper, 36; recruits men for settlement, 43-45; estimates of, 45, 80, 81, 82, 168-69, 234, 236, 238, 241-42; at site of Cincinnati, 46; founds settlements, 47-49; surveys for Virginians, 50, 50 n.; men of, in Indian attack, 51-52; goes to Va., 52; in Dunmore's War, 58-60; at Fort Gower, 65-66; returns to Ky., 68-76; faces opposition, 77-78; at first Transylvania Assembly, 81-84; humility of, 82, 211-12; attitude of, toward religion, 84, 219-20; helps new settlers, 84-86; is supported by newcomers, 86-87; is not at second meeting of Transylvania Assembly, 88; opposes Transylvania, 91-95; calls election, 93-94; visits Delaware villages, 95-96; rescues powder, 102; carries heavy defense burden in 1776, pp. 110-13; receives

INDEX

captain's commission, 113; quarrels with McGary, 116; leads Indian fight, 117; night hunts of, 118; hunts for meat needed by other settlers, 119; legendary adventures of, 119-20; disposition of, 119-20, 129, 148-52, 153-54; goes to meet John Bowman, 124-25; marries Ann McDaniel, 143-48; manner of, 144-51; moves into Fort Harrod with wife, 147; goes on salt journey, 149-53; gains partial victory over Transylvania, 154-55; defends John Bowman, 166; receives colonel's commission, 170; is elected to Va. Assembly, 170; favors Va. land law, 171-72; 185; establishes claims, 172-73; acts as guardian for stepson, 172-73; appears for relatives, 173; attacks Indians on Warrior's Path, 175; grieves over brother's death, 179; writes letter to William Clark, 180; is disturbed over attacks, 181-83; house of, at Boiling Spring is used as center, 183; relations of, with speculators, 183-86; petitions Continental Congress, 184-95; reaction of, to land disputes, 185; in Clark's 1780 campaign, 186-93; in Clark's 1782 campaign, 200-202; eastward journey of, 205-206; advances money to Clark, 207; reaction of, to Treaty of Paris, 208; doubts of, on statehood, 210-11; is made a trustee of Harrodsburg, 212; acknowledges Margaret as his daughter, 216; transfers land to Mahon, 216; desire of, for land as a symbol of his success at pioneering, 220; carelessness of, with money and papers, 220-21; in Clark's 1786 campaign, 226-30; and alcohol, 230-31; last hunt and disappearance of, 232-34; theories concerning death of, 233-35; last will and testament of, 238

Harrod, James (son of Thomas), land claims of, 173; signs petition, 184; remains in Ky., 239

Harrod, James (stepson of J. Harrod). See McDaniel, James, Jr.

Harrod, Jemima, 11

Harrod, John, Sr., 1, 9, 10; on Susquehanna, 4; death of first wife of, 4; marriage of, to Sarah Moore, 5; in N. J., 6; in Valley of Va., 5-7; in Pa., 7-9, 21; signs petition, 9

Harrod, John, Jr., early military service of, 1; background and birth of, 4-5; joins stepmother, 10; at Great Meadow, 3-4; is wounded, 4; remains loyal to Washington, 4; is wounded again, 15; is awarded pension, 15; sees Ohio Valley, 16; marries Rachel Shepherd, 25; lives at father's plantation, 25, 28; estimate of career of, 205; death of, 205-206

Harrod, Levi, an infant, 11; with J. Harrod, 48; cabin is built for, at Harrodsburg, 48; marries Rachel Mills, 69; in Ky., 104; protests fraudulent election, 239; is active in church affairs, 240; serves in Continental line, 240; serves in militias, 240; serves as first justice of Washington County, Pa., 240; asks for church transfer, 240-41; character and reputation of, 240-41; moves to Ohio, 241

Harrod, Mary, is wed to Evan Shelby, 21

Harrod, Margaret, birth of, 216; question of paternity of, 216-17; marriage of, to John Fauntleroy, 218; is victor in land suit, 223

Harrod, Nellie, is engaged to marry, 10

Harrod, Samuel, birth of, 1; in Md. militia, 10; serves under Washington, 14; sees Ohio Valley, 16; serves under Alexander Beall, 17; serves under Evan Shelby, 20; at Kaskaskai, 30-31; as fur trader, 30-31; tradition concerning, 125; draws lot in Louisville, 157-58; fondness of, for Ill., 158; death of, 178-79; signs Louisville petition, 179

Harrod, Sarah, 1, 9, 10; parentage and birth of, 5; marriage of, to John Harrod, 5; in Shingas' raid, 10-11; at Fort Littleton, 11; near Chambersburg, 15; refuses to flee, 18; moves to western Pa., 28-32;

INDEX

Harrod, Sarah, *continued*
question of second marriage of, 70-71; death of, 70-71

Harrod, Thomas, birth of, 5; is taken to Baltimore, 5; joins stepmother, 10; serves under Alexander Beall, 17; serves under Evan Shelby, 20; helps build road, 21; marries Hannah, 32; moves to N. C., 32; attitude of, toward Ky., 69; land claims of, 173, 222-23; moves to Tenn., 239; death of, 239-40

Harrod, Thomas (son of John), returns to Bedford, 206

Harrod, William, birth of, 1; early skills of, 10; appearance of, 10; native strength of, 11-12; wins fight, 12; first military service of, at Fort Littleton, 11-12; leads attack, 17-18; at Fort Frederick, Md., under Shelby, 20; serves under Burd, 23-24; serves in Ill., 25; serves under Piper, 26; returns home, 27; marries Amelia Stevens, 27; longs for Monongahela country, 27-28; moves to Ten Mile, 28-29; serves under Connally, 34; is commissioned a captain, 34-35; on militia duty, 36; in Ky., 40-41; in command at Ross's Fort, 54; serves as purchaser for fort, 53; recruits at Jackson's Fort, 53; recruits for McDonald, 55; respect of, for his commander, 56-57; joins Dunmore's army, 58; urges march to Chillicothe, 62; at meeting at Fort Gower, 65; receives letter from McDonald, 67; is enthusiastic over Ky., 69; arrives in Ky., 88; hears reports of attacks on Indians, 103; receives order from Pentecost, 104; returns to Pa., 104; purchases cattle, 104; is ordered to scout for Linn and Gibson, 104; builds fort at Grave Creek, 104, 131; character of, 104-109; estimate of career of, 104-109, 135; receives petition, 105; is proud of reputation, 107; is accused of embezzlement, 107-108; offers resignation, 107-108; Dunmore and Pentecost quoted concerning, 108; name of, is cleared, 108-109; abandons Grave Creek fort, 131; is made commander at Wheeling, 131; is wounded, 131; scouts with Foreman, 132; goes on furlough, 133; is visited by Clark, 133; is made captain under Clark, 134-36; takes men to Redstone, 135; fortifies Corn Island, 137; legend concerning, at Kaskaskia, 140; erects fort, 142; is elected one of first trustees of Louisville, 157; draws lots at Louisville, 157-58; escorts Gov. Hamilton, 160-61; returns to Louisville, 162; serves in John Bowman's campaign, 162-67; defends Bowman as commander, 166; is ashamed of his men, 167; returns to Monongahela, 167; argues with Col. Brodhead, 167-68; knowledge of men of, 167-68; scorn of pretense of, 167-68; remains on Upper Ohio, 177; letters of, to wife, 177-78, 180; is visited by Clark and urged to resume command at Louisville, 177-79; returns to home, 178-79; grieves over death of Sam, 179; gathers trophies, 180; visits Harrodsburg, 180; hunts in Ky., 196; seeks land granted for Ill. service, 196; is granted land on Ohio River, 221-22; town is named for, 222; assists widow of J. Harrod, 238; purchases of, at Muddy Creek store, 239; later years of, on Fish Creek, 239; death of wife of, 239; moves to Ky., 239; is active in civil matters, 239; death of, 239

Harrod's Creek, 172

Harrod's fort. *See* Fort Harrod

Harrod's Landing, 46, 73, 172

Harrod's men. *See* Appendix

Harrodsburg, Ind., 222

Harrodsburg, Ky., described, 47-49, 84; new arrivals at, 85; Settlers of, appeal to Va., 89-90; deserters arrive at, 138; Lord Hamilton is held prisoner at, 160-61; town of, is established, 211-12. *See also* names of individual settlers

Harrodstown. *See* Harrodsburg

Henderson, Col. Richard, 76; "treaty-purchase" of, 77; is opposed, 77-78;

INDEX 261

establishes "colony," 78-83; concern of, for good will of J. Harrod, 79; serves as intermediator, 81-82; comments of, on J. Harrod, 82; returns to N. C., 86-87; at Williamsburg, 93, 97-98; presents memorial, 154; receives Green River grant, 154-55

Henry, Gov. Patrick, 93-94; Clark's visit to, 98; supports Harrod, 98-99; fears for Ky., 110; appeal to, 126, 129, 133. *See also* Clark, George Rogers

Henton (Hinton), Evan, erects cabin, 51

Hite family, 6

Hite, Isaac, 244

Hockhocking River, 58, 62

Hogan, Henry, 243

Holsteiner, Michael. *See* Stoner, Michael

Holston River, is visited by J. Harrod, 32; rumor concerning, 42; men from, 44; news at, 49; J. Harrod at, 58, 60

Hughes family, 28

Hupp, George, 29

Illinois country. *See* Harrod, James; and Clark, George Rogers

Illinois expedition. *See* Clark, George Rogers

Illinois towns. *See* Clark, George Rogers

Indians, land claims of, 4-8; nature of warfare of, 13-16; attacks by, 53, 54, 175-76; attacks on, 103-104, 176-77; tactics of, 117-18, 150; friendly, 130; hostile, 127-28, 196-98; white men eat food of, 189. *See also* Treaties, and names of specific tribes, pioneers, forts, and towns

Iroquois Indian claims, 32

Jackson, Richard, fort of, serves as a recruiting center, 53

Jefferson, Thomas, supports Harrodsburg, 99. *See also* Clark, George Rogers; and Harrod, James

Johnson, Sir William, conference is planned by, 26-27

Jones, John Gabriel, serves as leader in revolt, 91-92, 96-100; is killed, 101-102; estimate of, 102

Jones, Mary, 240

Joppa, Md., 5

Kaskaskia, 133; is captured, 140

Keelboat, use of, 149-50, 158-59

Kenton, Simon, in Kentucky, 50; in powder rescue, 102; in attack at McClelland's Fort, 102-103; pilots families to Harrodsburg, 103; enlists under J. Harrod, 186-87; is mistaken for J. Harrod, 187

Kentuckians, love of, for titles, 170-71; petition of, 184; in 1780 campaign, 187; after defeat at Blue Licks, 199; show caution, 209-11; reaction of, to delays by Va., 224; reaction of, to proposed treaty, 224; adherence of, to legalities, 224-25; conservatism of, 237-38

Kentucky, a part of Fincastle County, 35-43; a county, 91, 109; divided into three counties, 185, 194, 195; constitution of, 237-38, 237 n.; population of 170-71, 183; weakness of, 209, 213, 226. *See also* Treaties and names of individual towns and pioneers

Kentucky rifles, 36-37

Kentucky River, 43, 46. *See also* Treaties; Harrod, James; and names of other pioneers

Kerr, James, 243

Kickapoo Indians, 96

Knox, James, 50, 244

Lancaster, Pa., 43

Land, Fairfax grant, 7; boundary disputes, 7, 8, 9, 12, 35, 134-35; speculators, 27-28, 33-35, 183-86, 211, 214-15; French and Indian War bounty lands, 33; settlement law, 34-35, 43, 170-72; land office, 88; commission, 171; prices, 171-72; warrants, 183. *See also* Bullitt, Thomas; Preston, Col. William; Harrod, James; Clark, George Rogers; Dunmore, Gov.; Washington, George; Henderson, Col. Richard; and Ohio Company of Virginia.

Landing Run. *See* Harrod's Landing

INDEX

Laurel Hill, 3
Lewis, Col. Andrew, under Dunmore, 57
Licking River, 162; attacks on, 181. *See also* Battle of Blue Licks
Lincoln County, Ky., created, 194; court in, 195-96, 222; charges against clerk of, 207; courthouse of, 208; militia of, 226-31
Linn, William, conveys powder, 106-107; serves as spy in Ill., 125-26, marries, 126
Liquor. *See* Pioneers
Little Meadow, Braddock at, 14
Little Miami River, 189
Little Sandy River, 233
Logan, Chief. *See* Mingo Indians
Logan, Benjamin, carries defense burden, 110; is made a captain, 113; keeps in touch with J. Harrod, 117; at Louisville, 158-59; with Bowman, 162-64; serves as a county lieutenant, 170, 194; in 1780 campaign, 186-93; offers gift of land, 196; reaches Blue Licks, 199; in 1782 campaign, 200; calls first Danville convention, 208-209; is made a trustee of Harrodsburg, 212; in 1786 campaign, 226-30; argument of, with McGary, 228; in court-martial, 229; soldiers take advantage of absence of, 230
Logan's Fort, defenses of, co-ordinated, 125; carries burden, 193. *See also* St. Asaph
Long Hunters. *See* Knox, James
Lottery cabins, 47-48
Louisa River, identity of, 43, 43 n.
Louisville, surveys at, 35, 89; is established, 142, 156-59; petition from, 179; is affected by division of county, 197; first dry goods store at, 214. *See also* Clark, George Rogers; Bullitt, Thomas; and Harrod, James
Loyal Land Company, 77
Loyalhanna, trail to, 22; Forbes at, 23
Loyalists in West, 138-39. *See also* Clark, George Rogers; and Pioneers
Lythe, Rev. John, 83, 126, 218

McAfee brothers, in Kentucky in 1773, pp. 37-41; meet J. Harrod, 73-74; in Dunmore's War, 74; religion and nationality of, 74-76
McAfee, Gen. Robert, comments of, on J. Harrod, 235-36
McAfee, William, death of, 192-93
McAfee's station, sends men to J. Bowman, 162; is attacked, 197
McClelland's Fort, on powder route, 102; is abandoned, 103; families from, move to Harrodsburg, 103
McColloch, James, 244
McCracken, Capt., is killed, 201
McCrea (McCra), Roderick, 244
McDaniel, Ann (Coburn). *See* Harrod, Ann (Coburn)
McDaniel, James, Jr., 215; inherits land, 144, 172-73; is killed, 144, 217
McDaniel, James, Sr., 143; is killed, 144
McDonald, Col. Angus, expedition of, 54-57; attitude of frontiersmen toward, 54-57; in Dunmore's War, 58; writes to William Harrod, 67; with William Harrod, 92
McDonald, James. *See* McDaniel, James, Jr.
McGary, Hugh, in N. C., 32; arrives in Ky., 88; organizes defense, 111, 113; in Indian fight, 117; quarrels with J. Harrod, 116; justice in court, 126; estimate of, 150, 198-99; at Louisville, 158-59; in 1780 campaign, 186; helps defend McAfee's station, 197; in Battle of Blue Licks, 197-99; is blamed for defeat, 198-99; in 1786 campaign, 227-30; kills Moluntha, 228-29; court-martial of, 228-29; brings charges, 229-30
Mackinac, British post at, 179
Mahon, ———, manager of J. Harrod's farm, 216; relations of, with Ann Harrod discussed, 216-17; land transfer to, 216
Marriage customs in Ky., 126-27. *See also* Harrod, James
Martin, Gov. Josiah, opposition of, to Henderson, 78
Martin, William, 243
Martin's Fort, attacked, 181-82

INDEX

Maryland, migration to, 5. *See also* Land; Harrod, James; and Shelby, Evan, Sr.
Mason, George, opposes Henderson, 99
Methodists in Kentucky, 220
Miami River, 182
Military titles. *See* Kentuckians
Militia, need for, 99. *See also* Pioneers; Harrod, James; and individual county and state names
Mills, Rachel. *See* Harrod, Rachel
Mingo Indians, at Fort Necessity, 4; with captives, 27; speech of Chief Logan, 63-64; Chief Pluggy attacks, 102
Miranda, Isaac, 238, 238 n.
Mississippi River, 179. *See also* Harrod, James; Clark, George Rogers; and Kentuckians
Moluntha, Chief. *See* Shawnee Indians
Monmouth, battle of, 205
Monongahela country, J. Harrod recruits at, 44; becomes crowded, 240; as population source for Ky., 244
Monongahela River, fort on, 3; Braddock's defeat at, 15; description of, 24; Harrod family moves to, 27; land disputes near, 34, 35, 134; settlers cross, 43; Indian hostility in area of, 131;
Monongahelans, show their enthusiasm over Bowman's expedition, 162; collect trophies, 163; eagerness of, for booty, 165; return home, 166-68; return to live in Ky., 166; land hunger of, 185; reverence of, for Tom Paine, 185
Monroe, James, letter of, to George Rogers Clark, 203
Montgomery, John, serves as captain under Clark, 136
Montreal, Quebec. *See* Harrod, James
Moon, Chief. *See* Cherokee Indians
Moore, James, Sr., 5
Moore, James Francis, cousin of the Harrods, 222; serves as land commissioner, 222; in Ky., 243-44
Moore, Sam, acts as spy in Ill., 125-26; is associated with J. Harrod, 166

Moore, Sarah. *See* Harrod, Sarah
Mortimer, William, 243
Moundsville. *See* Grave Creek fort
Muddy Creek store, 239
Muskingham River, 27
Myers, William, 243

Nash, William, 244
Nashville, J. Harrod at, 31
Nemacolin Trail, 3
New England, migration from, to Ky., 213
New Light, sect in Ky., 220
New River, as meeting place, 35
North Carolina, migration to, 7, 213; J. Harrod in, 31-32; radicals from, 237; as population source, 244
North Mountain, 20
Nourse, James, praises J. Harrod, 85

Ohio Company of Virginia, activities of, 2, 2 n.; forts belonging to, 3
Ohio country, lure of, 24; British supremacy in, 26; march to, 186; white settlements in, 226. *See also* Clark, George Rogers; Bowman, John; and Harrod, James
Ohio River. *See* Louisville; Harrod, James; Clark, George Rogers; and Bullitt, Thomas
Old Chillicothe. *See* Chillicothe towns
Oldtown. *See* Chillicothe towns and Harrodsburg
Ooley, Peter, 243
O'Post. *See* Clark, George Rogers
Ottowa Indians. *See* Pontiac, Chief
Owens, David, loyalty of men to, 105

Paine, Tom, 185
Pendergrass (Pendergast), Garret, 96
Pennsylvania, Little Cove, 7; Great Cove, 9, 10, 11; attitude of inhabitants of, toward Indians, 18, 19; land jobbers, 185. *See also* Land; Pioneers; Connally, John; Harrod, James; Forbes, John C.; Braddock, Gen. Edward; and Burd, James
Pentecost, Dorsey. *See* Harrod, William
Perry, ———, is killed, 177
Peters, Rev. Richard, serves as commissioner, 8, 9; petition of residents of Cumberland to, 18

Petitions of Kentucky, that of 1780 to the Continental Congress, stating the grievances of the Kentuckians and demanding statehood, 184, 195; that sent in 1786 by the third Danville convention to the General Assembly of Va., 223-24. *See also* Harrod, John, Sr.; Henderson, Col. Richard; and Court
Petry, Alexander, 244
Pickaway (Picqua) towns, 166, expedition to, 190
Piedmont. *See* Virginia
Pioneers, as soldiers, 13, 15-16, 22-24, 58-63; dress of, 13, 44, 71, 145-46, 214, 231; disregard for danger of, 42, 45-47, 121-22, 176, 186; attitudes of, toward Indians, 42, 45-47, 225; and authority, 54-57; songs of, 61; remedies of, 70, 148; philosophy of, 84, 90, 142; women, 113-14, 123, 148-49, 159, 195, 213; gossip among, 127, 216-17; generous natures of, 128; customs, marriage, 144-47; food of, 145-47, 187-89, 204, 214-15, 216 (*see also* Chapter XV; Ray, James; and Harrod, James); use of alcohol by, 146, 201, 230; dances of, 147-48; games of, 151; and booty, 165 (*see also* Monongahelans); fear of cannon of, 181-83; land hunger among, 186, 219-20; luxuries of, 214-15; scorn of, for classical education, 218. For homes of, *see* Harrodsburg
Pittsburgh (Fort Pitt), is established, 23-25; as place of rendezvous, 57-58; rumors concerning, 101. *See also* Forbes, John C.; Braddock, Gen. Edward; Clark, George Rogers; Harrod, James; and Fort Duquesne
Pluggy, Chief. *See* Mingo Indians
Poague, George, dream of, 51; land claim of, 173; in Ky., 243-44
Point Pleasant. *See* Dunmore's War
Pontiac, Chief, organizes rebellion, 25, 26
Population, on frontier, 74-75, 183; analysis of, 244
Potomac River, 1-7
Powell Valley, 88

Poytress, Rev. John, 219
Presbyterians, 219-20. *See also* Rice, Rev. David
Preston, Col. William, 35; attitude of, toward Bullitt, 43; sends surveyors to Ky., 49; on Transylvania dispute, 95
Princeton, battle at, 205
Prisoners, exchanges of, 27
Proclamation of 1763, pp. 28, 32
Proprietors. *See* Henderson, Col. Richard; and Transylvania proprietors

Quirk, Thomas, 243, 244

Ray, James, at Dick's River, 88; escape of, from Indians, 114-17; fights Shawnee, 117-18; night hunts of, 118; with Stagner, 122; kills Indian, 123; loyalty of, 165, 230
Ray, William, is killed, 114-15
Raystown. *See* Bedford
Redstone, Pa., 27; is reinforced, 131; boats taken to, 135; William Harrod returns to, 167
Rees, Azor (Azariah), 243
Religion. *See* Pioneers
Rice, Rev. David, 218-19
Richmond, Va., cases tried at, 195
Rivers. *See* names of individual rivers
Roads and trails. *See* names of individual roads or trails
Roanoke, Va., as original home of most of members of J. Harrod's company, 244
Ross's Fort, 54
Rowe, Adam and family, 177
Ruddle, Capt., 182
Ruddle's Fort, is attacked, 181-82
Russell, William, 42; station of, on Clinch River, 42

St. Asaph, settlement of, 81. *See also* Logan, Benjamin
St. Louis, 151
Salt, 149-54; danger at licks, 149; salt works, 152
Sanders, James, 243
Sandusky. *See* Sodousky, James
Scioto River, 39
Scotch-Irish, on frontier, 74-75; emigrate from N. C., 143

INDEX

Scott County, Ind., 221
Seneca Indians, 26-27
Separatism in Ky., 210-11, 223-24, 231
Settlement law. *See* Land
Settlements. *See* names of individual settlements
Seven Years' War. *See* Braddock, Gen. Edward; Forbes, John C.; Harrod, James; and Shelby, Evan, Sr.
Shakers, 220
Shane, Rev. John, 216; comments of, on J. Harrod, 219
Sharpe, Horatio, letter from, 21
Shawnee Indians, 4; rumored alliance of Pennsylvania with, 20; surrender of white prisoners by, at Whiteman Creek, 27; preliminary treaty of Bradstreet with, 27; Chief Cornstalk and, 38-39, 42, 62-63; conference of, with Bullitt, 38-39, 42; in Dunmore's War, 62-63; death of Chief Cornstalk of, 130-31; increasing hostility of, 103; campaign against, planned by Bowman, 162; Simon Kenton captured and tortured by, 187; unfairly blamed, 225; Chief Moluntha of, captured and killed, 228-29. *See also* Ray, James.
Shelby, Evan, Jr., joins father at Holston, 32
Shelby, Evan, Sr., family of, 5, 6, 20, 21, 22, 23; moves to Holston, 32; is denied pay allowance, 97
Shelby, Evan (son of Rees), marries sister of Harrods, 21
Shelby, Isaac, becomes first governor of Kentucky, 21; joins father, 32
Shelby, Rees, 21
Shelp, John, 243
Shepherd, Rachel, wife of John Harrod, Jr., 25
Shingas, Chief. *See* Delaware Indians
Shippensburg, 21
Sideling Hill, 15
Silver Creek, 221
Silver Hills, 221
Sinking Spring, 173
Six Nations. *See* Treaty, of Fort Stanwix
Slaughter, Thomas, brings party of land seekers to Harrodstown, 80; argument of, with J. Harrod over right to Kentucky lands, 81-82; helps J. Harrod, 99
Slavery, is opposed, 237
Smith, John, 243
Sodousky, James, 243, 244
Soldiers, regular, 13-15. *See* Pioneers
Soldiers, volunteer. *See* Pioneers
Southern tribes, 33
Spain, 179, 224
Speculators. *See* Land
Stagner, Barney, is killed, 122
Stanford, Ky., 196
Stanwix. *See* Treaty, of Fort Stanwix
Statehood. *See* Virginia, Danville, and Separatism in Ky.
Stations. *See* names of individual stations
Stevens, Amelia. *See* Harrod, Amelia
Stoner, Michael, is seen by Harrods in Tenn., 31; is sent to warn surveyors, 51; accompanies J. Harrod and Bridges up Kentucky River, 233-34
Stull, Martin, 243
Surveyors, methods of, 49-50. *See also* Land and Harrod, James
Susquehanna frontier, 4, 5
Swann, family, 28

Taylor, Hancock, as surveyor, 37, 39-40; in Ky., 244
Taylor, Richard, 244
Ten Mile Creek, Harrods move to, 27-29, 30, 31-32; rumors at, 34; as recruiting center, 53; in 1776, pp. 70-71. *See also* Harrod, James
Tennessee, is cut off from N. C., 224
Tennessee River, 31, 139
Thomas, Abraham, recollections of, 54-57, 241
Three Islands, 227
Todd, John, captain's commission is granted to, 113; serves as chief justice, 128-29; orders census, 129; serves as county lieutenant, 194; is killed, 198-99
Todd, Robert, marries J. Harrod and Ann, 144
Tories. *See* Pioneers
Town Fork, 84

Trabue, Daniel, quoted, 159
Traitors. *See* Pioneers
Transylvania Assembly, meeting of, 82-84, 88
Transylvania colony. *See* Henderson, Col. Richard; and Harrod, James
Transylvania proprietors, opposition to, 86-87; are awarded land, 87; move office to Harrodsburg, 88; failure of, 225
Treaties, 33, 43, 77-78, 185, 208
Treaty, of Lochabar, 33; of Hard Labour, 33; of Fort Stanwix, 33, 43, 185; of Sycamore Shoals, 77-78; of Paris, 208
Trenton, battle at, 205
Tutt, Benjamin, 244

Union, Camp (Greenbriar), J. Harrod at, 61
United States, loyalty of John Cowan to, 196; fails to maintain peace, 225; forbids punitive measures, 226; and separatism, 231

Valley of Virginia. *See* Harrod, James; and Virginia
Vandalia Land Company, 77
Vanmeter family, 5
Venable, William, 243
Vincennes. *See* Clark, George Rogers
Virginia, Valley of, 5-6, 43; House of Burgesses of, awards pension, 15; in land controversy, 35; Assembly of, 57, 93, 95, 207, 223-24; men from Piedmont area of, arrive in Kentucky, 85; Convention of, considers Harrod's petition, 97; Council of, awards powder, 97-98; House of Delegates of, helps Ky., 100; attempts of, to appease Ky., 185; favors statehood, 231; Valley of southwest Va., 244. *See also* Land; Harrod, James; Dunmore, Gov.; and Connally, John

Wabash campaign. *See* Clark, George Rogers, 1786 campaign of
Walker family, 6, 32
Warriors' Road, in Ill., 139; in Alleghenies, 175
Washington, George, mission of, to French, 1-2; expedition of, 2-4; with Braddock, 14; as speculator, 33
Washington County, 240
Waynesburg, Pa., 53
Westmoreland County, 34
Wheeling fort, 41; activity at, 131-35. *See also* Harrod, William
White Plains, battle of, 205
Whiteman Creek, surrender at, 27
Widow Harrod. *See* Harrod, Sarah
Wilderness Road. *See* Boone, Daniel; and Henderson, Col. Richard
Wiley, James, 243
William and Mary, College of, 35
Williams, David, 243-44
Williamsburg, reports from, 43; Dunmore at, 57
Wills Creek Fort 2-4
Wilson, Harrod, 127
Wilson, John, 243
Winchester, Indians at, 20
Women. *See* Pioneers
Wyandot Indians, Chief White Eyes of, 131; spies, 131, attack Foreman, 131-33; attacks of, along the Monongahela, 180

Yadkin River, J. Harrod visits settlements on, 32; Thomas Harrod lives near, 32
Yorktown, battle at, 205
Youghiogheny River, 14-15

Zane, Andrew, 243

www.ingramcontent.com/pod-product-compliance
Lightning Source LLC
Chambersburg PA
CBHW030317100526
44592CB00010B/468